Thetford Gleanings
Published 2003
by
David Osborne
107, Bury Road, Thetford,
Norfolk IP24 3DQ
Tel: 01842 753379
E-mail: david.osborne18@btopenworld.com

British Library Cataloguing in Publication Data
Osborne, David
Thetford Gleanings
ISBN – 0 9513484 3 4
Design and layout by David Osborne
Printed by:- Geo. R. Reeve Ltd.,
9-11 Town Green,
Wymondham,
Norfolk NR18 0BD

Front cover photograph by:-

Studio Five
▶ PHOTOGRAPHERS ◀

• 12 Bridge Street, Thetford, Norfolk IP24 3AD
• Tel: 01842 752265

Once again, I am t
help and much val‹
number of individu
allowing me the use
the archive at Thetford's Ancient House Museum, I wish to thank Oliver Bone the Curator and Norfolk Museums and Archaeology Service. Also Thetford Town Council, Studio Five Photographers for photographs, Amberley Working Museum, Sussex for allowing me to publish a print from their collection; Dr Tim Pestell, Curator of Archaeology at Norwich Castle Museum for allowing me to photograph Stephen Watson's gibbet; 389th Bomb Group Collection, Hethel, for allowing to publish photographs from their collection; Neville Lockwood for providing a vital photograph from a piece of cine film; Brian Jermy for providing additional material.

I also wish to thank the many different publishers who have given me permission to reproduce extracts from books published by them:- A. P. Watt Ltd, Blackwell Publishers [Basil Blackwell Ltd], Brian Hogwood & Leaf Publications, David & Charles Ltd, Hodder Headline Ltd, Lennard Publishing, Manchester University Press, Norfolk Archaeological & Historical Research Group, Norfolk Museums and Archaeology Service, Oxford University Press, Phillimore & Co Ltd.

I thank Doris Whalebelly for allowing me to publish the war time memories of her late husband, Clifford 'Jack' Whalebelly; Maxine Gower for her illustration on page 88 and Jennifer Bullock for reading through my first draft.

For allowing me to reproduce photographs from their family archives and personal collections, my sincere thanks are also extended to Wendy Brown, Michael Burton, David Fulcher, Norma Howard, Brian Jermy and John and Marjorie Keymer. Photographs not acknowledged are from the David Osborne collection.

Once again, I also wish to acknowledge the great editorial help, general comments and suggestions given to me by an Old Thetfordian but now settled in Yorkshire, my good friend Brian Carr.

Finally, but not least of all, I wish to thank Joy, my dear wife and friend for thirty years, for her patience, support and encouragement.

Contents

*T*hetford Gleanings is mainly, with one exception, a compilation of local history articles that I have written during the past fifteen years or so, either for one of our local newspapers, the *Thetford & Watton Times*, or various local magazines and newsletters. Between them, they touch briefly upon many aspects of Thetford's fascinating past.

Besides the inclusion of such well-known places of local interest as the Castle Hill, Town Bridge and Cluniac Priory, also featured are some of the more obscure and less known aspects of Thetford's past, such as the effects and treatment of small-pox, the 19th century temperance movement, the so-called 'Thetford Riots', military manoeuvres held in the surrounding countryside in the early years of the 20th century and the late 'Jack' Whalebelly's interesting account of his experiences in Thetford during the 1939-45 War as a Police War Reserve constable.

A variety of documentary and published sources have also been gleaned to provide additional information and evidence of Thetford's past. Moreover, many evocative and interesting photographs and drawings have been included. The photographs and other material featured in this publication are not necessarily those used when the articles were originally published.

For those who may wish to read further and deeper into Thetford's history than this modest book offers, I have included a Thetford bibliography. Although I can not claim this to be a definitive list, it is fairly comprehensive and includes most, if not all, of the books and other publications that I am either aware of or have come across whilst using or visiting local record offices, private and public libraries and museums. I have also consulted the University of East Anglia's *A Bibliography* of *Norfolk History*.

Nonetheless, information touching upon Thetford's distant and more recent past can also be found in a great number of other publications. Those covering the general history of England, East Anglia, Norfolk and the local, geographical region once commonly known as Breckland but now generally referred to as 'The Brecks'. There are also numerous guides, travel books, directories, maps etc that also contain facts and information about Thetford that seldom can be found elsewhere!

In addition to all this printed material, mention must also be made of the valuable detail that can be gleaned from the pages of local newspapers, published from the 18th century onwards. As a source for local historians it must be one of the richest, yet least valued. As such, I have endeavoured to include several items gleaned from a number of different local newspapers.

With such a wealth of printed material, covering so many aspects of Thetford's past, and the 'new world' that has recently opened to us all with the development of information technology through the world-wide web of the Internet, one may wonder if, indeed, there is a need for a publication such as this?

Apart from Alan Crosby's excellent *History of Thetford,* published in 1986 and still in print, much of what has been written and published has either been out of print for many years or is found only in specialist publications. I know also, from meeting and talking to a great number of fellow Thetfordians of all ages, that many share an enthusiastic interest both in the town's ancient and more recent past. Hopefully, for a wide range of people, this book will provide an interesting and valuable addition to what has previously been published.

However, despite all that we know or perceive to know of Thetford's history, our knowledge is still far from complete. In fact, our endeavours and efforts have barely scratched below the surface of over 1,000 years of history, notwithstanding much thoughtful research and recording by a number of dedicated archaeologists and historians over several centuries. Given the enormity of the task, perhaps it is not surprising that so much still remains shrouded in mystery. No doubt future archaeologists and local historians will continue to subject Thetford's past to further scrutiny and periodic reappraisal, while seeking new evidence and sources in the absorbing challenge of unravelling the past.

David Osborne,
Bury Road, Thetford

The Dark Deeds Of Sweyn Forkbeard
Thetford & Watton Times, 13 November 1987

A few yards from where I live on the Bury Road stands the 'gasworks', or to give its present designation - Thetford Transmission North Area Office, Distribution and Customer Reporting Centres. In 1957 archaeological excavations on the gasworks site revealed part of the foundation of an ancient church and a number of burials. The church is by tradition alone dedicated to St Edmund, the Saxon King of East Anglia [today's Norfolk and Suffolk]. In AD 869, King Edmund, in defence of his Christian faith and people, was executed by the Danes. His martyrdom resulted in a cult following.

Fifty years previous to the archaeological excavations, a stone coffin had been discovered by Mr Charles Snelling, the resident manager of the gasworks, while digging the garden of Gas Works House. The discovery was reported in the *Thetford & Watton Times, ...* *'On raising the lid the skeleton of a man was found inside, which was photographed. The news of the discovery quickly spread through the town and large numbers of townspeople visited the spot'*... *'The coffin measures 6 ft. 10 in. long and is of a width 2 ft. 7 in. at the head and 1 ft. 5 in. at foot'*... *'No evidence of identification was found either inside or outside of the coffin which is believed to be of Barnack stone'.*

It was decided that the coffin was to remain in the garden. There undisturbed it rested, with the skeletal remains of its undoubtedly once noble but now nameless occupant. During the early 1940s the coffin attracted the interest of a Dr and Mrs Jameson, who lived at the old Canon's House on the Brandon Road. After consulting various authorities recommended by the British Museum, they claimed that the coffin contained the remains of none other than Sweyn Forkbeard, King of Denmark, whose forces ravaged East Anglia and burnt Thetford in 1004.

In Denmark coins with a king's name begin with Svein Forkbeard, c.985-1014; in Sweden with Olaf Skötkonung, c. 994-1022; and in Norway either with Olaf Tryggvason, 995-1000, or St. Olaf, 1015-30 - probably the latter. English influence is strong. Svein is the first Scandinavian king to appear in some kind of portraiture, by way of a bust on a coin inscribed partly in Latin, partly in rough-and-ready Old English, Rex Addener, 'Svein king of the Danes'. **Source:** Gwyn Jones, *A History of the Vikings,* Oxford University Press [1973]. Reprinted by permission of Oxford University Press.

Following this claim, the coffin was removed from its resting place to the Priory of the Canons of the Holy Sepulchre, adjacent to the Jamesons' home. It was there, on the 6th July, 1943, that the Reverend R. Cooling, Vicar of St Mary's, conducted a service of re-committal, which included ancient rites used 900-1000 years ago.

Despite the claims made by the Jamesons, it is doubtful that Thetford is the resting place of King Sweyn. Most authorities give his place of death many miles from Thetford, at Gainsborough, on the 3rd February, 1014. One ancient story tells that his body was carried back to Denmark. However, accounts of King Sweyn's death, no doubt contrived by those interested in promoting the cult of St Edmund, tell of a sudden and mysterious end, *'Saint Edmund appeared to Sweyn in a vision and remonstrated with him on the misery he was inflicting on his people. The Tyrant, giving an insolent reply, the saint struck him on the head and he died of the blow immediately after'.* Sweyn's death gave the people of East Anglia cause to rejoice.

Today the memory of Sweyn Forkbeard survives in Thetford. The Town Sign erected in 1954 depicts his figure, a modern street his name and on a house in Icknield Way a wall plaque proclaims his deed of 1004. Perhaps more than he deserves.

The Thetford Town Sign was erected in 1954 and depicts King Sweyn on one side and Thomas Paine on the other. The carved, oak painted sign was made by the renowned craftsman, Harry Carter of Swaffham.

Viking raiders took winter quarters in Thetford in 869, the same year that King Edmund of the East Angles was killed after a battle with the Danes near the town. It is not known exactly when Danish Vikings actually settled in Thetford but it is likely to have been in the 880s. The town developed rapidly in the 10th century on both banks of the river Little Ouse to become a major Anglo-Scandinavian Settlement... **Source:** *The Viking Thetford Trail,* Norfolk Museums & Archaeology Service [2001]. Reprinted by permission of Norfolk Museums & Archaeology Service.

Danish raiding resumed in the 980s, and in 1004 a fleet commanded by the Danish king Swein sacked Norwich. The Danes went on to Thetford, which was also burnt, but somewhere near here they were confronted by the local militia led by the East Anglian earl, Ulfketal Snelling: 'and there was a fierce encounter and great slaughter on each side. There were slain the chief men of East Anglia, but if they had been up to strength the army would never have got back to their ships: as they themselves admitted, they had never met with harder hand-play in England than Ulfketal gave them'. The Danes returned in 1009, and in 1010 Thetford was sacked and the East Anglians defeated at the great battle of Ringmer, probably Ringmere in Wretham, north of Thetford. In 1013 all the people in the Danish-settled areas of England surrendered to Swein, and the English king Ethelred fled abroad. **Source:** *Tom Williamson,* The Origins of Norfolk, *Manchester University Press [1993]. Reprinted by permission of Manchester University Press.*

The stone coffin as it remained in the garden of the Gas Works house, until its removal to the Canons in 1943.

This is the stone coffin or sarcophagus discovered in the garden of the Gas Works House, July 1907, by Mr Charles Snelling who lived at the Gas Works House. It would be remarkable if Mr Snelling was a descendant of the East Anglian earl, Ulfketal Snelling, who fought the invading Danes in 1004 and again 1010. After the great battle near Thetford in 1010, the Anglo-Saxon Chronicle records that 'many fell slain on both sides. There the flower of the East Anglian people was killed'.

The Bury Road photographed about the time of the coffin's discovery. In the distance can be seen the retort house chimney of the Gas Works and beyond, in the far distance, the Thetford Union Workhouse.

Digging Up The Past Of Town's Historic Hill *Thetford & Watton Times, 26 May 1989*

Thetford's most famous historic site is probably the Castle Hill. It stands close to what was, and still is, an important river crossing, at the town's eastern extremity.

For many years, historians have differed in their opinion as to the origin of the Castle Hill and its defences. However, since an archaeological excavation undertaken in 1962 revealed evidence of Iron Age occupation, it is now generally accepted that it was built on a former Iron Age hillfort about the time of the Norman Conquest.

Thetford Castle Hill is said to have been formed by the devil scraping his boot after he made the Fen-dyke at Weeting by dragging his foot along the ground. A hollow north-east of the northern rampart and containing water is known as "Devil's Hole". **Source:** W. G. Clarke, *'Traditions, Customs and Ghost Tales',* In Breckland Wilds, Robert Scott [1925].

The Norman nobility directed and controlled the building of many similar earthworks, known as a motte and bailey. The word 'motte' is French, meaning a clod of earth, and 'bailey' is the fortified enclosure surrounding the motte.

The motte was a strategic military base which gave the Normans protection at times of insurrection and from the threat of attack from unconquered or foreign forces. For the indigenous population, the presence of a fortified motte was a sign of Norman authority.

To construct such a mound, as at Thetford, thousands of tons of earth, chalk, and flint were excavated with hand tools and then moved using bags, barrows, baskets, sledges and tubs - local labour providing the workforce.

The most practical method of construction would have been to first excavate the huge ditch that surrounds the motte, throwing the spoil inwards. A fascine, or causeway retained in the form of a ramp, connecting the motte to the outside of the ditch, would enable further material excavated from some distance away to be deposited upon the motte. Finally, to protect the motte from erosion, it was covered with a well-packed layer of chalk blocks and flint. Evidence of this can be seen at the base of uprooted trees on the west side of the hill.

Although it is called the Castle Hill, there is no evidence that a castle ever stood on the top. If there were, it was probably constructed of timber as no remains of stonework have been found. There is, however, an entry in a pipe-roll that Thetford Castle was dismantled in 1172-73. The Castle Hill is the most likely site of a castle at Thetford but another earthwork built about the same time stood at the western extremity of the town and is now called Red Castle.

Since the abandonment of the Castle Hill site, possibly in the late 12th century, part of the outer defences have been destroyed, and with the passing of time, the origin of the place is now obscure.

In September 1908, the Castle Hill and adjoining meadow was officially opened as a public park by Lady William Cecil, daughter of Lord Amherst of Hackney, whose estate included the Castle Hill and meadow. It was leased to the town for 99 years at £1 per annum and the freehold was bought by the Corporation for £25 in 1921.

The Castle Park has been the scene of numerous events. Perhaps the most unusual was that organised by the Breckland Motor Cycle Club in 1965. Watched by a reported crowd of two thousand spectators, Mr Ray Ward became the first - and hopefully the last - to conquer the Castle Hill by riding up the side on a motor cycle.

Other market or exchange sites might have been of a more temporary nature and not necessarily associated with settlements which may have had minster churches. Sceattas have been found in significant numbers at or in the close vicinity of hillforts in southern England, notably at St. Catherine's Hill, near Winchester, and Hod Hill. Such prominent sites may have provided obvious meeting places and locations for regular markets or fairs. The Iron Age fort at Thetford could conceivably have been used in the same way during the Middle Saxon period as it was a prominent landmark, next to an important crossing point on a major river boundary. No Middle Saxon coins have yet been found there, but excavations within the defences have been very limited, metal detecting is prohibited, and substantial disturbance was caused by the construction of the Norman castle on the site late in the 11th century. **Source:** Phil Andrews, *'Middle Saxon Norfolk: Evidence for Settlement, 650 - 850',* Norfolk Archaeological & Historical Research Group, The Annual [1992]. Reprinted by permission of Norfolk Archaeological & Historical Research Group.

The Borough Seal (commonly called the arms) represents a quadrangular castle embattled and surmounted by a tower...It probably dates almost in this form from 1148, and seems originally to have belonged to the Town Bailiff, and to have been made from the arms of the manorial lords. **Source:** W. G. Clarke, *Guide to the Borough of Thetford,* W. Boughton & Sons Ltd [1923].

A drawing of the Castle Hill from Thomas Martin's 'History of Thetford' published in 1779. The 18th century local historian, Thomas Martin [1696-1771], wrote of the Castle Hill... 'This may, however, with great probability, be ascribed to the Saxons'...
Archaeological discoveries made in the 1960s, however, suggest a hill fort was originally built on the site about 500 B.C. - 2,500 years ago.

The Castle Hill has been used as a commercial symbol or logo by a number of local businesses. It can be seen on this one pound note, dated 1820, and issued by the Norfolk & Suffolk General Bank, established in Thetford in 1801. Later, the Castle Hill was used on the screw-top of Bidwell's beer bottles. At one time the Bidwell's owned part of the hill.

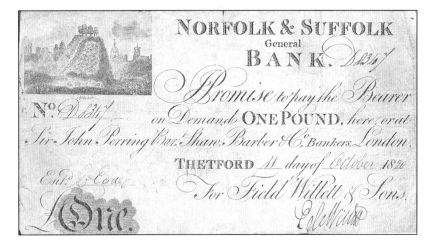

The Town Arms.

The Castle Hill in 1989, when trees uprooted in the 'great storm' of October 1987 could still be seen.
The hill is approximately 25 metres high and the largest earthworks of its kind in East Anglia. It was probably built in the decade immediately following the Conquest in 1066 when the Normans, using forced labour, built about forty castles in England. From these military bases, the heavily armed conquerors were able to suppress any local resistance, should it arise.

Relics of Saints...And Miracles At The Priory
Thetford & Watton Times, 10 August 1990

Anyone visiting the ruins of Thetford's Cluniac Priory, unaided by a guide or the knowledge of medieval architecture, monasticism and religion, would find it difficult to appreciate the history of the place and the communal life of its former inhabitants.

Monasticism had spread to many parts of England before the Norman Conquest, influenced from the north and west by the Celtic Church and from the continent by the Roman Church. The site we now call the Nunnery was originally a pre-Conquest Benedictine monastery, founded by the Abbot of Bury St Edmunds.

After the Norman Conquest, many new religious houses were founded by the new ruling class. One of these, the Earl of Surrey, founded the first Cluniac Priory in England. It was established in 1077 at Lewes, Sussex and dedicated to St Pancras.

A few years later, in 1103-04, a Cluniac Priory was also founded at Thetford by another Norman nobleman, Roger Bigod, a companion of King William I and lord of the manor of Thetford.

This new priory was established in the former cathedral church of St Mary. The site is now occupied by Thetford Grammar School. Soon after its foundation, Thetford's community of Cluniac monks moved their monastery from its original site, south of the river, to the place we know today as the Abbey or, more correctly, the Priory of Our Lady of Thetford. The foundation stone was laid in 1107 and in 1114 Prior Stephen and twelve monks moved into their new house.

Other Cluniac houses, all dependent on the great Abbey at Cluny, were established in Norfolk - most noticeably at Castle Acre and Bromholm, near Bacton. Bromholm Priory was famous for its relic of the Holy Rood and as a place of pilgrimage.

Thetford Priory also possessed relics of saints and attracted pilgrims. The 14th century monk, John Brame, wrote an account of their discovery and of miraculous events occurring at Thetford. The

The ruined priory church, looking through the nave towards the high altar at the east end of the presbytery. Photographed circa 1940.

relics were discovered in the head of an old image of the Blessed Virgin Mary, once kept in their original priory. The veneration of the saints and their remains is a fascinating aspect of medieval religion.

Many monasteries developed from being secluded communities, devoted to a communal life of prayer and worship, into very worldly or secular establishments indeed. Endowed with vast estates and properties, their influence extended into many parts of medieval life. Thetford's Cluniacs possessed over twenty manors, numerous churches and other privileges dispersed over several counties.

On the eve of the dissolution of the monasteries, many people continued to make gifts to them. In 1536 John Kent, a burgess of Thetford and probably the same person who was Mayor in 1512 and 1529, requested in his will... *'and my bodye to be buried in the monasterye of our Ladye of the monks in Thetford next the sepulcure of Robert Love sometymes Burges of this towne. Allso I will that the aforesayed monasterye shall have 8s in monye for breaking the ground for my sepulcure. Allso I geve and bequeth to my lord prior of the seyd monasterye 6s 8d'.* Perhaps more significantly that same year the King's natural son, Henry Fitzroy, Duke of Richmond, was buried at Thetford Priory.

Yet, so suddenly, the wealth of the monasteries came to an end. In the space of about four years, between 1536-40, their dissolution was complete. On the 16th February, 1540, William Ixworth, the last prior, and sixteen monks surrendered to the King's commissioners. The Priory was soon stripped of its wealth and by the middle of the following century it was a desolate ruin.

Though scant are the remains of Thetford Priory, we can be thankful that they did not suffer the same fate as that of St Pancras at Lewes. In 1845 the site was ploughed up and, where the high altar once stood, the railway between London and Brighton now passes over.

After the death of Roger Bigod, the founder, in 1107, his son Hugh was also an active patron of the priory. He was created the first earl of Norfolk c.1141, and the holders of that title, and later of the dukedom, continued to be patrons of Thetford. Hugh Bigod was buried there, as were also all his successors of the Bigod family. On the death of the last Roger Bigod in 1306, the Norfolk estates were passed to the Crown and were presented by Edward II to his half-brother de Brotherton, whose heirs held them till 1375. They then passed by marriage to John Mowbray, whose son, Thomas Mowbray was created the first duke of Norfolk. The third Mowbray duke was buried at Thetford in 1461, and his son, the fourth and last Mowbray duke, was buried there also (1476). The title and estates passed to the Howards, the present ducal family, in 1483, and the first Howard duke (killed at the battle of Bosworth fighting for Richard III), who was first buried at Leicester, was translated to Thetford as the proper place of burial for a duke of Norfolk. His son, the second Howard duke, won great fame by his heavy defeat of the Scots at Flodden in 1513, and on his death in 1524 was buried with magnificent pomp in front of the High Altar at Thetford. **Source:** F.J.E. Raby & P.K. Baillie Reynolds, *Thetford Priory*, DOE Official Handbook [1979].

Thetford Priory was excavated by the Ministry of Works in the mid-1930s and the ruins renovated. Although, from the surviving evidence, it is difficult to imagine and fully appreciate the appearance of the Priory before dissolution, the ground-plan of the monastery can be clearly seen.

Monastic houses were, generally, built to the same plan. The conventual church aligned east-west and, abutting the nave of the church, the covered and arcaded cloister, forming a rectangle or square around a central garth. It is in the cloister where monks would read, write and meditate. Directly off from the cloister was the chapter house, where the monks would gather daily to discuss monastic business.

Perhaps the most impressive surviving part of the Priory is the 14th century gatehouse once the main entrance into the Priory. It stands to the north-west of the Priory and is faced with knapped flint, with stone dressings. At one time, three sides of the Priory precinct must have been enclosed with a wall or some other form of fence to secure the privacy of its community. The Little Ouse river formed a natural boundary to the south.

The interior of the Chapter House. The east wall was rebuilt in the 1930s.

The gate house photographed circa 1910. Weather-moulding for a high-pitched roof of a building, perhaps an almonry, that once abutted the east wall of the gatehouse can be seen. It was from the almonry that alms or gifts were distributed to the poor and sick.

Between 1536 and 1553 there was destruction and plunder in England of beautiful, sacred and irreplaceable things on a scale probably not witnessed before or since. First, those hundreds of often massive and glorious buildings which had housed monks and nuns for centuries were razed, gutted or left without windows, roofs and stairs, for the elements to claim or new lay owner or local folk to despoil at their leisure; the inmates gone, the landed possessions seized by the crown, the lead and bells stripped, the cattle and household goods like beds, tables and kitchenware and everyday linen auctioned on site, the more valuable vestments, altar frontals, mitres and staffs, the plate, jewels and 'objects d'art' sent off to London'... **Source:** J.J. Scarisbrick, *'The Reformation and the English People'*, Basil Blackwell Ltd [1984]. Reprinted by permission of Blackwell Publishers.

St Mary-the-Less is the largest of Thetford's three surviving ancient churches. It is also the only one standing on the south side of the Little Ouse river in what was the Suffolk part of the town.

During its long history, which possibly pre-dates the Norman Conquest, St Mary's Church has undergone numerous changes to its appearance. We can appreciate, without knowing the exact details, that during the turmoil of the Reformation in the 16th century, when parish churches throughout the nation were stripped of their elaborate furnishings, decorations and wealth, drastic changes were made to the fabric of St Mary's in order to accommodate a profound change in religious practices.

Parts of the present structure of St Mary's Church are believed to date from the 12-15th centuries but a large proportion is the result of work carried out in the 19th century. This work was undertaken to replace defective structures, rather than for aesthetic considerations.

In 1802, at the very beginning of the 19th century, the brick-built chancel that we see today was constructed. Leading parishioners helped to pay for its construction despite a convention, developed after the Synod of Exeter in 1287, that the patron or rector was responsible for the upkeep of the chancel, while the parishioners maintained the nave.

Some of these same parishioners also made a contribution towards new chancel seats or pews, thus securing for themselves and their families at service time, a place of privilege in the parish church. It is also interesting to note that the ownership of certain houses in the town possessed the right of a pew in St Mary's Church.

Substantial alterations and repairs continued throughout the 19th and into the 20th century. In 1850 the thatched roof was replaced by one of slate and an old north gallery, known locally as the 'cooler', was replaced by a new north aisle. At the same time, new seating was placed in the nave and a new east window was installed. Then, for the first time, the church was illuminated by gas, supplied from the Bury Road 'works' of the Thetford Gas Company.

Further changes continued 16 years later, when the old organ gallery at the west end was removed, revealing the tower arch and west window. This allowed the ancient west entrance to be re-opened. A new east window was also installed and dedicated, *'to the memory of the late Rev W. Collett, Perpetual Curate of St Mary's 1828-62'*.

Many of St Mary's ministers, but not all, served as Master and Preacher of the Thetford Grammar School. The school and a row of almshouses, situated near-by, was founded by Sir Richard Fulmerston, who died in 1566/67 and was interred in a tomb on the north side of the nave. Sir Richard's will requested, *'The maintenance, of a learned man to preach the word of God in the parish church of St Mary's aforesaid, four times in the year'*.

Towards the end of 1878 the church was closed for several months while the old nave roof was replaced by one of pitch pine. According to the historian Thomas Martin [1696-1771], the nave roof had been destroyed and the church used as a stable by Parliamentarian soldiers during the Civil War. The 1640s was a period when Puritan zealots damaged churches and destroyed many of the images of 'popery' that had survived a century earlier.

At the same time as the nave roof was replaced, the south porch was also restored. The church porch was once used for several important functions, particularly in the medieval church. It was from the church porch that alms were doled out to the poor of the parish by those important lay officials, the churchwardens and overseers. In the 17th and 18th centuries, the poor of St Mary's received an assortment of gifts - bread, meat, lengths of cloth, clothing and money.

Is the only parish church now standing in the Suffolk part of the borough, meanly built, having a square tower with six bells. On the corner of the steeple were placed the symbols of the evangelists in freestone; but, being thought too heavy for the building, they were taken down...The church, chancel and porch, are neatly thatched with reed. **Source:** Thomas Martin, *History of Thetford*, J. Nichols, London [1779].

The church, however, is not just the name we give to a building used for religious worship. It must be remembered that it is also a body or gathering of people who share the same religious beliefs and practices. It continues to play an important part in the religious and social lives of many people.

Countless generations of people, driven by religious devotion and affection for their place of worship, have striven to maintain the fabric of their parish church. While the Church, for its part, has helped to provide spiritual guidance and material welfare for its parishioners.

Sadly for St Mary's, the stone, brick, wood, glass and other materials that form this sacred place, have now become redundant. As each year passes, its uncertain future becomes more precarious.

A True and Perfect Account of All and Singular the Goods Books Ornaments and Utensils belonging to the said Church of Saint Mary aforesaid.
First an organ, also one silver flaggon, one silver cup and stand, and one silver plate, the weight unknown,
The Name and Arms of James Mingay Esquire the Donor are engraved on all the above Communion Plate -
Also one pulpit cloth
Also one large linen Cloth and Napkin for the communion table
Also two common Prayer Books
Also one large Bible of the first translation
Also six Bells with their frames and roppes
Also one large Surplice of Holland
Also one Carpet of Green Cloth for the Communion table
Source: St Mary's Church Terrier 1801.

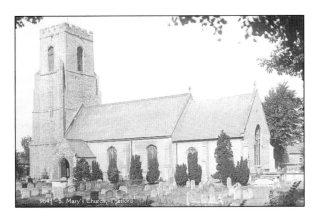

St Mary's Church, circa 1925. For much of the 20th century the maintenance and repair of St Mary's Church continued, aided with funds provided by parishioners. Even so, the six bells, one of which was cast in 1615 by Thetford bell founder John Draper, ceased to peal in 1954 because the tower was so weak. Just over a decade later, the belfry was demolished leaving the tower as it can be seen today.
In the mid-1970s the church ceased to be used for regular worship by the Anglican community but in an effort to keep the church in use, it was later leased to the Roman Catholic Church, for the annual payment of a rose.

St Mary's Church shrouded in a blanket of snow, January 2003. It must have been unimaginable to parishioners before the middle of the 20th century that the ancient church of St Mary-the-Less would ever become redundant, unwanted and uncared for. Now this once sacred edifice, stripped of fittings and furnishings since the late 1980s, presents a sad, desolate scene of neglect and decay.

Whereas reorganisation is the term which most happily applies to the history of the parish church in Norwich, decline is the word which most readily springs to mind in Thetford. Out of a total of twenty-two medieval parish churches, only three remain today; the remaining nineteen have been all but obliterated. From a population of about 4,500 in the 11th century, the town's diminishing prosperity resulted in a population of about 1,500 by the 16th century (Crosby 1986, 49), and the history of its parish churches is a small catalogue of closure. Great St Mary's became the new cathedral in the 1070s; St George's, St Martin's, and the church excavated at St Michael's Close had all gone out of use by the end of the 12th century; St Benet's, St John's and St Margaret's by the end of the 13th century; St Helen's and All Saint's by the end of the 14th century: St Lawrence's, St Edmunds, St Michael's and St Giles' by the end of the 15th century; and four in the 16th century, St Andrew's, St Etheldreda's, St Nicholas's and Holy Trinity. Although the town has expanded greatly since 1958, the three surviving parish churches seem sufficient for present day needs. Source: Neil Batcock, The Ruined And Disused Churches of Norfolk, East Anglian Archaeology 51 [1991]. Reprinted by permission of Norfolk Museums & Archaeology Service.

Passing through the iron gateway leading into the churchyard, St Mary-the-Less stands neglected and desolate in the pale, wintry daylight. Now redundant, through a persistent decline in the number of Thetfordians attending church, the fabric of St Mary's has once again been damaged, mutilated and scarred by the deeds of mindless men.

In keeping with this scene of decay, the surrounding church or graveyard resembles an ageing and forgotten place, even though it stands so close to a busy road and the present-day world.

Moss and lichen cling to the rough, weathered headstones and while many inscriptions have faded along with the memory of those whose names they once proclaimed, others have survived the test of time. Perhaps the stone is of a better quality or the mason cut a deeper groove with his chisel. Or is it that a broad-leafed tree or the closeness of the church has given shelter from the vagaries of the weather?

Of all those inscriptions that are still legible, none is much older than 200 years and few date after the 1850s, when a municipal cemetery was opened beside the London Road. By then, the three local Anglican churchyards had become so overcrowded, if that's the correct word, after centuries of countless interments and the small graveyards of the Dissenters chapels were rapidly filling too.

But amongst the uncared-for headstones, some leaning askew or lying broken on the ground, there is a kind of living past; a story to be told from the brief inscriptions that mark the resting place of those departed and from other fragments of their past lives that have survived, recorded on some document or other.

Wandering through the graveyard studying the headstones, some names appear unfamiliar to me but many others are instantly recalled. Side-by-side, just inside the gateway stand two, small, unpretentious headstones. One is inscribed, *'In memory of Mary the wife of Benjamin Burrell who died 6th April 1807 aged [?] years'*. The inscription on the stone beside Mary has completely faded but it is almost certainly that of Benjamin, her husband who died 14 years earlier.

Mary, whose maiden name was Bull, had married Benjamin on Monday 30th May, 1757, in her local parish church of St Mary's, Bury St Edmunds. Benjamin, a whitesmith and blacksmith by trade, then lived in the parish of St Cuthbert's, Thetford and it was here that they set up their home, in a house between the Dolphin Inn and Spread Eagle Inn, facing what was then the Market Place.

Within 10 years of their marriage, Mary and Benjamin had been blessed with three sons: Joseph, William and James. All three became skilled tradesmen but Joseph in particular, who was apprenticed to his father in 1773, is remembered as being the founder of Thetford's famous engineering firm, Charles Burrell & Sons Limited. But now, like the graves of their Burrell descendants in Thetford's cemetery, their resting places appear to mean little to us. But we must now leave this story, of which there is much more to tell, and look at others from the past who lie at rest in St Mary's churchyard.

Besides the Burrells, who were to feature prominently in local life, there are members of the Bidwell family, whose deeds as brewers, maltsters, merchants and members of the Corporation are well recorded amongst local documentary sources.

Another old Thetford family, well represented in St Mary's churchyard, are the Tyrrells. Like the Bidwells they also have a strong brewing tradition but unlike their close rivals, they appear not to have become deeply entangled with local politics.

Another surname that means little in Thetford today is that of Spendlove but in the 18th and 19th century they were renowned locally for the quality of their clocks and watches. Amongst the Spendloves buried in St Mary's is John Simpson Spendlove, the last member of the family to work as a watchmaker, trading from a small shop in Bridge Street, where he lived with his sister Hannah, until his death in 1852. Hannah died a few years later and now shares her brother's tomb.

It is etched on Robert Ward's headstone, that when he died he was *'deeply lamented'*. I wonder if this sentiment was shared by his former pupils at the Thetford Grammar School. The Reverend Robert Ward, M.A., was master there from 1822 until his death in 1848, at the age of 50 years. There was then only a handful of boys attending the solitary school building. Opposite stood *'a house with a Garden containing by estimation Two Acres and one Rood for the School Master'*. Unlike many people, we know roughly what the School Master earned, *'a Stipend of Twenty Six Pounds Thirteen Shillings and Four Pence'*. We don't know what affliction claimed the life of the Reverend Ward but many of those who died suddenly, without any apparent explanation, were often cited to have suffered *'a visitation from God'*.

There are three inscriptions, however, that instantly remind us of life's tragedies. That of James Arbon, aged 9 years, *'who was drowned while bathing'* on the 15th June, 1842. And by coincidence, the following day two Thetford anglers, John Goodboy of the King's Arms Inn and Edmund Craske, Jnr., a baker, both in their thirties, were drowned when their fishing boat capsized on Fowlmere, near Croxton. I suspect there are many more interred in St Mary's hallowed ground who, after danger caught them unawares, suffered similar tragic deaths.

Mystery shrouds a large, ancient, stone coffin lid that lies overgrown, between the north wall of the chancel and the vestry. It appears to have been re-used in 1826 to mark the resting place of *'William Wright, alias William Jaggard Postman'*, a fact uncovered in the 1920s by the Reverend Tyrrel Green. But like his tombstone, William's life remains a mystery.

St Mary the Less...In the middle of the church, by the pulpit, lies a flat stone, about nine feet six inches long, and about four feet four inches broad: it had a slip of brass once inlaid upon it.
By the font a small stone with a figure in brass gone.
The step before the font is part of a raised grave-stone.
In the chancel, without the rails, two coffin lids, supposed to have originally covered two fine stone coffins now in the belfry. Two smaller were taken up 1770, in the yard, at the east end of the church, one of whose lids serves as a head stone. These four coffins being found at different times are supposed to have belonged to one family. Another reversed lies in the yard by the vestry, over the grave of Edmund Clarke, late clerk, who begged it for this purpose and his name is cut on it... In the chancel is a stone, joining to the north wall; under which are interred, William Tyrrel, gentleman, and Bridget his wife; the Reverend Mr. John Tyrrel their eldest son, sometime schoolmaster of the free-school in this parish, and rector of Santon in Norfolk: also Mr George Tyrell, their second son, who was baptised Jan. 7, 1668, and died Oct, 25, 1732.
On a mural monument, with a pyramid over the south door of the chancel: "In a vault under this place lie the remains of Mrs Frances Le Strange, daughter of George Cook, gentleman, who lies in the same vault. She was

first married to John Monk, esq. of Bokenham-house in Sussex, by whome she had issue two son and three daughters; of whom Anne and Frances, the only two surviving, in great respect to the memory of their dear mother, caused this to be erected. She died Feb. 19, 1725-6, aged 49 years. In the same fault lies Mrs Frances Monk, who died Nov. 14, 1751. In memory of Mrs Anne Monk, who died Jan. 11, 1763."
Extracts from a Register of this church, beginning 1593, ending 1639:
Nicholas Greene, burgess, buried 25 Apr. 1594.
Richard Diggon 28 Septemb. 1594...
Names of some persons who by will requested to be interred in St Mary's church-yard:
Johannes de Sculton 1328.
Johannes Spendlove 1328.
Adam le Sadeler 1328.
Henricus Alstan 1351
Herveus de Runhale 1359...
Source: Thomas Martin, *History of Thetford*, J. Nichols, London [1779].

There are countless numbers of people buried in St Mary's churchyard, indeed in many other places as well, whose lives have left no trace. Lives that have been completely erased by time, as if they had never existed at all. No stone marks their resting place, not even a name in the parish registers or in an ancient will or deed. If anything, St Mary's Church and its neglected graveyard might remind us of those forgotten generations who have gone before.

Finally, ought we to heed the poignant words inscribed upon the tomb of one Thomas Southgate, buried in the yard on the north side of the nave:

'Always suppose thy death is nigh And seek to be prepared to die'.

Undoubtedly one of the most photographic views of Thetford is the tower of St Peter's Church with the 'Bell Corner' in the foreground.

One of the earliest descriptions of St Peter's Church is found in the Reverend Francis Blomefield's historical account of Thetford, published in 1739, ... *'St Peter's Church is now standing on the Norfolk side, in the most public part of the town, and is reckoned the Head Church of the three that are now in use'... 'The present building is of Freestone and Blackflint, and by the appearance of it, don't seem to exceed the time of Edward III [1327-1377]. It hath six bells in a square tower so cracked it seems very weak'...*

Burrell was paid £111 9s. 11¾d. for his painting and glazing work. Subscriptions amounting to £1,239 had been raised, leaving a balance of £846, which was to be paid by means of an annual rate, levied against the principal inhabitants of

St Peter's Church photographed from the Bell Corner in the early years of the 20th century.

achievement but their efforts were stopped by an official of the church, perhaps anxious that the new bells should not become a focus of contested rivalry.

It is now 200 years since the old tower was demolished. Times have indeed changed, so much so that St Peter's Church is no longer used as a place of regular worship. Nevertheless, occasionally the merry peal of St Peter's bells can be heard across the town.

Once again the tower is in need of repair. In 1987 an appeal was launched to raise funds for the renovation of the tower of St Peter's and St Cuthbert's Church so that they may be preserved, not only as a part of our local heritage but for the enjoyment and use of future generations.

The tower survived until 1789 when it was demolished and work began building the tower that is so familiar to us. Undertaken at the same time were many other alterations and repairs to the church and churchyard. These included the demolition of the old south porch, re-roofing of the chancel and nave, a new peal of eight bells and a new east window designed and erected by Mr George Bird Burrell, plumber & glazier, who is best known for his map of Thetford published in 1807. Mr Burrell's window was replaced in 1870 by one paid for by Mr Shelford Bidwell.

The Churchwardens' Accounts reveal that the cost of all this building work was an expensive operation. The total amounted to £2,085 1s. 5d. The new bells, cast by Thomas Osborn at his Downham Market foundry, cost £364 0s. 9d. [old bell included]. Mr

the parish, until the debt and all interest was fully discharged.

One benevolent parishioner, Mr James Mingay, paid for the erection of a cast-iron palisade around the churchyard and a new chandelier above the middle aisle of the church.

The new tower and refurbished church were completed and opened in March 1791. Bell ringers from many parts of Norfolk, Suffolk and Cambridgeshire travelled to Thetford to hear the new bells.

Later that year it was reported that St Peter's bell ringers rung 5,040 changes of bob majors in 3 hours 20 minutes and that the Bury St Edmunds ringers rung the same bells to the general satisfaction of the town. The following morning the Bury ringers had prepared themselves for an attempt at beating the Thetford ringers'

St Peter's - This church, which has been closed for restoration since August last year, is now approaching completion...The old gallery has been removed, and the organ enlarged and rebuilt in the north aisle. The nave roof is entirely new, while the ceiling has been taken away from the roof of the north aisle, and the open woodwork restored. The chancel arch has been rebuilt. The vestry has been doubled in size and very much improved, with an entrance to the outside through the kindness of one who has helped us very liberally. A new lobby has been built at the north side entrance...The east end of the chancel still remains unfinished for a time. A new mode of warming the church will be adopted before winter. **Source:** Thetford & Watton Times, 6 May 1893.

The peal of eight bells, cast by Thomas Osborn of Downham Market in 1790, was tuned and rehung in 1875 and again in 1937. The peal is made up of:-

No.	Note	Inscription	cwts.	qrs	lbs.
1	F	"Cum Voco Venite" Thos. Osborn Fecit 1790	6	0	26
2	E	Thomas Osborn Founder 1790	6	1	8
3	D	Thomas Osborn, Downham, Norfolk, Fecit 1790	6	3	16
4	C	"Our voices shall with joyful sound make hills and valleys echo around."	7	2	10
5	B	"In wedlock's bands all ye who join with hands your hearts unite, so shall our tuneful tongues combine, to laud the nuptial rite."	8	1	1
6	A	Thos. Osborn Fecit 1790.	9	3	6
7	G	Thos. Osborn Founder 1790	12	3	21
8	F	"Percute dulce cano" Town of Thetford 1790 T. Osborn Fecit	18	0	1

Source: Anon., *St Peter's Church Thetford*, H. Green, Thetford, [1953].

This invaluable and interesting drawing of St Peter's Church was made circa 1750 by Thomas Martin. It allows us to appreciate something of the appearance of St Peter's Church and south churchyard prior to the restoration work carried out between 1789-91. A small turret can be seen on the south east corner of the tower. This probably allowed access from the nave into the tower and belfry. Below the turret can be seen the old south porch, once the main entrance into the church by way of the churchyard. At the east end, on the south side of the chancel, can be seen the chantry chapel dedicated to the Virgin Mary and St Katherine and endowed by William Tyllis, a gentleman landowner of the town, who was interred there in 1501. Almost from the moment of William Tyllis's death, a trental - a series of masses - would have been celebrated over his body for the next thirty days. This, of course, was before the Reformation when the whole interior of the church was a colourful scene of painted images and ornaments, stained glass windows and lighted candles. The chancel was separated from the nave by a richly decorated screen. Stairs, of which there is still some evidence, led to the roodloft where the Holy Rood or Cross was in full view above the chancel screen. In 1511 Robert Love, who was Mayor of Thetford in 1506, gave 40s. to the rood-loft, most likely for the provision of lights or candles. Before the Reformation, at the east end of the middle aisle, there was also another chapel, as described by Blomefield. It was dedicated to St Anne, 'in which there was a gild, to the honour of that saint'. In 1483 Thomas Reynberd was buried in this chapel and gave a sum of money to new glaze the windows, and for painting St Paul's tabernacle' - a tabernacle is a niche in an interior wall displaying the image of a saint. Money was also given to sustain the religious Gild of St Anne.
[Drawing courtesy of the Ancient House Museum, Thetford]

Although there were several religious houses in medieval Thetford, inhabited and administered by monks, friars or canons, there was only one such place for women. Perhaps this is not surprising in a society that women played mainly a domestic role.

A community of nuns was first established at Thetford in about 1160, at a site close by the Little Ouse river, south-east of the town. This came about after the Abbot of the great Benedictine Abbey at Bury St Edmunds allowed a cell of nuns to leave Lyng Nunnery, near West Dereham, and settle in Thetford.

This wasn't the first time, however, that a religious community had been established at this site in Thetford. Uvius the first Abbot of Bury St Edmunds is said to have founded a Benedictine monastery there about the year 1020, to commemorate those killed in a great battle between King Edmund and the Danes that took place near-by.

Thetford's parish church of St George, in which the monks once officiated, became the nuns' conventual church. Moreover, in order to provide the nuns of Thetford with a source of revenue, the Abbot also gave them the local parish churches of St Benedict, and All Saints and whatever other possessions belonging to Bury St Edmunds Abbey that remained in Thetford. In return, the nuns were to make an annual payment of 4 shillings to the Abbey infirmary.

At first the nuns' provisions were supplied from the Abbey at Bury and delivered each week by cart but this routine was stopped after the supply cart was robbed on several occasions along the highway between the two towns. According to a 13th century Customary, 35 loaves and 96 gallons of beer [a seemingly over-generous allowance] were sent weekly to Thetford. However, this practice ceased in 1369 when it was agreed that each year the Abbey would grant an adequate supply of corn, barley and 62 shillings in money.

Like their male counterparts, the nuns' daily routine was divided between a regular order of services, contemplation, study and the necessary work of the convent, although servants were probably employed for some menial tasks. The first service of the day was at 2 am when Matins was sung. This was followed by Lauds at 4.30 am, Prime at 6 am, Terce at 9 am, Sext at noon, Nones at 3 pm, Vespers at 4.30 pm and Compline at 6 pm. Mass was also sung each day.

Regular inspections, known as 'visitations', were made by the Bishop or his representative to ensure that each religious house was in good order and well maintained. The visitation in 1514 noted that the books required repairing and, after questioning the Prioress and eight nuns, it was found that two of the nuns expressed a fear that the Prioress was about to receive as nuns, certain unlearned and even deformed persons, particularly one Dorothy Sturghs, who was both deaf and deformed.

The visitation of 1520, undertaken by the Bishop in person, simply resulted in an entry that the nunnery was very poor. There was clearly nothing amiss. Nor was there anything to correct after the visitation of 1526 when there were four novices, in addition to the Prioress.

After the Nunnery was dissolved in February 1537, the last Prioress, Elizabeth Hothe, was given a pension as some compensation. Elizabeth was certainly blessed, for 16 years later she was still enjoying her pension, *'as a good and catholic woman'* at the age of 100 years.

After dissolution, the Nunnery was acquired by Sir Richard Fulmerston, who converted the church of St George into his personal residence, a house called The Place. After Sir Richard's death in 1566/7, his son-in-law, Sir Edward Clere, inherited the estate and it was here, at The Place, that Queen Elizabeth was entertained in 1578.

Fulmerston's former home later became known as Place Farm, an agricultural estate that contained 700 acres early in the 18th century. It was probably about this time, after a new farmhouse was built, that the nuns' former conventual church of St George was converted into a barn.

By the early years of the 20th century, Place Farm had come to be known as The Nunnery, while the old conventual church was used as a grain store. It later served as a stable for racehorses and, during the 1939-45 War, as a billet for Indian soldiers. After many years of disregard, the substantial remains of St George's Church have regained something of their former glory and prestige, having recently been converted into the library of the British Trust for Ornithology - its future preserved.

Seal of the Benedictine Nunnery.

Sir Richard Fulmerston, died 1567

This worthy knight flourished at the Reformation period. Ipswich and the Norfolk village of North Lopham are alike claimed as his birthplace in the early sixteenth century. From about 1535 Fulmerston made Thetford his permanent residence. He was Master of Horse to the Duke of Norfolk, together with whom he came into possession of much Church property in the town, at the dissolution of the monasteries. Sir Richard built the dwelling-house described in his epitaph as the Place Farm, on the site of the ancient nunnery thought to be the earliest religious establishment in Thetford. Sir Edward Clere, High Sheriff of Norfolk and member for Thetford, married Frances, Sir Richard's only daughter...As a pioneer, however, of Protestant charities, Fulmerston deserved well of Thetford. His will contains directions for founding the present grammar school....A further gift to the town, arising from spoils of old religious foundations, were Fulmerston's almshouses for aged and infirm poor..Fulmerston also provided for a preacher, to be paid ten shillings for each of four sermons to be delivered annually in St Mary's Church. Sir Richard represented Thetford in Parliament in 1563. His bones are buried in a vault under the church just mentioned. An imposing memorial to this local benefactor and to Alice his wife occupies a considerable space on the south wall of St Mary's. **Source:** J.L. Smith-Dampier, *East Anglian Worthies,* Basil Blackwell Ltd., Oxford [1949]. Reprinted by permission of Blackwell Publishers.

The interior of St George's Church, once the conventual church of Thetford's community of Benedictine Nuns.
It had been converted into a barn by the time that this drawing was made in the first quarter of the 19th century. Only the nave and south transept of the former church survives today, incorporated into the premises of the British Trust for Ornithology.

This vaulted building was possibly the nuns' chapter house - where the Prioress and nuns would meet each day to discuss the business of the nunnery.
When this drawing was made, in the early years of the 19th century, it is believed the building was used as a brewhouse.
Most nunneries in this country were very small institutions. While monks appear to have come from all classes of society, nuns were generally from the wealthier sections.

Great Inns Of The Past Recalled *Thetford & Watton Times, 21 July 1989*

The Christopher, Fleece, George, Half Moon, Spread Eagle, and White Hart are the names of a few inns that once traded in Thetford. From an early time, the inn provided accommodation and refreshment for the traveller. On busy main roads the inn was often a substantial house that catered for large numbers of travellers and their horses. Elaborate assembly and banqueting rooms were provided for entertainments, social gatherings and the transaction of business and trade.

For the reconstruction of old inns and their function in former times, details can be found in newspapers of yesteryear and other documentary sources. In the 18th and early 19th centuries there were six inns situated in White Hart Street and Bridge Street, Thetford's main thoroughfare. They were the Anchor, Bell, Fleece, George, King's Head and White Hart.

The Bell Inn, circa 1885. The timber-framed Bell Inn dates from at least the end of the 15th century and has probably been Thetford's premier hostelry from that time. Part of the present building, the range running alongside King Street, dates from the late 15th/early 16th century.

The Anchor, which probably succeeded the Christopher Inn before the end of the 18th century, still stands close to the Town Bridge and the Little Ouse river. It once had stabling for 40 horses and in 1804 it was reported, 'a great trade of corn is carried on in this

Their route from Cambridge was through Newmarket (13 miles from Cambridge), Barton Mills (10 miles from Newmarket), and Thetford (10 miles from Barton Mills). They baited their horses at the Bull at Newmarket, dined at the Bull at Barton Mills, and supped and slept at the George at Thetford. 'A great many soldiers at Thetford going on to Norwich. Prodigious fine road from Cambridge to Thetford.'
Next day, May 23rd [1776], they went from Thetford to Attleborough (15 miles from Thetford) where they dined at the Cock and from Attleborough to Norwich - another 15 miles, where they supped and slept at the Kings Head. **Source:** James Woodforde, *The Diary of A Country Parson 1758-1802*, James Beresford, [Ed.], Oxford University Press [1978]. Reprinted by permission of A.P. Watt Ltd on behalf of B.W. Beresford, J.C. Beresford and Rosemary Beresford.

house'. In the Anchor yard, regular auctions of agricultural implements and livestock were also held. In the late 18th century, general auctions were also held at the King's Head, built in 1778-79 with stabling for 25 horses.

The Bell has traded for at least 500 years and continues as Thetford's principal hostelry. In the so-called 'coaching days', the Bell was a stopping place for most of the important scheduled coaches that passed through the town. It was also noted for its hospitality and as a popular meeting place for the local aristocracy and lesser gentry.

A close rival to the Bell was the George Inn, known today as Bridge House, a private residence. The George hosted the first Thetford Wool Fair, founded in 1793 by Norfolk's famous agriculturalist, Thomas W. Coke, of Holkham Hall. After the George closed in 1815, the annual wool fair was moved to the Bell. Among the many social events held at the George was a 'Rejoicing Ball' to celebrate Nelson's great naval victory at the Battle of Copenhagen in 1801. The tickets cost 5s, tea and coffee included.

BELL INN, THETFORD, NORFOLK
ELIZ. RADCLIFFE respectfully informs the nobility, gentry and her friends, customers of her late husband, that she means to carry on the business of the said Inn. She returns her most grateful acknowledgements to her late husbands friends, and most humbly solicits a continuance of their favours, assuring them that nothing shall be wanting on her part to render the accommodation in every department such as to merit their countenance and support.
The mail coach passengers breakfast and sup at the above inn every day. - Also a coach sets out from the above inn at Six o'clock on Tuesday, Thursday and Saturday mornings, for the Saracen's Head, Snowhill and returns from London on Mondays, Wednesdays and Fridays, and arrive at Thetford at Six o'clock in the evening. **Source:** *Bury & Norwich Post, 31 October 1792.*

Another inn which once rivalled the Bell and has given its name to a street, is the White Hart. The 'great dining room' of the White Hart Inn was a popular venue for cock-fighting in the 1770s. Situated at the north end of White Hart Street was the Fleece. When offered for sale in 1830 it had stabling for 30 horses.

At Thetford the decline of the inn began from the middle of the 19th century, as many travellers deserted the turnpike roads to take advantage of a new mode of transport - the railway. By the end of the 19th century the Fleece had closed, while the King's Head and White Hart had declined in status to that of a public house. The Bell and the Anchor both survive to cater for a later form of traveller - the motorist.

JAMES CRAIGS

Late butler to Sir Geo. Jernegham, Bart. now gives Notice, That he has taken the WHITE HART INN at THETFORD in Norfolk, to enter upon immediately; so that the same inn (which is large and commodious) may be fitted up in the best Manner against the next Thetford Assizes, for the Reception of the old customs, or any others; who in return for the Favour of their company, may at all Times depend upon meeting with the most decent and obliging Behaviour, and of being constantly supplied with the neatest Beds, Provisions of all Kinds, (well dressed and served up in a genteel Manner) great Variety of Wines and other Liquors, with handsome Post-Chaises and able Horses; also good stables for Horses, which will be well taken care of, and provided for with the best Hay and Corn; and whatever else may be necessary will be had, for the convenient and agreeable Accommodation of such may oblige him with their custom. **Source:** *Ipswich Journal, 3 March 1759.*

This large house that once stood at the north end of White Hart Street is another of Thetford's old inns. Although it has a fairly modern facade, in the early years of the 18th century it was known as the Fleece Inn and sometimes the Golden Fleece Inn. Beer was probably brewed on the premises until the late 1820s when a quantity of brewing equipment was offered for sale on the premises. The Fleece then had stabling for 20 horses and finally closed in the 1880s. Photographed circa 1910.

The Dolphin stands on what was once the north side of Thetford's medieval market place, before it was moved to a new site in 1786. A deed of 1510 describes an inn on the north side of the market place, 'called of old tyme the Dolphyn, now the Grffyn'...

In the early years of the 19th century, the Dolphin was one of four Thetford public houses owned by local brewer Thomas Vipan. In 1837 the Dolphin, containing extensive stabling, barn, piggeries, granary, yards and garden, was purchased by Mr Bidwell of Thetford. It was also described as, 'well worth the attention of Jobbers and Dealers, it having long been frequented by Drovers to and from Norwich and Downham Markets'. The Dolphin is the only public house surviving in this old part of the town. This photograph dates from the 1880s. [Photograph courtesy of the Ancient House Museum, Thetford]

The Anchor, decorated for the Coronation of King Edward VII in 1902, almost certainly stands on at least part of the site of an ancient inn known as the Christopher. The Town Bridge, standing close by, was once known as the Christopher Bridge. It is not known exactly when in the 18th century that the Christopher closed but the Anchor appears for the first time in 1775 with a notice advertising coals at 3d. per chaldron at the 'Anchor Key or Wharf'.

A newspaper advertisement in 1804, also tells us something of the Anchor Inn, 'The great trade at this house in Wine, Ale, Spirits &c., has been well known for the last 20 or 30 years...A great trade in Corn &c., is carried on at this house...it also has stable room for 40 horses'. Moreover, newspapers in the early years of the 19th century carry advertisements for the sale of livestock, agricultural equipment and other goods from the Anchor yard. It is interesting to note that 3 dozen spittoons were included amongst the contents of the Anchor when sold in 1861.

What we today would probably consider to be 'heavy' or excessive drinking, was a common and accepted way of life for many from all classes of society in the 19th century. The consumption of alcohol in the form of beer, wine or spirits was not an option that could easily be refused, for it was strongly embedded in the culture and traditions of a male dominated society.

Besides the popular activity of drinking purely for pleasure, drinking could be found, often in a very ritualised form, in the work place, in business life and at the numerous clubs and societies that were established and pursued in the rooms of inns and public-houses. Moreover, alcoholic drinks were used extensively for medicinal purposes and were considered a safe alternative to most public water supplies at a time when there were few non-alcoholic beverages.

Although the wealthier classes of society were able to consume liberal amounts of alcohol in their private homes without complaint, authority had long associated the public-house as a centre of disorder, drunkenness, immorality and as a cause of poverty amongst the lower classes. After the Beer Act of 1830, opportunities for consuming beer considerably increased. Before the 1830 Act, all public-houses were licensed through the local Justices and publicans had to find sureties for good behaviour on the premises. After the Act, virtually any householder who paid a small Excise fee, could sell beer on the premises. This effort by the Government to reduce spirit consumption and encourage a more sober society by promoting what they considered to be *'a harmless and wholesome beverage'*, appears to have had little effect in reducing intemperance.

It is against this background that temperance reform began in the 19th century. Despite frequent attacks on the public-house from various sections of society, there was no common organisation, until the emergence of the temperance movement, to discourage the population from the apparent evils of intoxicating liquors. The temperance movement, which initially advocated abstinence from spirits while permitting beer and wine in moderation, has its origins in America before appearing in Ireland in the late 1820s and then Scotland and England. The first English temperance society was formed in Bradford, Yorkshire in 1830.

The more radical form of temperance, known as Teetotalism, really began two years later when

> *It was very common for many of our public houses to be open all night, as Bruces Act for closing them, as now at 11 o'clock was not in force. Drunken brawls and fights even in our own streets were a common occurrence. I have seen many a drunken man dragged to gaol by our old parish constables...* **Source:** extract of a letter from Robert Nurse of Thetford, to the Editor of the *Thetford & Watton Times, 3 July 1888.*

John Livesey and a group of friends, known as the 'Seven men of Preston' - most of whom were Methodist lay preachers - took a pledge of total abstinence *'from all liquors of an intoxicating quality, whether ale, porter, wine or ardent spirits, except as medicine'.* From there, along with other teetotallers, they set out across the country to rescue the intemperate and to check some of the evils of indulgence. Within a decade, Teetotalism had extended its influence over the country, including the towns of East Anglia, particularly those that held a strong Nonconformist interest.

The first temperance organisation formed in Thetford appears to have been a Teetotal Society established in January 1839. They celebrated their first anniversary the following

year, with a dinner for seventy members, at the Wesleyan School Room [now Nether Hall] in Nether Row. Teetotalism very probably came to Thetford after a visit of a Teetotal missionary who was most probably a Methodist. Indeed, Thetford's leading temperance advocators at this time are known to have been either Primitive or Wesleyan Methodists. One of the most active was Stephen Oldman [1815-1901], a total abstainer and a Wesleyan Methodist, whose late father had helped to establish the Methodist Church in Thetford. Stephen Oldman later severed his links with the Wesleyan Church for what he considered their apparent indifference to temperance, by not embracing Teetotalism.

Although it would appear there was work for temperance reformers in Thetford, it is difficult to assess the extent of intemperance amongst the layers of Thetford's society. A report of the Borough in 1834 stated, *'Great complaints are made, and we think justly so, of the state of the public houses which are often disorderly'.* In 1845 there were twenty inns and public-houses and at least fourteen beer houses, giving an approximate population ratio of 116 inhabitants per public house. With so many retail outlets selling intoxicating liquors it is not surprising that Thetford had its drunkards. One has only to look at the number of cases appearing before the local magistrates. There must have been others too, while not habitual drunkards, who spent a large portion of their income on alcohol, leaving their families without basic necessities.

The call for temperance gained a lot of interest and became a subject of much local debate, ranging around biblical quotes, moral and social ethics and the growing interest in medical and scientific knowledge. Nonetheless,

Thetford's temperance reformers encountered plenty of forceful opponents, certainly during its early years. At many public temperance meetings in the town, disturbances erupted as drunkards and others with an interest in the drink trade attempted to break-up the proceedings. One such meeting affected was a lecture given in the Town Hall by one of the first nation-wide Teetotal missionaries, James Teare, a Methodist minister and one of the 'Seven men of Preston'. Teare spoke with Bible in hand and later claimed that, *'he had been convinced of the evils of beer by his visitations of the poor'*.

It was at these meetings that people were encouraged to sign or make some kind of pledge, either simply to abstain from ardent liquors or from all alcoholic liquors - the more radical pledge of Teetotalism. Pledges could be made for a short or long term, ranging from a few weeks to a lifetime. Some people were understandably reluctant to pledge themselves, believing it would imply that they had been drunkards. Although many preferred moderation, and along with a hard-core of habitual tipplers, scorned the cry of teetotalism, an unfaltering resolve and persistence amongst Thetford's leading temperance advocators appears to have made gradual progress, as more and more pledged themselves.

Besides frequent lectures, some of which were held in the open on the Market Place, attacking the drink trade, illustrating the effects of alcohol on the body and generally tempting the inebriate to a life of total abstinence, there were all sorts of temperance galas and other entertainments, *'to draw young men from the enticements of the public-house, too much frequented in this borough on Saturday evenings'*. So wrote a reporter of the Bury & Norwich Post in 1862. Tea, coffee and other non-alcoholic drinks were served at these functions. After a new Primitive Methodist Chapel was built and opened in Guildhall Street in the early 1860s, the former Primitive Methodist Chapel on the edge of Melford Common was utilised as a temperance hall, a special meeting place for the growing number of abstainers.

The former Primitive Methodist Chapel and Temperance Hall.

It was in the Temperance Hall in 1872 that agricultural labourers, who for a long time had been criticised more than others for their intemperance, held one of the first local branch meetings of the National Agricultural Labourers' Union. After the meeting, several labourers are reported to have taken the pledge, reinforcing the Union's ties with the Primitive Methodists and the temperance cause.

From the late 1860s there were further significant developments, followed by two decades that were some of the most active and successful for Thetford's temperance reformers. The Beer Act 1869 once again placed the licensing of public-houses in the hands of the Justices and in 1872 the opening hours for public-houses was regulated and reduced, something for which Thetford's Teetotallers had petitioned for years. Pubs were now required to close at 11 o'clock rather than stay open all night as they often did.

Thetford:- Sunday Closing of Public Houses
The publicans of this town are busy inducing people to sign petitions against closure of public-houses on Sundays. **Source:** *Bury & Norwich Post, 27 June 1862.*

A number of different temperance organisations were formed in the town during the 1870s and 80s. The Town Hall meetings of the Gospel and Blue Ribbon Association, in particular, were very often packed to capacity. As many as one hundred and fifty people at a time are reported to have come forward to take the pledge and don a blue ribbon as a sign of their new-found temperance. Members of the Church of England Temperance Society also wore a blue badge. A blue and white one was worn if they had also taken an additional pledge to abstain from tobacco.

Perhaps the progress made by Thetford's temperance reformers can best be gauged by the appearance of a Temperance Hotel at the bottom of Well Street in 1874. The Temperance Hotel or 'British Workman' as it was sometimes called, provided accommodation without the sale of intoxicating drinks. The £500 necessary to purchase the house was raised by an issue of £1 shares. So successful was the venture, that

Driven From Drink

The Melbourne Hotel, Well Street, circa 1965. This building was formerly The Temperance Hotel or 'British Workman'.

within a few months, plans were put forward to extend the hotel.

However, despite the fervent activities of local temperance societies over a period of four decades, bringing the subject of intemperance into the open, apparently without any serious opposition from Thetford's extensive brewing interests, something had seriously retarded the impetus of the temperance interest by the early 1890s. Apart from the Temperance Hotel and the Bands of Hope attached to the different Sunday schools, all the different temperance organisations had almost ceased to function by the mid-1890s.

Why had the loud call for temperance faded to a whisper? Could it be that everyone in Thetford had signed the pledge and the public-houses were empty? Of course it wasn't the answer. There were still just as many public-houses, although the ratio of public houses to inhabitants had slightly improved to 1 to 148 at the end of the 19th century. In the whole of England it was 1 to every 326 inhabitants. Drunkards were still appearing before the local magistrates and even a few who had taken the pledge were once again consuming alcohol. Part of the reason for the decline in local temperance activities can be found in the absence of staunch, outspoken radicals such as Stephen Oldman. The formation of so many different temperance groups may also have created a fragmented cause, rather than a united one.

But there are much wider issues, resulting from social progress and reform. A new society had evolved, generally much better educated and one that was able to enjoy more leisure time and participate in a wide-range of sports and pursuits. Hard work, respectability, sobriety and family life had also become important values in many more Victorian homes. It is arguable that social changes in the 19th century had made a greater impact on people's drinking habits than the endeavours of the temperance movement, valuable as they were.

Another point to be considered is the greater availability of a wide-range of non-alcoholic beverages such as tea, coffee, cocoa and sparkling drinks. The Artificial Mineral Waters Company sold over two million bottles of their soft drinks at the alcohol-free Great Exhibition in 1851. Safer drinking water was also obtainable in Thetford after 1877 when the Water Works began supplying the town from a deep artesian well just off the Mundford Road. Whatever the cause of its decline, the temperance movement had become unfashionable in a more affluent and self-determined society. Even attempts by a few life-long abstainers to establish a local temperance society in the early 1900s failed.

Today, with so many places in the town from where alcohol can be purchased and consumed, one might consider the temperance cause to have been a complete failure. In fact it is difficult to appreciate that such a popular movement ever existed, especially as there are so few memorials to remind us of those solemn pledges taken by many of our ancestors. The old Temperance Hotel was demolished in the mid-1960s and the former Temperance Hall in Melford Bridge Road is now divided into three cottages [numbers 18, 20 & 22]. However, in the cemetery, almost completely hidden by a large bush, there is a fine marble stone:

RAISED BY SYMPATHIZING FRIENDS
IN MEMORY OF
WILLIAM BUXTON MILLER
WHOSE LIFE WAS SUDDENLY CUT SHORT IN THE MIDST OF HIS LABOURS AS A TEETOTALLER
AND A PRIMITIVE METHODIST
ON JANUARY 7th 1877 IN THE 52nd YEAR OF HIS AGE

HIS PLEDGE FAITHFULLY KEPT AND EARNESTLY RECOMMENDED FOR THE LAST 13 YEARS OF HIS LIFE
"I ABSOLVE TO ABSTAIN FROM ALL INTOXICATING DRINK, AND TO DISCOUNTENANCE THE CAUSES AND PRACTICE OF INTEMPERANCE".
THE CAUSE OF HIS UNTIMELY DEATH
AN ACCIDENT
AT THE TWO MILE BOTTOM WORKS

On The Thetford Public House Signs

*I feel griev'd for the people and in truth well I may
When there are so many objects which lead me to say,
What a pretty menagerie we have in our town,
First with tame beasts then wild beasts and birds of
renown.*

*There's a fine old 'Spread Eagle' that bird of renown,
Which so long have been kept by the men of the town,
And some men will keep it though they ever suppose,
As it don't eat their children, it ne'er swallows their
clothes.*

*We next see two horses one 'White' and one 'Black'
Which never as yet had a man across their back
But put them in harness, whether single or pairs,
And they'll soon trot away with your table and chairs.*

*A fine old 'Red Lion' is the next beast that follows,
But I never yet heard whether Nero or Wallis,
It is not in their nature to live upon stones,
When they've eat up your meat they'll roar for your
bones.*

*A 'Dragons' the next brute held up to be seen'
Tis' so long since George slew him he may well be turned
'Green'
Though such a strange creature, take it granted from me
That the men who support him are greener than he.*

*There's a stag that has run til It's called a 'White Hart'
Though it can't run fast now, tis still doing its part,
With the 'Fleece' 'Bell' and 'Chequers' and others
combined
To take off your comforts & injure mankind*

*There's a very fine 'Partridge' that's kept with a 'Dog'
Which can beat all the sportsmen, and e'en squires can
flog,
But men who love sporting and attend much to this
Will soon find there is something amiss.*

*There's a 'Dukes Head' and 'Kings Head' whose 'Arms'
once were 'Chains',
If their dupes' heads are like these heads they've not
many brains,
What queer things men fancy to help on their trades,
Cutting Kings into pieces putting 'Queen' in the 'Shades'.*

*There are men in the 'Moon' so some people say,
But they who keep outside are wiser than they,
To live in such air, make most men feel strange
And lucky they'll be, if they don't loose their change.*

*There's a fine 'Coach' and four, who'er wish to drive
All their comforts from home, and their children deprive,
With their wives of the pleasure their presence should
bring,
Turning joy into sorrow their fond hearts to wring.*

*There's the 'Albion' we find though the nam'es rather
new,
With a fine red brick 'Castle' built up in full view,
That King Alcohols subjects may call in and stay
When appetite's passion shall prevent saying nay.*

*As a King they do crown him, and it's right they suppose
So they find him a 'Crown' that's decked with a 'Rose',
A 'Prince' to his aid, binding fetter on fetter,
While his victims insist they could not do better.*

*But what'er his poor dupes may think in the rancour
It is strange that the landsmen should e'er want an
'Anchor',
But lest they should lose her they will splice her cable
Though they have no bread to put on their own table.*

*As the tide of intemperance injures the brave,
A life boat puts out, poor drunkards to save,
But the makers of drunkards have out-stepp'd the mark
By erecting instead, a counterfeit 'Ark'.*

*Lest I tire your patience and think me to blame
I'll be leaving off now though there's more I might name,
Just allow me one more to finish the dish,
We have a 'Good Woman' who'll cook your fish.*

*Don't misunderstand me, I'm ready at call
What is said upon one sign applies to them all,
The strong drink that is sold is Britain's great curse
It will strip both your person & empty your purse,
Though my Rhyme be a poor one, don't blame it amiss,
Had I not lov'd the drunk'd I'd ne'er written this.*

P. Ellis Thetford, Nov. 1868

Source: the original of this amusing rhyme, mocking Thetford's pubs and their patrons, can be seen at Thetford's Ancient House Museum. It was printed and published on a single sheet of paper. The writer, P. Ellis, was most probably, Phillip Ellis, the manager of Thetford's Temperance Hotel, situated in Well Street, in the early 1880s.

What we today call the pub, or public-house, has been a centre of social activity and the sale of alcoholic drink for consumption on, or off, the premises for countless generations.

In earlier times the pub was known as the ale, beer or tippling house. Please note, a tippling house was a place where ale or beer was sold and does not imply excessive drinking. The ale or beer was, very often, brewed on the premises.

There was certainly a great increase in the number of beerhouses after the Beerhouse Act of 1830 which permitted any householder, assessed for the Poor Rate, to obtain a justices licence for two guineas a year, allowing the sale of beer from the house, to be consumed on or off the premises.

At Thetford, as elsewhere, beerhouses were to be found mostly in the working-class areas, in the back streets and on the fringes of the town. Two good examples of former beerhouses are the Albion, Castle Street and the Ark, Norwich Road.

But not all public-houses originated as beerhouses. Among Thetford's pubs there are a number once described as inns: the Angel, Black Horse, Dolphin, Green Dragon, Kings Head and Red Lion. The inn not only provided alcoholic refreshment but also food and accommodation. The inn was most likely to be found in the town centre or beside a main road.

Many pubs began their lives as ordinary dwelling houses and, prior to the 1920s - in some instances much later - there was little to distinguish the exterior of the pub from an ordinary private house. Most pubs lacked any form of commercialism, apart from a signboard displayed outside. The name on each signboard can reveal a wealth of knowledge and history.

For example, it is perhaps no coincidence that an old pub called the Chequers stood in King Street, adjacent to the King's House, what is believed to be the site of an ancient manor house. The heraldic arms of Thetford's medieval manorial lords, the De Warenne family, is a chequered field of 'or' [gold] and 'azure' [blue].

An evocative photograph taken outside the front of an unidentified local pub towards the end of the 19th century. The gentleman on the left is William 'Bill' Stroulger, licensed victualler of the Albion beerhouse circa 1895-1915. [Photograph courtesy of Norma Howard]

Chequers: Pubs with many stories explaining their names can all be correct no matter which story they adopt for their particular pub. The Romans would emblazon a chequer sign on the outside of a Taberna to signify that games such as chess were played therein. The arms of the 'Great Earl Warenne' who was given the power of granting licenses to sell beer are 'simply cheqy or and azure'. **Source:** Paul Corballis, *'Pub Signs',* Lennard Publishing [1988]. Reprinted by permission of Lennard publishing.

During their history, one or two of Thetford's pubs have had several different names depicted on their signboard. The names have been changed to commemorate important events, people, the whims of fashion or that of the landlord. The Prince of Wales, a former pub in St Nicholas Street, was once the Prince of Wales' Feathers, the Prince Albert, [in 1871] and before that the Red Cow. In 1984 the Bridge Tavern was renamed Flints and is now called The Bridge.

Albion: This ancient and poetic name for England is Gaelic in origin. Legend says this son of Neptune discovered England and ruled it for about a half century. Another story is that Albion was a Roman and, having come to Britain became the first Christian martyr here. **Source:** Paul Corballis, *'Pub Signs',* Lennard Publishing [1988]. Reprinted by permission of Lennard publishing.

I can only guess at the location of several local beerhouses and pubs which appear in documentary records. Where in Thetford was the Admiral Keppel [in 1780], the Engine and Tender [in 1853], the Golden Lion [also in 1853], the Queens Head [in 1846] and [in 1776] the Six Bells?

Pubs certainly come and go. Of the thirty-one licensed houses which traded in the early 1900s, many have been converted into other uses or have completely disappeared, leaving little to remind us of their existence. Even recently a modern, purpose-built pub, The Rights of Man, named after the famous book written by Thomas Paine [1737-1809], a native of Thetford, was opened in 1968 by Mr Michael Foot, MP. It was renamed The Warrener in 1979 and earlier this year was closed.

Lot 2 A FREE PUBLIC HOUSE CALLED "THE GOLDEN LION" adjoining the above cottages (Back Street), with good stabling for four horses; warehouse, detached, a commodious loft; and good yard, with cartway to the road, and every convenience for a private Brewhouse, now in the occupation of Thacker, at the rent of £14 per annum. Also 2 newly erected cottages adjoining the said public-house, now in the occupation of Webster and Mott, at the rent of £5 each. The public-house is well situated and commands a good trade of not less than 3 barrels per week. **Source:** *Bury & Norwich Post, 22 June 1853.*

Petty Sessions - John Carter of the Horse Shoe Inn applied for an extension of one hour before 6 am, so that his customers could have refreshment before they went to their work. Inspector Simpson opposed the application, and the Bench refused it, as they did not consider beer was necessary so early in the morning. **Source:** *Thetford & Watton Times, 8 June 1893.*

This small, flint cottage that stood in Croxton Road [now Old Croxton Road], was a 19th century beerhouse known as The Plough. Its signboard depicted seven stars - the constellation Ursa Major and commonly known as the Plough. The Plough beerhouse closed sometime soon after 1883 and in 1988 the cottage, number 20, was demolished. Photographed 1975.

The Albion public house, situated at number 93 Castle Street, displays a date-mark '1820' on the west gable. The adjoining land was once known as Gallows Close. The Albion appears to have begun as a beerhouse about the middle of the 19th century. The 1861 Census records Abraham Woolsey as 'beerhouse keeper, Albion beerhouse'. By 1874 Woolsey's son-in-law, George Oldfield, had taken over. In those days, the Albion was numbered 73 Castle Street but must have been renumbered later after a terrace of new houses was built and others demolished on that side of the street in the late 19th and early 20th century.

Suffolk brewer Greene King purchased the Albion beerhouse for £600 in 1888 and since then the premises have undergone several refurbishments and alterations, reflecting changing fashions and social trends. The adjoining cottage at number 95 was added to the pub premises in the mid-1970s. The signboard now depicts the Albion, the only surviving Norfolk wherry. Photographed 2003.

For a number of years in the 19th century, this cottage, number 6 Mill Lane [once Garden Place], was the Flower Pot beerhouse. In the middle of the century it is known to have been a popular haunt of poachers and probably other local criminals. It was then kept by John Spalding who described himself as a 'brewer' and it is likely that a small volume of beer was brewed on the premises or in an adjoining outhouse. The Flower Pot appears to have closed by the end of the 19th century. This narrow alley, leading off from Mill Lane, is still known by some locals as Flower Pot Alley. Photographed 2002.

Bygone Days When Street Was 'Great' *Thetford & Watton Times, 25 January 1991*

Magdalen Street is one of six streets that radiate from the Market Place. In the 19th century, it was known as Great Magdalen Street, while Castle Street was often referred to as Little Magdalen Street. In the late 1950s and early 1960s, Magdalen Street was extended at its northern end with the construction of new houses and bungalows. Until then it terminated with a sharp left turn into Lime Kiln Lane, then a narrow, hedge-lined by-way.

At one time, exactly when is not clear, Magdalen Street continued in a straight line northwards, joining the Norwich Road somewhere near the present roundabout. It may have been the old road known as Wrethamgate.

Magdalen Street's most interesting feature is its shape. Anyone standing at Doran's Corner and looking northwards will immediately notice that the street gradually widens until it becomes quite broad and spacious. Here it is bisected by Grove Lane [once Botany Bay Lane] and Melford Bridge Road. At this junction stands the Black Horse public-house, from where the street gradually becomes narrower as it continues towards Lime Kiln Lane.

A street with this cigar-shaped characteristic often indicates an early site of a street market or fair. Thetford's *'Charter of Incorporation'*, granted in 1574, mentioned *'one Market Fair yearly to be held and kept there on Mary Magdalen Day and to continue for two days'*. It was probably reaffirming an ancient custom that may date back to the 13th century when, it is believed, a local church dedicated to St Mary Magdalen was founded. However, although it is tempting to suggest that Magdalen Street was once the site of Magdalen Fair [or Mawdlin Fair as it was also known], there are other alternative venues.

> *St. Mary Magdalen.*
> *Was a parish church before it was converted into an hospital...*
> *This hospital was founded by John de Warren, earl of Surrey, and had the church or chapel of St. Mary Magdalen annexed to it, from which it takes its name. It stood some distance from the town near the road to Norwich. The piece of land upon which it stood is called Mawdlin [Magdalen] Acre. Opposite to it stood Magdalen-cross, at which Shropham hundred court was sometimes kept, after it was granted from the crown.*
> *The founder endowed it with several parcels of land to a considerable value. By degrees it became possessed of 260 acres of land, and 604 acres of pasture and heath, and liberty of four fold-courses in Thetford, Kilverstone, Croxton, and other places.*
> **Source:** Thomas Martin, *'The History of Thetford'* J. Nichols, London [1779].

In the time of the historian, Francis Blomefield [1705-1752], before the Market Place was moved to its present site, Magdalen Fair was held at the end of Magdalen Street, in the area between the Green Dragon public-house and St Cuthbert's Church. In the 19th century it was held on the Market Place and adjoining streets, not as one would expect on Mary Magdalen Day [July 22nd] but on August 2nd and 3rd.*

In 1849 Magdalen Fair was reported to be *'the largest known for 40 years past'... 'so densely crowded it was difficult to pass. There was much done in the way of amusement as well as business'*.

Magdalen Fair survived in Thetford until it was abolished by the Corporation in 1876. By then, the original purpose of a fair as a trading centre had declined. Many of today's annual leisure fairs are the remnants of medieval fairs, once important for the trading of merchandise.

Besides its interesting shape, Magdalen Street is lined with an interesting mixture of buildings which reflect the diversity of Thetford's past and present society. Some are humble dwellings, such as the row of almshouses founded by Sir Charles Harbord, in 1679, for six poor men. Others are substantially built and in between are many modest, terraced cottages and houses, built in varying proportions of brick and flint. Some of them are older than one might imagine.

One house, which now forms numbers 16 and 18, was bought by the Corporation in the 1760s and converted into the Borough Workhouse or House of Industry. Soon after the Union Workhouse was built, just off the Bury Road in 1836, the old Borough Workhouse was sold to a local brewer and converted into four cottages.

The 1851 Census, taken on the night of 30th March, recorded 322 people resident in Magdalen Street. An analysis of their ages, sex, marital status, relationship within the household, occupations, place of birth and household size would make an interesting comparison with today's population.

Later this year we shall be taking part in another national census - perhaps many years from now, historians will be making those comparisons.

* By 1582 the Julian calendar had become 10 days adrift of the solar year. In that year, Pope Gregory XIII adjusted the Julian calendar by 10 days, to make it more accurate. This new Gregorian calendar, or reformed Julian calendar, was accepted by most of Catholic Europe in 1582. In Protestant England, however, it was 3rd September 1752, before the change was made. It resulted in the immediate loss of 10 days when introduced, so that the 3rd September 1752 became the 14th. September. Mary Magdalen day, traditionally celebrated on the 22nd July came to be celebrated on 2nd August.

Magdalen Street looking towards the Market Place in the very early years of the 20th century. It is in the immediate foreground, where the street is at its widest. Most of the properties that line Magdalen Street are residential, including the flint cottages in the left foreground, some of which were built as early as the first quarter of the 18th century. Notwithstanding the Black Horse public house and one or two small shops, it is at the end of the street nearest the Market Place, however, where most of Magdalen Street's commercial premises have traditionally been found.

A view of Magdalen Street, looking north, in the early years of the 20th century. On the right, but just out of view, stands the Black Horse public house. In the far distance, across the line of the roadway, is a row of flint cottages, now demolished. The left or west side of the street is lined with a variety of houses. Perhaps, as a group of dwellings, it stands among the most interesting in Thetford.

On a warm, sunny day you may often find octogenarian Dorothy 'Dot' Mutum watching the world pass by outside the front of her Bury Road home in Thetford. Just a few feet away, heavy lorries and other motor vehicles roar past, filling the air with noise and pollution so that it is impossible to hold a conversation without shouting.

What a different scene from that of nearly 87 years ago when Dot was born, just a few doors away from her present home. Traffic noise was then almost non-existent on a minor highway like the Bury Road, particularly as most travellers on local roads were pedestrians.

Many local businesses and working-class people relied upon 'shank's pony or mare', as well as a variety of hand-carts to move all manner of wares and goods about the town. What traffic sounds there were came from the 'clip-clop' of horses, the gentle clatter of a steam-powered traction engine or, at worst, the very rare reverberation from *'the obnoxious motor car'*, as it was described by one town councillor in the early years of the 20th century.

As Dot gazes across the road, to the familiar outline of St Mary's Crescent, she remembers her early childhood. No houses stood there but a field used by the Boys' Grammar School. From time to time sheep were put out to graze on the field to keep the grass down to a playable level. One of Dot's youthful errands was to slip into the field to collect bucketsful of sheep droppings for her father's tomato plants. *'Dad used to grow some lovely tomatoes'*, she recalls.

The dwellings that form St Mary's Crescent are Thetford's first council houses, built by the Borough Council between 1912 and 1914 for *'working-class families'*. They were officially called 'Corporation Dwellings' but were soon nicknamed the 'White City', a name that has stuck, perhaps because of the light-coloured paint treatment on their rendered exteriors.

Almost opposite Dot's house, running west alongside the old Grammar School field, was a rough track that now forms the line of the modern Icknield Way. It led to allotments and smallholdings where Nelson Crescent, St Margaret's Crescent and Saxon Place now stand.

Dorothy 'Dot' Mutum [1905-2000]
at the front of her home, 85 Bury Road.

Another old track that led off the Bury Road, nearly opposite the workhouse, had a wooden gate that was always kept shut. This was the entrance to Thetford's Isolation Hospital, a small group of corrugated-iron buildings that stood a quarter of a mile from the main road, close to where the Fulmerston Road Christian Fellowship Church stands today. The hospital, built in the early 1900s for smallpox cases, was partly destroyed by a fire in 1916 while occupied by troops. It was rebuilt in 1925 and finally dismantled 10 years later.

Like many Old Thetfordians, Dot clearly remembers the numerous tramps or 'roadsters' who passed along the Bury Road and who, in winter time, use to warm themselves in front of the coke furnace at the Gas Works. Once past the Gas Works there was nothing but fields and Barnham Cross Common, apart from the austere and grim shape of the Thetford Union Workhouse or 'Spike' as it was known. The Spike was an overnight shelter for tramps and a final refuge for many of the aged and infirm poor from Thetford and the surrounding district.

In the early years of this century, the small shops and businesses that lined the Bury Road included Tom Clarke's post office and general store, a branch store of the Thetford Co-op, the Star and the Trowel & Hammer public-houses, Simons' dairy farm and, for a time in the 1930s, Alice Goddard's small shop selling groceries and home-made cakes.

Alice still lives on the Bury Road, that part of it known as St Mary's Road until the late 1960s, when the north-east corner of St Mary's churchyard was disturbed to allow the Bury Road to be diverted towards the London and Brandon Road junction. The road just south of the Fulmerston almshouses was then blocked off, creating Old Bury Road.

When Alice married Gerald Simons in 1939 she became a member of a family who had farmed in the Bury Road area for many years. As recently as 1961, Simons' herd of cows were driven daily, except in winter time, from their field [now occupied by Nunsgate] or Barnham Cross Common, along Mill Lane, nicknamed Cow-Pat Alley [or words to that effect], on to the Bury Road and into the milking parlour of Simons' dairy farm - a rural scene so distant from our Bury Road of today.

Retracing our steps into the town, and passing the Girls' and Boys' Grammar Schools, about one hundred yards before reaching the Town Bridge, a fine yew tree marks the beginning of Bury Road, the opposite corner being the site of the ancient cockpit. On this road, just before reaching St. Mary's Church, are four almshouses with curious brick chimneys, erected in 1612 at the expense of Sir Richard Fulmerston, and built of black flint and ashlar, the latter the spoils of some of the monastic foundations whose possessions had enriched their founder. A slab nearly in the centre bears the following rendering of Hebrews xii.14:- "Follow peace and holiness with all men; without the which no man shall see the Lord," and there are also numerous initials, said to be those of former occupants, carved on the freestone blocks. At the south end are remains of a sundial dated 1612, with inscriptions, including "God bless the founder of this work". In the garden opposite, the western planes are considered to be the finest in the country. **Source:** W.G. Clarke, *Guide to the Borough of Thetford,* W. Boughton & Sons Ltd., [3rd edition 1923].

The Bury Road of Dot Mutum's early childhood. On the left a hedge marks the east boundary of the Boys' Grammar School playing field. Opposite stand newly built, semi-detached and detached, bay-windowed, brick houses. Just a few years later, the 'Corporation Dwellings' were built on the old playing field.

Tranquil scenes, such as this, taken in the early years of the 20th century, seem so remote from today's Bury Road, the daily route for thousands of motor vehicles. The Thetford Co-operative Society branch store had yet to be built on the corner of Mill Lane. On the opposite side of the road junction, the signboard of the Trowel & Hammer public house can be seen. In the distance, yet another signboard, that of the Star.

Another of Thetford's old streets and the memories which it evokes is recalled in this historical *Thetford Dateline*. It is the thoroughfare which leads eastwards from the Market Place, past the Castle Hill and ramparts, on towards Melford Bridge. In the middle of the 19th century it was known as Little Magdalen Street. Today it is called Castle Street.

Later, during the Second World War, which brought about a new meaning to the term 'normal life', my mother was employed at a popular Castle Street venue, the Castle Hill Café, serving countless cups of tea to servicemen and women from the neighbouring camps and airfields.

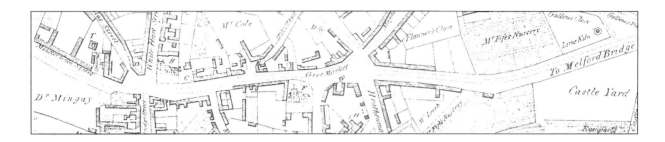

Source: extracted from *'A Plan of the Ancient Town of Thetford'* drawn by G. B. Burrell. A.D. 1807.

It is evident, from studying George Bird Burrell's map of Thetford dated 1807, that there was more open space and fewer houses bordering Castle Street in the early 1800s than today. The oldest surviving houses stand closest to the Market Place. Only recently the structure of numbers 3 and 5 was revealed as a 15th century timber-framed Wealden house. Many of the buildings which line the street are attractive, 19th century cottages and houses, built of local brick, chalk and flint.

Castle Street holds many memories for many Old Thetfordians - not only events of local importance but also some of the ordinary happenings of day-to-day life no longer practised. One such old custom is that recalled by octogenarian, Mrs Gladys Carter. As a child Gladys remembers seeing oak bark from the local tannery being strewn across the street in the front of a house where, inside, an elderly woman lay dying. The bark was provided so that the woman's peace was not disturbed by the sound of passing wagons and carts. I am told that when bark was not available, straw was used as a substitute.

Another Old Thetfordian, Mrs 'Dot' Mutum, recollects that, for a special childhood treat, she was allowed the hire of a cycle from Mr William Lambert's 'works' in Castle Street. The hire charge, recalled by Mrs Mutum, was 9d. for the first hour and 6d. for each subsequent hour.

My mother, who as a child lived in Castle Street in the early 1930s, remembers the weekly errand of carrying the wireless accumulator across the street, to be recharged at the premises of another well-known trader, Mr Frank Clarke, cycle repairer and ironmonger.

Castle Street, circa 1910.

My father, John Osborne, who was born at number 38 Castle Street in 1912, remembers the once familiar cry of 'Rag-a Bone' from Henry 'Henny' Knights, as he walked along the street on his rounds, collecting rags and rabbit skins. Also 'Dod' Dickson who sold fresh watercress harvested from local rivers; Billy Gill the fish merchant; the knife sharpener; tinkers mending pots and pans; organ grinders with their monkeys and many others who pedalled and hawked their wares about the town in the old, accustomed manner.

Castle Street circa 1920.

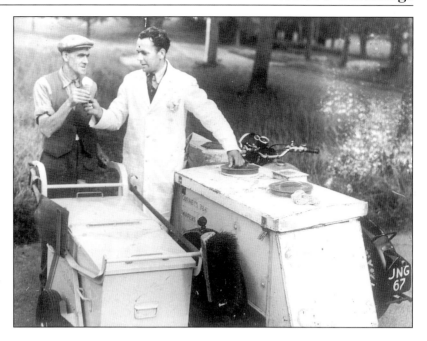

One of the most popular and frequently seen street traders, even today, is the ice cream vendor. This photograph, taken in Castle Street in the early 1950s, captures Thetford Borough Council road sweeper, Charlie Loynes, buying an ice cream cornet from Bumshee ice cream roundsman, Gordon Fulcher of Coney Weston. In the summer months, Mr Fulcher regularly toured around Thetford and the surrounding villages selling ice creams from his motorcycle and specially adapted side-car. Cornets were 6d or 3d and a sign displayed on the end of the side-car reads, 'Sports and Fetes Catered For'. [Photograph courtesy of David Fulcher]

A memory of Castle Street now lost with the passing of time is this one, viewed through an arch erected in the Market Place and decorated for the Norfolk Show held in Thetford in 1912. The show was not only a great attraction but a highly regarded privilege for the town. The showground was on fields near the Bridge Station and just off the Euston Road on the eastern extremity of the town. As the main route from the town centre to the showground, Castle Street is festooned with coloured flags and bunting. [Photograph courtesy of the Ancient House Museum, Thetford]

Although King Street is Thetford's principal commercial street, its early history remains vague and enigmatic. Early documents describe it simply as, *'the way leading from Briggate to St Cuthbert's Church'.* It appears on Thomas Martin's map of Thetford drawn about 1760 and G. B. Burrell's map of 1807 but it is not named. The earliest newspaper reference I have found of 'King Street' is in the year 1821*.

*The earliest reference to Thetford's 'King Street' appears to be that found in Frederick Accum's, *'Guide to the Chalybeate Spring of Thetford',* published in 1819.

The name King Street, it is assumed, is associated with the King's House, a building of medieval origin which stands at the west end of the street, adjacent to St Peter's Church. The King's House has a well-documented history which includes visits made there by King James I while on hunting trips at Thetford.

The oldest commercial premises in King Street are that of the Bell Inn, trading there at least from the late 15th century. Two other hostelries were once situated in King Street, the Chequers and the King's Arms. Both failed to survive the economic conditions of the 1920s.

King Street's commercial value increased after the old Market Place, situated at the east end of the town, was moved to its present central position in 1786. King Street then linked the new Market Place with Bridge Street and White Hart Street, the main commercial thoroughfare of 18th century Thetford.

Before the 1830s, it is difficult to determine the number of shopkeepers and the full extent of commerce transacted in King Street. Nevertheless, by the mid-1830s, several shops and other places of trade are recorded. William White's Directory of 1836 lists twenty-one different traders in King Street. These include chemist, confectioner, cooper, draper, grocer, hairdresser, innkeeper, milliner, publican, veterinary surgeon, watchmaker and wheelwright. There was also a post office, a timber yard and possibly an iron foundry.

Miss M. Barnes
James Cole, King's House
Mrs S. Fison
Rev. T. Methold
S. Mills, printer, bookseller & auctioneer
J. Whistler, chief constable
A. Turner, King's Arms ph.
J. Hambling, Chequers ph.
S. Clarke, academy
T. Breeze, chemist
S. Pratt, confectioner
G. Thompson, cooper, joiner & builder
G. Green, grocer & draper
W. Newstead, grocer & draper
W. Whistler, hair dresser
J. Burrell & Son, founders & mach. makers
J. Hambling, joiner & builder
H. Clark, milliner
S. Norman, plumber, painter & glazier
H. Best, surgeon
J. Brett, draper
W. Howard, veterinary surgeon
J. Carley, watch maker
J. Huggins, wheelwright
Rd. Chambers, postmaster
R. Edwards, Bell Inn
Source: King Street's traders and residents extracted from *William White's Directory of Norfolk 1836.*

One shop, which stood in King Street, was converted into a place of worship by the Society of Particular Calvinistic Baptists, in 1861. Three years later, this chapel was demolished and the present Baptist Chapel erected on the site. Like most Nonconformist chapels it was built to a plain, functional design.

A directory of 1937 lists only one additional trader in King Street than was recorded a century earlier. Their names will be familiar to Old Thetfordians: D. Adderley, baker; R. J. Bantock, photographer; Bell Inn; L. Broadly, hairdresser; H. Broomhall, chemist; E. Brown, ironmonger; P. Brown, cycle maker; J. Clarke, newsagent; E. Cozens, dental surgeon; H. Ellis, fishmonger; Gooch & Son, bootmakers; H. Green, printer and bookseller; International Tea Company Stores, grocers; E. Nunn, nursing home; R. Osborne, pork butcher; A. Petchey, watchmaker; O. Revell, butcher; M. Rudling, women's hairdresser; Savage Bros., grocers; L. Smith, wool repository; A. Starling, tobacconist; W. & E. Turner, boot and shoemakers.

Since the mid-1960s most of King Street's old established businesses and the premises they occupied have been replaced. Today, King Street's pedestrianised appearance reflects many of the recent changes in architecture, commerce and our consumer society.

...The walk through King Street, which together with a few shops in Guildhall Street and White Hart Street, comprised the business centre, furnished ample evidence of the lack of prosperity.
A large house, which had been used as a private Nursing Home but which had become unoccupied and partly demolished, stood on the site now occupied by the Woolworth store in King Street and with other vacant sites gave the town centre a somewhat forlorn appearance. Very few of the multiples had considered it worthwhile to open branches but one undoubted blessing, much loved by Thetfordians, was the family business of Savages which occupied a large portion of the north side of King Street, next to the Post Office. Savages sold practically everything

from sheets to semolina, from rugs to ribbons. The store, like Topsy, had "just growed" and it was characteristic of the lay-out that one had to squeeze past the bacon slicer and along a narrow passage in the Provisions Department in order to gain access to the large internal room, with little or no natural lighting, which served the purpose of the Gentlemen's Outfitting Department. Each customer could rely upon personal service and an old world courtesy which, in retrospect, seems to be centuries away from the atmosphere of modern supermarket shopping. **Source:** Ellis Clarke, 'The 30 years Following the Second World War', *Thetford Antiq Burg,* Leaf Publications [1985]. Reprinted by permission of Brian Hogwood and Leaf Publications.

The emporium of Savage Bros., photographed circa 1910. In the last quarter of the 19th century the shop was occupied by George and Henry Durrant. They traded as high-class grocers and drapers, selling a wide-range of foods and non-perishable goods and were amongst Thetford's principal shopkeepers. In the 1870s and early 80s, the Durrants employed at least eight shop assistants and apprentices.

About 1883, the Durrants' shop was taken over by Harry 'Hotty' Webster, another draper and grocer, and in 1904 it was purchased by Messrs Savage, later Savage Bros. In 1962 Savage Bros., closed and soon afterwards the shop premises, much enlarged since 1904, were demolished. Swept away were the old furnishings, the long, polished wooden counters, the brass fittings that adorned the countless drawers, the cabinets that held their special items and the general aura and customs of a shop that had, somehow, become so unfashionable and a victim of progress.

This view of King Street was published on a picture postcard, postally used in 1932. In the right foreground is Ye Olde King's Arms Tea House, which had been the King's Arms public house until closure 1927. The site was redeveloped in 1936.
Opposite is the premises of auctioneers, house and business agents Harry Hawker & Witton.

Narrow Street Spans The Centuries *Thetford & Watton Times, 4 March 1988*

Of Thetford's principle thoroughfares, White Hart Street is the least altered by recent modernisation and development. It is often referred to in medieval documents as Briggegate. In this context, 'gate' is derived from the Old Norse word 'gata' - a way, a path, a street.

It carried travellers to and from the Great Bridge spanning the Little Ouse. By the late 18th century, it had come by its present name, after the White Hart, an important coaching inn which occupied the building that still stands adjacent to St Peter's Church. When closed in 1914, the White Hart was a mere public-house of no importance.

Besides the old White Hart, many other interesting buildings form the narrow confines of the street. These exhibit a variety of architectural styles and building materials that give an appealing appearance. The most historic is St Peter's Church.

Mansard [1598-1666], who did much to popularise it. The King's Head has stood there from about 1779 when it was described as a *'new erected messuage or inn'*. In 1837 it was one of four public-houses in the town owned by Thomas Vipan, whose brewery occupied land between Ford Street and the river.

A private house, number 14, that stands opposite the King's Head, was once a theatre. This is said to have been one of a number of theatres built, or adapted from existing ones, by the Fisher family

A few yards from the old theatre is an attractive, part Jacobean and part Georgian house called the, 'Chantry'. A tunnel, now concealed, once linked the Chantry and King's House. It is possible that this was a secret passage provided for King James I, who often resided at King's House whilst hunting in the district.

At the north end of the street, an ancient church dedicated to St Andrew, once stood where is now The Wilderness. A modern bungalow has been built on part of the site and only a few carved stones lying in the garden give any clue to a church having stood there.

White Hart Street, looking south towards the river crossing, in the early years of the 20th century. On the left is Wereham House and, just beyond, The Chantry. On the right is a house called Cintra and in the distance the King's Head public house and other commercial properties.

Opposite is a hotel named after Thetford's famous son, Thomas Paine [1737-1809]. He was born in a house that stood in White Hart Street. During his eventful life, he published a number of influential political pamphlets that have established him as a great revolutionary thinker of international renown.

A church of that name was recorded in the Domesday Book as one of four local churches appendant to Thetford's cathedral church of St Mary-the-Great. Nothing of the present structure is known to date beyond the 14th century.

The Ancient House is a fine example of Tudor craftsmanship, believed to have been built about 1500 as a detached dwelling for a wealthy merchant. Since 1924 it has served as Thetford's museum.

Adjacent, stand the King's Head public house. It is one of the few buildings in the town with a mansard roof, named from the architect Francois Mansart or

of actors and comedians who toured Norfolk and Suffolk in the early years of the 19th century. In 1819 it was described as, *'rather small, but has a good company of performers during the Lent Assize and some excellent actors have trod its narrow stage'*.

After the Lent Assize ceased to be held at Thetford in 1833, it was reported as being, *'Nearly deserted since the removal of the Assizes to Norwich'*. Once, six sculptured busts of Roman nobilities adorned the outside of the theatre. One of these, the Emperor Tiberius, is displayed in the Ancient House Museum.

Over the centuries, White Hart Street has been the scene of a great variety of trade and commerce. Gone are the baker, blacksmith, cobbler, currier, grocer, muffin maker, stay maker and straw hat maker, to name but a few. During the 1950s and 60s, traders and shopkeepers complained of trade losses caused by heavy motor traffic passing through the narrow street. Since being created a cul-de-sac in 1980 it has now become almost traffic free. How happy those traders would be today!

This photograph was published on a picture postcard in the early years of the 20th century, but was originally taken circa 1880.
It reveals a row of cottages that once stood at the north end of White Hart Street, where Thetford's most famous son, Thomas Paine [1737-1809], is believed to have been born.
The house named Cintra stands in the left foreground.

Photographed in 1983, the grand facade of the former Theatre conceals a building that is, generally, of a much more humble construction.
It was one of a number of theatres built or adapted by David Fisher [1760-1832], who founded the famous Fisher company, that presented an unbroken succession of plays, operas, pantomimes and other entertainments in towns all over Norfolk and Suffolk for over fifty years. The theatre at Thetford closed soon after 1833.

The Star Supply Stores is just one of a great number of shops that once traded in White Hart Street. The Star Supply Stores traded from number 5 from the 1920s and into the 1950s.

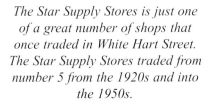

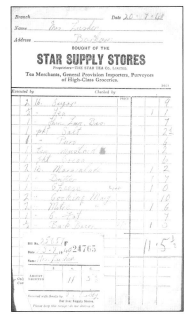

Timber-framed or half-timbered buildings are one of our most loved and cherished forms of building construction and design from an earlier age. Large house or hall, tiny cottage or even a barn, their architecture and style evokes in us a sense and feeling of the past.

Although many of Thetford's old, timber-framed houses have been demolished over the past centuries and in recent years, a few, some of them dating back to the 15th century, have fortunately survived. One of the best known of these is the Ancient House Museum, in White Hart Street, once the main thoroughfare and one of the principal commercial streets.

The Ancient House is a fine example of late 15th or early 16th century architecture and craftsmanship and it is these features that we have to rely on to understand something of its origins. It is not until the late 18th century that documentary sources begin to provide us with real evidence of the house, its owners and occupiers. The earliest that the Ancient House can be positively identified is 1794 when it was conveyed by deed to Elizabeth Juler and Mary and Ann Tyrrell, daughters of the late John Tyrrell, a woolcomber. The house then had one occupier, James Mills, a carpenter.

While the interior of the house has been restored to its original floor plan, over the centuries there have been numerous alterations to the building. Perhaps it was James Mills who, early in the 19th century, inserted the familiar and attractive bow window, the sash windows and Georgian door facing White Hart Street.

At some time, the house was converted into two separate dwellings which later came to be known as 21 and 23 White Hart Street. The house appears to have

Thetford's Ancient House Museum, circa 1925.

already been converted into two separate dwellings by 1801 when it was offered for sale by public auction at Thetford's Bell Inn. After being sold at the Bell, perhaps it is not surprising that the new owner of the house was Mrs Elizabeth Radcliffe, who had been running the inn since the death of her husband Alexander in 1792. The house was conveyed to her for the sum of £300 in March 1802.

Mrs Radcliffe, or 'Betty' as she was widely known, appears to have lived in one part of the house, perhaps as a convenient retreat away from her busy hostelry, but near enough to assert her authority and control if necessary. After her death in 1829, she bequeathed the house to two local businessmen, Joseph Gifford and James Fison in trust for her nephew, Edward Gifford.

In 1849 the house was again offered for sale by public auction, this time at the Red Lion Inn. It was then described as, *'all that freehold double dwelling-house, with the outhouses and stables and gig house'.* Furthermore, it was advertised as a house *'of the Elizabethan Age'.* The house was purchased by Thetford tanner, Edward Frost for £360.

In the second-half of the 19th century, number 21 was occupied by Henry R. Tyrrell, a farmer and maltster, and later by Robert Brown, a master plumber & glazier. Next-door at number 23, in the 1870s and 80s, lived a spinster named Sabina Matthews, one of many women in the town occupied as a dressmaker. A few years before the Great War, number 21 became the retail premises of John Kemp Main, watchmaker and shopkeeper.

The house was given a new lease of life after it was sold in 1921. Its new owner was an enthusiastic historian and collector of local ephemera, Prince Frederick Duleep Singh, of Blo' Norton Hall, who bought the house as a gift for the town, to be used as the Thetford Town Museum.

Structure and Plan
Although the house is mainly timber-built, the cellar, foundations and some walling are of flint, chalk and bricks, and the west gable is of flint and brick. The nogging between the oak uprights appears to have been mainly "clay-lump" but in some cases is chalk, and in others narrow bricks inserted herring-bone fashion. The street front block is roofed with a modern flat pitched slate roof with ridge running parallel to the street, and about 17 feet from front to back. This block originally contained two rooms on the ground floor and two on the first floor. **Source:** W.G. Clarke, *Description of the Ancient House, Thetford,* Thetford Corporation, [circa 1925]

On the ground floor, to the right of the front entrance passage, is this room, the largest and most elaborate in the house and once the hall. The ceiling, perhaps the finest feature of the building, is constructed of oak, finely decorated with intricate carvings and mouldings.

Also to be found in this room is a fireplace with part of a carved lintel.

A recent architectural study has revealed five major phases of alteration to the house since it was first built circa 1500. Coincidently, these changes took place at roughly 100 year intervals, beginning in the early years of the 16th century. [Drawing courtesy of the Ancient House Museum]

The familiar, timber stud-work that forms the facade of the Ancient House was concealed for many years and was not revealed until 1867, during maintenance work. The discovery was recorded by A. L. Hunt in his history of Thetford published in 1870, 'Two interesting Elizabethan studded houses discovered in White Hart Street, upon the removal of the external plaster'.

Recent expert examination of the building suggests that the front was once brightly coloured and not the contrasting black and white we have come to associate with such buildings today.

Although several drawings were made of the Ancient House in the second-half of the 19th century, this photograph, taken about 1914, is probably the earliest, when it was partly occupied by watch & clock repairer, John Kemp Main. In 1912, he advertised as being in 'Tanner Street, King Street'.

48066. THETFORD: ELIZABETHAN HOUSE.

After the recent visit to Thetford by the Queen, it was wrongly thought by many people that it was the first trip to the town by a reigning monarch since the first Queen Elizabeth in 1578.

If we discount the occasions when Edward VII and George V passed through the town on their visits to Elveden Hall, it was Elizabeth's cousin and successor James I who was the last sovereign to visit the town.

King James owned a house in Thetford and frequently visited the town so that he could enjoy the pleasures of hunting the great variety of game to be found in the surrounding countryside. Besides, with his love of horse racing, it was not too far from Newmarket.

It was after one such visit in April 1614 that the churchwardens of the Suffolk town of Mendlesham paid John Shepherd, the chief constable, the sum of 6 shillings for *'removinge of the Kinge from Thetford'*. It was then the custom for all parishes in a region where the King was in residence or travelling to pay a sum or levy for provisioning the royal household.

King James' former palace in Thetford, fronting King Street, is now appropriately called King's House. Moreover, not only is it a former royal residence, but enjoys the reputation of occupying the site of the medieval manor house, once belonging to the Lords of the Manor of Thetford. If this is so, it is no coincidence that adjacent stands the ancient parish church of St Peter.

The exterior of the King's House that we see today is basically a mid-18th century construction. Very little of earlier buildings [and I imagine there must have been several] appears to have survived. Drawings made by Thomas Martin [1696-1771] give us some idea of the house before rebuilding in the 18th century. They reveal a very different house, making it difficult to associate it with the present one.

However, much of its long and interesting history has been uncovered by one of its former occupants, Mr Henry Fison Killick, who retired to the King's House at the end of the 19th century. Although unable to discover anything of its very early past, he was able to trace the ownership of the house from King James to King Charles who in 1628 granted the house to Andrew Pitcairne. By

The King's House, the home of the Fison's c.1885. [Photograph courtesy of Thetford Town Council]

1630, however, Sir Thomas Wodehouse was in possession of the King's House. Members of the Wodehouse family represented Thetford in Parliament and served as Borough Recorders. They continued as owners of the King's House, apart from a few years in the 1740s, until it was conveyed to Thomas Wright of Thetford in 1763.

It was almost certainly during Thomas Wright's ownership that the King's House was rebuilt and modernised, creating much of the architecture that we are familiar with today. After Thomas Wright's death in 1778 the King's House and his other substantial estates, which included the near-by manor and parish of Santon Downham, were offered for sale. The King's House was then described as, *'consisting of three large parlours, dining room 40 feet long and seven lodging rooms, besides garrets, a spacious modern staircase and two others; study, coach house, dove house, stables for 15 horses, dog kennel, court and other yards, gardens and six acres of old pasture adjoining, all walled and well planted'.*

Two years after Thomas Wright's death the house was conveyed to James Cole. Perhaps the upkeep of such a large house eventually became too much for James Cole's heirs, who had certainly divided it into two separate dwellings by the late 1850s, and possibly from the early 1840s when James Cole, jnr., dealer in foreign wines, traded from the King's House at the same time as the Misses Rogers were running a private school there.

Very often the owner, or owners, of the King's House have not resided there, but leased or rented the house to someone else. Of course, being such a large and valuable property, it only attracted the wealthiest and most prominent members of local society. One such tenant, who appears in the early 1850s, was Henry Best, a local surgeon and general practitioner. Best resided at the King's House with his wife and eight children, and a small retinue of domestic servants: one housemaid, a cook, two nurse maids and a groom.

By 1859 the King's House was owned by Cornell Henry Fison, the senior member of a local family of merchants, whose business interests included malting, milling and the manufacture of artificial manure. Cornell H. Fison resided there until 1886 when he moved into the more secluded Ford Place, another of Thetford's 'Big Houses'.

After Cornell H. Fison's death in 1895 the house was administered by the Trustees of his will. Eventually, however, it came into the possession of George Wild Staniforth, a retired Yorkshire businessman. His generosity and love for the town of Thetford was fully revealed after his death in January 1947. He had bequeathed to the town his King's House and its spacious gardens, a valuable library and other gifts.

In 1952 the King's House replaced the Guildhall as the Thetford Borough Council chambers and offices. From 1974 it also served as offices for Breckland District Council, but their recent departure to Breckland House, officially opened this year by the Queen, has made way for the Wayland District Registrar's office - so beginning another chapter in the long history of the King's House.

Female members of the Fison family can be seen in this rare interior view of the King's House in the 1880s. Compare this spacious and opulent room with that, then found, in the small, terraced, flint cottages found in many parts of the town.
[Photograph courtesy of Thetford Town Council]

The Royal Arms of King James I sit high upon the parapeted facade of the King's House. The Wodehoue Arms are also displayed, carved in stone, at the front of the house and on the east gable a very old sun-dial.

The manor house of Thetford was traditionally said to have been on the site of the Kings House, on the north side of King Street immediately east of St Peter's church, and since the present house does have vestiges of medieval work in its cellars this seems a reasonable assumption. The location beside the church implies that this site was of considerable importance from an early date. The grounds of the manor house seem to have extended north and east as far as Earls Street, formerly known as Earls Lane - a street name which in this context assumes a great significance for it presumably relates to the Earls Warren, lords of the manor. Medieval documents contain occasional references to land and buildings called Earls Barn and Earls Yard, situated near to the present market place in the angle formed by King Street and Earls Street. **Source:** Alan Crosby, *A History of Thetford* Phillimore & Co Ltd [1986]. Reproduced by kind permission from *A History of Thetford* by Alan Crosby, published in 1986 by Phillimore & Co Ltd., Shopwyke Manor Barn, Chichester, West Sussex, PO20 2BG.

The King's House in 2003. Several large pieces of dressed and decorated stone, no doubt salvaged from the ruins of Thetford's former medieval religious houses, can be seen incorporated into the flint-faced walls of the house. Similar pieces of stone can also be found laying in the gardens.

Thetford's Earls Street follows a gentle curve from its junction with the Norwich Road at one end, to the Market Place at the other. It is believed by some archaeologists and historians that this curve follows the line of what was once part of the town's northern defences - a system of ditches and embankments that surrounded much of the Saxon town one thousand years ago.

In the 18th and early 19th century, Earls Street or Lane was more commonly known as Alice's Lane, although its present name probably comes from a past association with Thetford's medieval manorial lords, the Earls of Warrene. The main entrance to their manor house, now called King's House, once led off the highway we now call Earls Street. The Earls of Warrene are also reputed to have owned a barn that stood against the road.

Most of the buildings that now form Earls Street are cottages and houses. Sandwiched in between what was originally a Late Victorian cottage hospital and Thetford's earliest chapel for dissenters, erected in 1817 for the Independents [Congregationalists], there is an equally interesting building that represents a meaningful, yet immeasurable part of Thetford's past. As a monument to the 19th century endeavours of Thetford's working classes, it has, as yet, received little attention from historians. High above the street, on its red-brick and stone gable is carved, *1891 Oddfellows Hall*.

The Oddfellows is just one of at least six benefit or friendly societies formed in Thetford about the middle of the 19th century. Some of these societies were purely local but others such as the Oddfellows, were national institutions with lodge branches in most cities, towns and even in many villages.

Lodge meetings were usually held in local inns and public-houses, except when funds allowed the use of a permanent room or even the construction of a purpose-built hall.

Membership of Thetford's friendly societies in the 19th century was formed from a fairly broad spectrum of the male working-class: skilled artisan craftsmen, small shopkeepers and the more prudent labourers. A weekly subscription provided each member with financial and sometimes medical help in times of sickness, unemployment or death.

Thetford: The ninth anniversary of the Loyal East Anglian Lodge of the Manchester Unity of Oddfellows was commemorated by about 40 members and friends dining together at the Town Hall, on Friday last, Mr J.S. Banyard in the chair. D.G.M. Daynes explained the usefulness of provident societies, shewing that the members could by such unity be independent of parochial relief... **Source:** *Bury & Norwich Post, 6 November 1850.*

In the days before the birth of the Welfare State, self-help organisations such as friendly societies, funeral societies and savings clubs were essential in providing members with some independence from what was then considered by many as the shame of poor relief.

From its formation at Thetford in 1859, the Phoenix Lodge of Oddfellows Manchester Unity, to give its full title, proved both popular and successful - by 1882 it boasted two hundred and ninety paying members. Besides providing assistance in times of distress, each lodge fostered a close brotherhood and a lively social atmosphere. For the Oddfellows, this culminated in June each year with the lodge anniversary, an exciting and colourful occasion that always drew large crowds of spectators.

Dressed in their full regalia, carrying flags and banners, and often accompanied by a brass band, the Oddfellows would parade the town before attending a special service at one of the town's three Anglican churches. Afterwards they reassembled, and again paraded the town before returning to the lodge for a celebratory dinner, numerous toasts and musical entertainment.

One other friendly society also had close links with Earls Street. For many years the Ancient Order of Foresters celebrated their anniversary with a fete on Hatches Close, a piece of land on the east side of Earls Street, stretching across to Grove Lane [formerly Botany Bay Lane]. Their only memorial in the town is a row of houses built on Hatches Close in the early years of the 20th century, and known today as 'Foresters Row'.

The Foresters: On Tuesday last the Thetford Oak Lodge of Foresters held their fourth anniversary dinner at the Bell Inn. There were in the procession seventy or eighty members, each wearing a green sash and various other decorations. Robin Hood on a powerful grey horse, rode in front, followed by mounted attendants; next came the sax-horn band, with flags and banners, followed by a long line of attendants on foot and horseback. The members attended Divine Service at St Peter's Church, at 12 o'clock, where an appropriate sermon was preached by the Rev. E.H. Gibbon, the Rector, from Gal. vi 7. They then paraded the town, the streets of which were thronged with spectators. At 2 o'clock they returned to the Hotel and sat down to a substantial dinner. The chair was occupied by H.W. Bailey, Esq., surgeon of the Club...The Society appears to be in a prosperous position. **Source:** *Bury & Norwich Post, 1 July 1862.*

*THETFORD ODDFELLOWS.
WHITSUNTIDE FESTIVITIES
ON WHIT SUNDAY, JUNE 3rd,
1900, a PROCESSION, headed by
the Band of G Company 4th
V.B.N.R. (by the kind permission
of the Officers Commanding) will
parade the Town at Two o'clock,
and attend a Special Service at the
Oddfellows' Hall at Three o'clock.
Preacher, the Rector of West Tofts.
Collections en route and at the
Hall in aid of the Thetford
Hopital.
On WHIT TUESDAY, JUNE 5th,
ATHLETIC SPORTS will take
place on the Heath adjoining the
Bridge Station (by kind
permission of W.H. Jillings, Esq.),
when 45 Prizes and a Cup
presented by the Licensed
Victuallers of the town will be
competed for. For particulars
apply to G. Gathercole, G.J. Fife,
or J. Forster.
In addition to Steam circus,
Archery, and other Amusements,
there will be a grand Balloon
Ascent and Parachute Descent by
Professor Fleet with his
Mammoth Balloon, "Princess
Maud," 115 feet high and 200 feet
in circumference. Concluding
with a Grand Display of
Fireworks by Mr. H.B. Sullings,
including all the latest
Pyrotechnic Novelties.
Refreshments by J. Carter at town
prices. A few stalls allowed on
application to R. Tilley before
May 24th. No Scent Fountains
allowed.
Admission Tickets up to Saturday,
June 2nd, 6d. each. Children
under 12, 2d. - after that date 1s.
each. No Re-admission...A
SOIREE will be held at the Hall at
Ten o'clock. Admission 1s.
each...***Source:** *Thetford & Watton
Times, 12 May 1900.*

*Thetford's Oddfellows Hall, now the Thetford Snooker Centre, was
erected and opened in 1891. It was built on the site where a school for
infants had stood for much of the 19th century.*

*Thetfordians celebrate the Coronation of King George V in June 1911.
Displaying their coloured sashes, members of Thetford's friendly
societies, follow the Boy Scouts as they parade from the Market Place to
a special service at St Peter's Church.*

Oddfellows'
*"Loyal Phoenix" Lodge, No.4790, M.U. Approved Society under National
Insurance Acts, 1911.*
*Meetings of this Lodge are held at the Oddfellows' Hall, Earles Street, every
fourth Saturday at 7.30 p.m. Medical Officers, Dr. A.G. Minns, Bridge
Street, Dr. G. Cowan, King Street, and Dr. A. Oliver, Market Place;
Secretary, G.R. Blaydon, 37, Croxton Road; Assistant Secretary, Mr F.
Hensby, 65, Castle Street; Treasurers (Voluntary Section), Mr E. Burrell, 55
Bury Road; (State Insurance Section), Mr A.S. Law, Capital & Counties
Bank, Ltd., London Road.*
*A Juvenile Branch of the Lodge also meets every fourth Monday at 5.30 p.m.
Secretary, Mr R. Tilley, The Homestead, Castle Street; Treasurer, Mr H.
Flack, 31, Earles Street.* **Source:** *Thetford & District Almanac 1923.*

Guildhalls or Gildhalls, once meeting places for the craft, merchant and religious guilds which existed in pre-Reformation England, can still be found in many of our cities, towns and villages. Thetford's Guildhall, standing in the centre of the town beside the Market Place, is believed to occupy the site where a guildhall has stood from at least 1337, when it belonged to a religious guild dedicated to St Mary the Blessed Virgin.

The religious guilds, fraternities or brotherhoods [the terms are interchangeable]· were lay-bodies of men and women who gathered together for religious and social activities. Members may have belonged to a wide-range of social and occupational backgrounds. Each guild was dedicated to a revered saint and, among other things, was much concerned with the intercession of the saints, purgatory, providing a decent burial and praying for the souls of deceased brethren.

...the Guildhall is a fine old building of black flint, when it was first built I cannot learn. It had a noble kitchen under it, (now turned into a stable) where they made ready for the corporation at their guilds and other public times. **Source:** Francis Blomefield, *'History of Thetford'* [1739].

The large, important guilds were closely associated with the local oligarchy, whereby the guild officials were to be found among the leading citizens. Moreover, in towns such as Thetford which before the Reformation had yet to achieve incorporation, the guilds gave some corporate identity where none would otherwise have prevailed. If surviving ordinances from religious fraternities elsewhere are anything to go by, Thetford's Guild of St Mary would attend a special annual service in its

chapel, followed by a procession to a general meeting and feast held in its guildhall. This was held on the 15th August - the feast day in honour of the translation to heaven of the Virgin Mary [Feast of the Assumption].

It is because of their religious rituals that the guilds were suppressed by the Chantries Act of 1547. Following this Act, it appears that Thetford's Guildhall escaped seizure by the Crown. The Mayor and leading burgesses had, somehow, acquired it when the Borough of Thetford was granted its Charter of Incorporation in 1574. It recited *'the Gildhall shall be their Common Hall or place of meeting for all manner of pleas and causes as shall seem necessary'.* The Guildhall, therefore, became a public Town Hall. Not only was it to be used by the corporation for its aptly named 'halls' or assemblies, but also for many other purposes. Perhaps the foremost of these, however, was the annual King's Court or Assize for dealing with serious crimes. It was because of the importance of the Lent Assize and the prestige it brought to the town that the medieval Guildhall was improved and enlarged in 1680 through the benevolence and influence of Sir Joseph Williamson [1633-1701], MP and Borough Recorder.

At this Assembly it was ordered that a good turret clock be erected on the Town Hall and that Mr John Spendlove do provide the same. **Source:** *Corporation of Thetford Minute Book, 16 January 1800* [T/C2/8].

More than a century later, between 1799-1800, the Guildhall was again rebuilt, *'for the better accommodation of the public at the Lent Assize for the County of Norfolk'.* On this occasion it was paid for by the Corporation, which was then resisting appeals from many parts of the county for the removal of the Assize to Norwich.

The improvements to the Guildhall were an attempt to retain the Assize at Thetford - a bid that proved successful until 1833 when it was finally moved to Norwich.

The structure of the Guildhall had deteriorated so badly before the end of the 19th century that a decision was made to demolish it and build a new hall on the same plan as the previous one. It was opened in 1902.

This fine Guildhall, opened in February 1902, consists of basement, fire engine house, kitchen, scullery, Mayor's parlour, Hall 52 ft. x 27 ft., council chamber, magistrates' room, county court, entrance hall & grand jury chamber. Surmounting the whole is a dome & clock visible from many parts of the town & immediate neighbourhood. The clock bell was cast in 1800 by Thomas Osborn of Downham Market. In the council chamber are stained glass windows displaying the arms of Sir Joseph Williamson, the Borough and King Charles II, and a portrait of the 2nd Duke of Grafton. **Source:** W. G. Clarke, *'Guide to the Borough of Thetford'* W. Boughton & Sons Ltd., [1925].

Since the last quarter of the 16th century, Thetford's Guild or Town Hall has been used as an art gallery, auction room, banqueting room, bingo hall, canteen, church, club-room, concert room, dance hall, election polling station, exhibition hall, fire engine house, mechanics' institute, meeting hall, music hall, sale room, school, temporary jail, theatre, workhouse, workshop, wrestling booth, and possibly many more besides. Nonetheless, one important event continues to be held there - the Mayor making ceremony - a tradition which has lasted over four hundred years.

Thetford: Our Town Hall has been greatly improved by lighting the courts, council chamber and entrance hall with gas. The work has been ably executed by Mr Pank of Norwich. **Source:** *Bury & Norwich Post, 24 March 1852.*

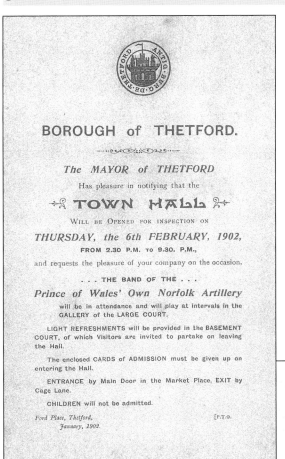

The antiquarian Francis Blomefield described the Guildhall in his History of Thetford published in 1739, ...'a fine old building of black flint, when it was first built I cannot learn'. It was demolished and replaced by a new Guildhall, erected between 1799-1800.

Well before the end of the 19th century the Guildhall [see photograph page 49] was in need of major refurbishment. Eventually it was decided to completely demolish the Guildhall and erect a new one. A number of old memorial tablets and other interesting fixtures from the previous building were incorporated into the new Guildhall. The new Guildhall opened to the public in February 1902 at a cost of about £10,000. For many locals, however, it was an extravagant expenditure, provoking much criticism from some of Thetford's ratepayers. Although it was then something of a bold, costly and controversial decision, the money lavished on the Guildhall has since proved to have been worthwhile.

It is quite probable that the Guildhall served as the offices and chambers of the Corporation from the time that the town was granted its charter of incorporation in 1574. In 1952 the Corporation offices were moved to the King's House.

High above the north gable of Thetford's Guildhall stands a stone figure of Justice, blindfolded and holding the traditional scales in one hand and the famous sword of justice in the other. Nearby, is the grim edifice of the old Gaol, built of black flint and brick. Both buildings are reminders of the important Lent Assize, once held in the ancient town.

Justice - as in the administration of the law - has no doubt been practised in the town from the earliest times. Thetford's feudal manorial lords, the Earls of Warenne, were responsible for law and order within the town, through the offices of their bailiff or steward and the manorial Court Baron and Court Leet. A deed relating to a shop in the market of Thetford at the end of the 13th century, describes its location *'near the prison of our Lord Earl Warenne'*. This was probably the same site occupied, today, by the old Gaol.

Towards the end of the 12th century, however, a new legal system evolved which took away the most serious crimes from the manor court. This was the 'assize', whereby itinerant or travelling justices, appointed by the King, presided and gave judgement over such felonious crimes as murder, robbery, larceny, arson and forgery. The word 'assize' comes from the Latin *assideo* meaning 'I sit'. About the same time the procedure evolved of trial by a definite form of jury, a 'grand jury' as it was known. The role of the jury was to bring local criminals before the King's justices for trial. In those early days the jurors were prosecutors rather than deciders.

It is not known when an assize was first held in Thetford, but it may well have been as early as the 12th century. An annual assize was certainly being held in the town by the 15th century, when the Paston family of Norfolk made numerous references to them in their now famous letters. According to one letter, the assize was held in Thetford's 'Shire-hall' but it is not known where, in the town, it was situated. From the latter part of the 16th century until the 19th century, the assize was held in the Guildhall, on the site of the present building. In 1800 the Guildhall was rebuilt ... *'for the better Accommodation of the Public at the Lent Assize'*... The Thetford Lent Assize was held in February or March. Such was Thetford's early importance in Norfolk that, besides Norwich, it was the only assize town in the county. The Norwich Assize was held in August.

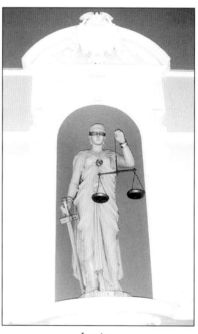

Justice.

From the 17th century onwards there are many more accounts, from a variety of sources, giving all sorts of detail of the Thetford Lent Assize. Some of the most descriptive and interesting are those from contemporary local newspapers. The assize was certainly an important local event, attracting the county gentry and many other folk. There are reports of the town full of visitors, creating a scarcity of lodgings. Innkeepers were accused of charging exorbitant prices for rooms, stables and feed for horses.

The visiting Assize judge, along with his servants, was among those who lodged in the town. In 1823 a mansion house, situated in White Hart Street, was offered to be let ... *The Judges have always been accommodated with lodgings on this estate at the Lent Assizes'*... It is also said, by tradition alone, that the Assize Judges lodged at the King's House, but there appears to be no written evidence to support this statement.

No doubt, on arriving at the outskirts of Thetford, the judge's coach was met and escorted into the town by the High Sheriff of Norfolk and Thetford's Mayor. On the Sunday prior to the commencement of the Assize [Size Sunday as it was known locally], the Judge, accompanied by the High Sheriff of Norfolk, Mayor, councillors, officers of the Corporation and court officials, many bewigged, dressed in ceremonial gowns and displaying the insignia of their office, proceeded to St Peter's Church for a special service. During the service, a sermon of some significance to the occasion would be delivered from the pulpit by the High Sheriff's Chaplain. It was all part of the spectacle - the pageantry, theatre and tradition that surrounded this important event.

A few days prior to the Judge and other officials publicly reaffirming their faith and beliefs, male and female prisoners standing trial at the assize were transported by cart from the various bridewells or gaols situated about the county, such as Swaffham, Wymondham and Norwich. Finally, on reaching Thetford, the prisoners were led, manacled and chained, into the Gaol. There they joined others already confined there, miserably awaiting their trial. The administration of law and order was a lengthy and slow process, and it is likely that since their arrest, some prisoners had already spent several months incarcerated in the most wretched and squalid conditions imaginable. The numbers of prisoners indicted to stand trial at the Lent Assize varied. The local historian, W.G. Clarke [1877-1925], estimated that in the period 1731-56 the average number of prisoners for trial was about twelve; the numbers increasing to sixteen between 1757-80; twenty-four between 1781-1806 and forty-four between 1807-1831.

The Assize usually began on a Monday, the Judge having been carried in his personal coach from his lodgings to the Guildhall. Both civil and criminal cases were dealt with at the Lent Assize. Once the civil proceedings were dealt with, the criminal cases followed. The court room would often be packed to capacity with members of the general public, especially if there was a particularly shocking and widely reported crime to be heard. On a few occasions civil cases, involving persons of some local fame and distinction, attracted as much attention as the criminal proceedings.

As they were due to stand trial, the manacled prisoners were brought from the Gaol and held in cells under the court room [stairs from the Guildhall basement once led directly into the Assize Court]. Eventually, each prisoner would stand at the bar to hear the charge, and come face-to-face with the Judge and Grand Jury. The Grand Jury, having been sworn in, then consisted of between twelve and twenty-three 'law-worthy' men selected both by and from amongst the local aristocracy. Of course, they would all have been owners of property and men of some influence and power in the county. As very few prisoners could afford to have legal counsel, justice was quickly dispatched. As many as 40

prisoners might be tried and sentenced within the space of a week.

The former gaol in Old Market Street. On the top floor, iron bars still secure the cell windows

For much of the 18th and early years of the 19th century, an extraordinary number of capital crimes, well over two hundred, were punishable by death. The French writer, Voltaire [1694-1778], was well justified in saying, *'the English were a people who murdered by law'*. Of course, punishment was particularly brutal for those found guilty of murder, but it was equally so for offences against property and the Game Laws. Nonetheless, W. G. Clarke also reckoned that between 1731 and 1831, about one third of all prisoners were acquitted at the Thetford Lent Assize. The severity of punishment depended much on the seriousness of the crime, but there is ample evidence that Justice was never consistently pronounced. For stealing a rabbit, one man might hang while another receive a much lesser sentence.

For centuries, public executions had been carried out in the town and continued well into the 19th century. They were an annual, public spectacle, often attracting large crowds and great interest. The Assize judge was frequently moved

to place the sinister and ritualistic, black cap upon his head immediately before pronouncing the death sentence.

Between the 16th and 18th centuries, a gallows was sited on the northern extremity of the town, just off the Mundford Road. The area is still known today as Gallows Hill. Thomas Martin's rough sketch map of Thetford, drawn circa 1760, also depicts gallows situated close to the site known later as 'Gallows Pits' on the edge of Melford Common and the Castle Yard. The last executions carried out in Thetford took place in April 1824, when Robert Gibson and James Reeve were hanged for sheep stealing and Miles Wiseman for wounding a game keeper. At that time, according to Alfred Leigh Hunt whose history of Thetford was published in 1870, the place of execution was *'gallows latterly fixed across the roadway in front of the gaol'*.

At Thetford Assize, John Painter, John Johnson, alias Black Jack, and Henry Reynolds, received sentence of Death for horse stealing; and Henry Wright for robbing on the Highway. One for stealing Hats, and a Boy for robbing his Master, were ordered for transportation. **Source:** *Suffolk Mercury or Bury Post, 14 March 1736/37.*

A map of Thetford, drawn early in the 19th century, also shows 'Gallows Pits' the area where 'Castle House', Castle Street, stands today. This is probably the burial site of those executed at Thetford, whose bodies were not claimed by family members or others in the late 18th and early 19th century. However, not all executed prisoners were buried in the town. After John Rye was hanged at Thetford in 1777, his body was carried to Norwich, where it was to be anatomised or dissected by surgeons practising their skills. There are also accounts of dissections being carried out at Thetford. Following an Act in 1752, the dissection of a small number of corpses was officially allowed. In 1834 an Act was carried which discontinued the practice of dissecting executed murderers before exposing the body to public view.

Not all of those sentenced to death at the Thetford Lent Assize were executed in the town. Some were hastily transported to Norwich for public execution, before large crowds assembled in the Castle Yard. A few prisoners, those found guilty of particularly brutal murders, were dealt with in an even harsher method than simply being hanged. At the assize of 1795, William Bennington was found guilty of murdering his master, John Filby. He was executed at Thetford and afterwards his body was drawn on a sledge to West Dereham, near Downham Market, where the murder had taken place. There, close to the spot where the murder was perpetrated, his body was *'hung in chains'* - a punishment known as gibbeting. Twenty years later, his weather-beaten skeleton could still be seen hanging there. The locality came to be known as Gibbet Lane.

At the same assize, a similar fate fell to Stephen Watson of West Bradenham, near Dereham, who was found guilty of murdering his wife. Watson's gibbet can be seen today, hanging in Norwich Castle Museum. The gibbet was a frequently used instrument of punishment, intended as a deterrent, a grisly warning to all and was even said to be feared by many hardened criminals. The use of the gibbet, only officially legalised as late as 1752, was abolished in 1834, following reforms by Robert Peel.

It was 1868 before public executions finally ceased and from then on, only two statutory capital offences remained - murder and treason. A century later, the sentence of death by hanging was ended.

The iron-hooped gibbet in which Stephen Watson's body was suspended at West Bradenham in 1795. It is now on display at the Castle Museum, Norwich.

Many other forms of punishment were administered at the assize. During the 18th century, an increasing number of those convicted of capital offences at the Thetford Assize, escaped the death sentence when others faced 'the fatal drop'. Some convicts were transported to far away places, for seven or fourteen year periods and even for life. From the early 17th century, convicts were transported to remote American colonies such as Virginia and Maryland. But after the American War of Independence, the more distant Antipodes was the destination of thousands of British convicts, including a number who had been sentenced at the Thetford Lent Assize. The first convicts, numbering about 750, arrived in what is now the city of Sydney, New South Wales, in January 1788. And even if a convict somehow managed to escape and return from a distant colony, his freedom and life was still in jeopardy. At the

Thetford Assize in 1775, William Stratton was sentenced to death for returning from transportation. By the 1840s, the transportation of convicts to Australia had virtually ceased.

There are also a few accounts of convicted male prisoners, particularly during times of war, who were given the 'King's Pardon' on condition they went into His Majesty's Service. In the 1770s this was often as a soldier, but in the 1790s it was most likely to serve on a fighting ship, such as a 'man-of-war', where there was a high risk of being maimed or killed in action against the enemy. After 1776 some male convicts were incarcerated, for periods of 2 or 3 years, in prison hulks moored on the river Thames, where they were put to hard labour... *'raising Sand, Soil and Gravel from, and cleansing the river Thames'*. By 1850 the prison hulks were rotting on the Thames and ceased to be used soon after. Before the 19th century imprisonment was generally a rarely used form of punishment for serious offences, but by the 1850s it was an accepted and common form of punishment, very often with hard labour for men and women, in one of the new prisons situated on the British mainland.

Other punishments noted at the Thetford Lent Assize include, branding and whipping. In 1756, Jane Shinn, was branded on the hand for bigamy and exactly twenty years later, Ann Aldridge was branded with a hot iron for stealing. For petty larceny in 1732, Elizabeth Crick was ordered to be publicly whipped around Thetford market place on the next market day. Thetford's market place was then situated just east of the gaol. In 1740 a sheep stealer was ordered to be whipped on three market days at Thetford and four men were publicly whipped in 1773, three of them for stealing a solitary rabbit from a warren at Weeting. Branding

SENTENCES

Of the Prisoners, that were tried at the Lent Assizes, at Thetford, on Saturday, the 20th day of, March, 1830, before the Right Honourable Lord Tenterden, and the Honourable Sir John Vaughan, Knight, one of the Barons of our said Lord the King, to deliver the aforesaid Gaol of the Prisoners therein being.

Charles Salmon, aged 22, Committed September 5, 1829, by Kerrison Harvey and John Herring, Esqs. charged on the oath of Ann Littleboy, of Happisburgh, with having broken the window of her dwelling-house, and stolen one cotton shirt and one cotton handkerchief. *Death Recorded.*

John Cadman, aged 22, and *Robert Diver, aged 18,* Committed October 2nd, 1829, by John Wright, Esq. charged on the oath of George Fuller, of the parish of St Cuthbert, with having stolen a black mare. *Death Recorded.*

Elizabeth Addison, aged 36, Committed November 3, 1829, by J. Thurlow Dering, Esq. charged on the oath of James Watson and George Riddle, with bigamy. *2 years.*

William Garrod, aged 35, John Culling, aged 43, and *James Melton, aged 21.* Committed February 18, 1830, by John S. Patteson, Esq. charged on the oath of James Asten, with having broken into his dwelling-house, and stolen therefrom four pounds of bacon, two pints of butter, and a silver tablespoon. *7 Years Transportation.*

N. B. Wm. Brooks, in attempting to escape from prison, has so seriously injured himself as to be incapable of removal.

THETFORD GAOL.

William Howard, aged 22, Committed March 1, 1830, by Henry Best, Esq. charged on the oath of William Spalding, on suspicion of having, stolen from his person the sum of Thirteen pounds three shillings. *No true Bill.*

Thomas Tuck, for breaking into a dwelling house, and stealing 3 sovereigns, a 5£. note and a 10£. note. *Death Recorded.*

Source: just 7 out of 33 proceedings extracted from an official notice printed on a single sheet of paper by *'WALKER, PRINTER, NORWICH'.* It can be seen displayed in the Ancient House Museum, Thetford.

was virtually ended after an Act of 1779 and the judicial whipping of women ceased in 1820 but for men it was much later.

Thetford's former Gaol stands at the east end of the old market place, in what is now Old Market Street, at its junction with Ford Street [once Gaol Lane]. Very little is known of the gaol's history until the 18th century. It is needless to say, that prior to reforms in the 19th century, conditions in any gaol were extremely harsh, unsanitary and very often over-crowded. Thetford's Gaol was described by John Howard, High Sheriff of Bedfordshire and penal reformer, in his *'The State of Prisons in England & Wales'* published in 1780.

'Thetford Town Gaol': 'Is also the town bridewell. The ground floor for the keeper. On the first story, are four rooms for debtors; and two for delinquents. For felons, a dungeon down a ladder of 10 steps; 18 feet by 9½, and 9 feet high: a window 18 inches by 14: and an aperture about 2 feet square, lately opened into the passage.

At assize once a year, from sixteen to twenty prisoners brought hither from Norwich castle are confined in this dungeon, men and women together, four or five nights. Court not secure. No water. Keeper no salary. No fees: only the house to live in'...

Thetford's Gaol was *'repaired and considerably enlarged'* in 1796, six years after John Howard had died of gaol fever in the Crimea. Moreover, a plaque outside the gaol also tells us that, once again, *'THIS GAOL was Enlarg'd in the Year 1816'.* No doubt, this was to hold the increasing number of prisoners being brought to Thetford for the Lent Assize and at other times.

Well before the end of the 18th century, however, many in Norfolk were continually calling and petitioning for the Thetford Lent Assize to be moved, to the more conveniently situated city of Norwich. Despite the efforts of Thetford's most prominent inhabitants and a few supporters to keep the assize at Thetford, the assize of 1832 was the last to be held in the town. Its demise ended centuries of prestigious tradition and custom in the town. As some

recompense for the loss of the assize, the Borough was soon granted a new Court of Quarter Session, to be held in the Guildhall, which also continued as a court room for the Borough Petty Sessions, where more trivial cases were heard, and the annual Brewster Sessions for the licensing of Thetford's public houses.

The old gaol continued as a Borough Gaol and as a House of Correction. In 1834 it was described as *'a large and ill-contrived building...The number of prisoners when we visited the gaol was 3 males and 1 female. The men were all regularly employed on a tread mill erected in the gaol. The woman was confined day and night in the same room...The gaol was clean and appeared to be well kept'.*

In 1858, it was ordered that the treadmill and bean mill be removed after it ceased as a House of Correction. By then the old Gaol had become the Borough Police Station, while the assize and all it entailed was but a distant memory. Yet another era in the town's history was already in the making.

Ancient Privilege Of Market Place *Thetford & Watton Times, 4 June 1993*

Thetford has a long tradition as a chartered market town, a privilege that almost certainly goes back continuously to the early 11th century when Thetford was an important Anglo-Saxon town.

Although the site of the original market place is now lost, it was probably south of the Little Ouse river, where most of Anglo-Saxon Thetford was situated. One possible site suggested by Alan Crosby in his, *History of Thetford,* is the convergence of roads just south of the Town Bridge. Another likely site, one only a few hundred yards away beside the Brandon Road, is the area known as the Grammar School Plains. One of Thetford's ancient annual fairs was held here until finally abolished in the early 1870s. Even today, it remains an open space, beside the former Priory of the Canon's of the Holy Sepulchre.

After the decline of the south-bank town, it would seem Thetford's market place was re-sited, on what had become the more populous north bank, in the area east of St Cuthbert's Church, towards what is now the Green Dragon corner and Guildhall Street - Castle Street junction. Once known as the 'Grassmarket', it resembles a site often associated with an early market place, close to an ancient church near which several roads converge.

Alan Crosby also tells us that the Grassmarket probably pre-dates another market place established on the extreme east of the town, *'probably in the century after 1173'.* Moreover, Crosby has shown that this market place stretched from the gaol, eastwards along what is now Old Market Street, to just beyond where the Dolphin public-house now stands. The south side of the street was open ground, sub-divided into areas for the sale of different goods:

cheese, corn, fish, meat and timber.

In 1786, this market place finally became redundant when the market was moved to a more central but equally confined position, back to the site of the old Grassmarket. A new covered market building, known as the Shambles, was erected opposite St Cuthbert's Church. As this was such a confined area, it is likely, however, that on busy market days, stalls were allowed to encroach into the Guildhall Yard, now the present Market Place.

Our present Market Place began to take shape in 1837 when the Guildhall Yard was cleared and modernised. The old Red Lion Inn, which belonged to the Corporation

Borough of Thetford: At a Meeting of the Tradesmen in this Borough, held this day, at the BELL INN, it was unanimously agreed to prosecute as the law directs, all Hawkers and Peddlers who shall hereafter sell or expose to sale, any goods, wares or merchandise whatsoever, in any other place within the said Borough, than in the Market Place, and on a Market Day. **Source:** *Bury & Norwich Post, 22 June 1791.*

and stood on the north-east corner of the Guildhall Yard, was demolished along with the Shambles erected in the 1780s. A new brick-built Red Lion Inn, the one that is familiar to us, was then erected on the site of the Shambles. A new Shambles was built below the north gable of the Guildhall. The new Market Place was completed with the erection of livestock pens on the south side, between two fire-engine houses, while trees were planted along the east and north side.

The appearance of our Market Place was again altered in 1887 when the livestock pens on the south side were demolished, to make way for a Mechanics' Institute [until recently a wine bar], built to commemorate Queen Victoria's Golden Jubilee.

The following decade, the old Shambles was demolished and a new Shambles [the present building] erected as covered market accommodation.

At different times in the 20th century, the Market Place has again been modernised and refurbished. As recently as 1986, new Victorian-style lamp standards and traffic bollards were erected. Moreover, the Late Victorian Shambles lost its identity after conversion into four shop units.

Not only has the location and physical appearance of Thetford's Market Place changed, so has the prescribed day or days for traders to set up their temporary stalls. Thetford's ancient market charter granted a Saturday market. However, in addition, a weekday market was established on Wednesdays some time in the 1950s but as recently as 1970 this market day was changed to a Tuesday.

Yet, despite competition from permanent shops, the recent growth of newly established Sunday markets and occasional car boot sales, Thetford's Market Place continues to flourish as a centre of commerce and trade.

Thetford:- On Saturday morning our market place presented a scene of activity. The steam horses, swinging boats, shooting galleries, stalls etc from Mildenhall were built up, when a meeting was held in the Guildhall - present Major Marsham, Rev. W. Dalley, and Inspector White, to take steps, if possible to prevent it. Mr Pye, the lessee of the tolls and of the Red Lion was sent for and remonstrated with, but he maintained his right to allow them, it being market day, thus bidding the authorities defiance. **Source:** *Bury & Norwich Post, 16 July 1878.*

Some historians have suggested that the Grassmarket, once situated in the open area between St Cuthbert's Church and the Green Dragon public house, may have Saxon origins. Although its origins are obscure, it is mentioned in a 14th century deed. When the Bailey End Market Place [now Old Market Street] closed in 1786 the area once occupied by the Grassmarket served as Thetford's market place until 1837. This photograph was taken in 1953.
[Photograph courtesy of Studio Five, Thetford]

The Guildhall, Market Place and Shambles prior to 'modernisation' of the Market Place in the mid-1880s. The Shambles seen here was erected in 1837 and replaced by the present Shambles in the 1890s.
The market and other tolls were let by tender, for a seven year term, for much of the 19th and into the 20th century.
In 1881 the Town Council agreed to discontinue the use of the Market Weights. These are now displayed in the Ancient House Museum.

Besides the presence of market stallholders, the Market Place has also been the scene of numerous celebrations, displays, parades and other events. This photograph is of a Civic Week celebration in the late 1920s. Numerous decorated vehicles can be seen and in the foreground, the Borough of Thetford Fire Brigade with their horse-drawn steam fire engine.

Postal Roots Go Deep In Our Town's History
Thetford & Watton Times, 31 March 1989

As it almost exactly 50 years since the present post office building was opened, I thought it appropriate to research Thetford's postal history, an undertaking that has revealed many interesting facts. For instance, Lord Arlington, who was responsible for building the near-by Euston Hall in the 1670s, was at one time the Postmaster General. His secretary, Sir Joseph Williamson [1633-1701], became one of Thetford's greatest benefactors.

About this time Thetford's postmaster, Isaac Osborne, was succeeded by his illiterate son Charles, an appointment which, not surprisingly, often caused frequent misdirection of the mail. The Bell Inn then served as Thetford's Common Post House for the receipt and dispatch of all letters. Post-boys on horseback carried the mail along the post roads between towns and cities, a journey often made hazardous by armed highwaymen, the poor condition of the roads and the weather. In the mid-1750s a postboy was found frozen to death while carrying the mail between Norwich and Thetford.

Despite these hazards, delivery of the mail was expected to be reasonably punctual. However, delay occasionally occurred for other reasons. In 1776 the Mayor of Thetford committed a postboy to jail for 14 days with hard labour for *'loitering and misspending his time on the road, whereby, the arrival of the mail to Lynn was retarded almost six hours'*.

From 1785 the post was carried between Norwich, Thetford and London on the famous Royal Mail coaches. Thetford's postmaster was then James Parker, who was also employed as a land surveyor until his death in 1798. John Theodrick followed as the postmaster, a position that he held until 1826.

The Post Office was then situated in King Street, possibly the building now occupied by the Halifax Building Society [in 2003 a coffee shop]. It was certainly this building which served as the Post Office from about 1840 until 1850 when William Christopher was postmaster.

This was Thetford's Post Office when the Penny Post, a uniform penny postage rate covering all places in the British Isles, was introduced in 1840. Thetford's postmaster was then William Christopher, a master tailor. This was probably the same Post Office auctioned in 1826. There is some evidence that earlier in the 19th century the Post Office was situated in Tanner Street, in a cottage now demolished.

*All that valuable FREEHOLD ESTATE, late the property of Mr James Theodrick, deceased; comprising a convenient dwelling house, now used as the "POST OFFICE", in King Street, Thetford...it contains a parlour and shop in front, a good back keeping-room, 4 chambers, an attic, a cellar, a detached backhouse and a good workshop over the same...***Source:** *Bury & Norwich Post, 23 August 1826.*

In January 1846 the last of the horse-drawn mail coaches operating between Norwich and London passed through Thetford.

About 1850-51 Jacob Howard, a boot and shoemaker was appointed as Thetford's postmaster and the Post Office was established in his small cottage opposite the Market Place. Jacob Howard was succeeded as the postmaster by his son Harry in 1882. The staff then consisted of the postmaster, two sorting clerks telegraphists, two female clerks [the postmaster's two sisters], four town postmen and three rural postmen.

POST, MONEY ORDER, SAVINGS BANK, and TELEGRAPH OFFICE, Market Place; Mr Harry Howard, postmaster. Open week days from 7am till 9pm; Sundays from 7 till 10am. Letters arrive from London and all parts at 7am., and from London, Norwich, Brandon and Cambridge at 12.55pm. Out going mails marked* are not made up on Sundays:- *London,, Brandon, and Cambridge, 11.20am; *Attleborough and Norwich, 11.20am; *London, 5.20pm; London and all parts, 10pm. On Sunday there is only one delivery, at 7am. **Source:** *William White's Directory of Norfolk 1883.*

In the 1880s, the size of Thetford's Post Office became inadequate for the needs of a town with a growing population and an increasing number of postal services. In 1894 Harry Howard's cottage was demolished to make way for a new purpose-built post office.

Forty years after opening, Thetford's Late Victorian Post Office, like its predecessor, had become too small for the size of the town. In the late 1930s another purpose-built Post Office was constructed at a cost of over £8,000, adjacent to the existing Post Office and opened in May 1939.

Today, Thetford's sorting office manager, Peter White, who began working there as a telegram boy in 1946, controls a staff of thirty-seven postmen, four higher-grade postmen, six part-time postmen and two cleaners. There is also a counter staff of eight clerks.

A rare photograph, taken about 1890, of Thetford's Post Office in the days when Harry Howard was Postmaster.

Postal deliveries in Thetford probably became much easier for postal staff after the town's houses were ordered to be numbered in 1871. Even so, complaints were being made in 1900 that 'some persons were refusing to have their houses numbered'.

[Photograph courtesy of the Ancient House Museum, Thetford]

Postmen can be seen departing from Thetford's first purpose-built Post Office, erected in 1894. It was built on the site of Harry Howard's boot shop and post office.

What must have been one of Thetford's first post or pillar-boxes was erected outside the Bell Inn booking office in 1860.

2511   Post Office and St. Cuthbert's Church, Thetford

The present Post Office, built at a cost of over £8,000, was officially opened in May 1939 by Mr Somerset de Chair, M.P.

Designed by H. M. Office of Works, the ground floor contained the public office, with a mahogany panelled service counter 21 feet [6.4 m] in length at the east end, and two recessed telephone boxes at the west end. There was also a waiting room, sorting office and staff room.

Mr Somerset de Chair was the first person to send a telegram from the new Post Office, while another invited guest, Lady Fisher of Kilverstone Hall, made the first purchase of postage stamps.

Coach Travel Was A Real Marathon *Thetford & Watton Times, 22 March 1991*

In the 1820s, at the peak of the 'coaching days', it is estimated that over 1,500 scheduled stage coaches departed daily from London, including ten to Norfolk.

Public coach travel had gradually increased during the 18th century, although it was an uncomfortable and often long and dangerous undertaking. Not only was coach travel important for transporting passengers, but it was also a vital means of communication between cities, towns and villages. Furthermore, the carriage of London and provincial newspapers informed the public both of world and local news and opinions.

In 1769 it took thirty hours [sometimes more] to travel by coach from the Maids Head Inn, St Simon's, Norwich to London, stopping over-night at Thetford; a total distance of 112 miles. The fare to London, travelling inside the coach, was then 22 shillings [110p], a large sum of money considering an agricultural labourer was then earning only 7-14 shillings [35-70p.] a week, depending on the season. A half-price fare was offered, however, for those prepared to face the hazards of the weather on the outside of the coach.

The Norwich-London coach service improved with the introduction of a *'new coach on steel springs'* in 1771. The journey time was then reduced to one day and included a parcel collection service from the King's Head, Wymondham; Crown, Attleborough; Angel, Larling; Bell, Thetford and Red Lion, Newmarket.

At the same time, conditions on the main roads were improving through the work of the turnpike trusts. The road or turnpike between Norwich and Newmarket was repaired and maintained by two separate trusts, each financed by tolls collected from travellers at strategic points along the route. Toll gates were erected in the nearby parishes of Elveden and Kilverstone.

Further improvements continued with the introduction of Royal Mail coaches. Heavily guarded against highwaymen and exempt from tolls, they provided a speedier service and also travelled at night. The Royal Mail coaches began passing through Thetford early in 1785, just a few months after they first began operating between London and Bath.

Norwich Coaches: The proprietors of the Mails, the Expedition thro' Newmarket, and the Post Coach thro' Bury, respectfully acquaint the public, that from the extravagant price of Hay, Corn and other articles, they are under absolute necessity of advancing the fares, Inside 4s, Outsides 3s, and Carriage of Parcels above 6lb. weight, to 2d per lb. from Norwich, and in the same proportion on the roads; assuring them, that whenever an opportunity offers, they will be ready to reduce them again. Norwich Jan./13, 1800 **Source:** *Bury & Norwich Post, 15 January 1800.*

As the number of coach services increased, particularly from the 1780s, so did competition between rival coach proprietors and their servants. Occasionally, coach drivers attempting to be punctual and getting the first chance of travellers on the road, were charged with reckless driving. In 1823 the drivers of the 'Day and Times Coach' were summoned before the Mayor of Norwich, who threatened them with the treadmill after their coach had travelled at a dangerous speed, covering the 112 miles between London and Norwich in less than 11 hours. Even so, most drivers were respected for their skills.

An integral part of coach travel was the large inns that developed along the main coaching routes, providing fresh horses and stabling and food and refreshment for travellers [if time allowed]. Some of the more important inn proprietors established their own scheduled coach services. In 1843, Robert Edwards, of Thetford's Bell Inn, introduced the 'Prince Albert Coach', daily [except Sundays] between Thetford and London in 7 hours.

By now, however, the short-lived 'coaching era' was already in decline as the newly constructed railroads made their impact, not only upon the landscape but also the way in which people travelled. The arrival of the railway at Thetford in 1845 was followed the next year by the passage through Thetford of the last scheduled coach between London and Norwich.

COACHES. [from Thetford]
From the Bell Inn. To London, 1/4 before 6 mg., 1/2 before 11 morning, and at 11 night. To Bury, 1/2 past 10 mg.; to Cambridge, 2 afm; to Norwich 1/4 before 4 mg; and at 1 and 3 afm - daily, except Sunday. Also to Bury, Wed. 10 mg; & Tue. Thu. & Sat. 8 evg; and to Lynn, Tues. at 7, & Thu. & Sat. at 8 morning.
From the White Hart. Mail, to Bury, Newmarket, &c. at 8 night; and to Norwich 6 morning.
From the Kings Head. To Lynn, Tues. 7, & Thu. & Sat. at 8 mg.; & to Bury, same evenings at 8. **Source:** *William White's Directory of Suffolk 1844.*

Nonetheless, a public coach service between Bury St Edmunds and King's Lynn continued through the town for some time afterwards. Moreover, local carters and carriers flourished, transporting goods and passengers to and from the surrounding villages and the new railway system, in their horse-drawn vehicles.

No doubt, at the turn of the century, many years after the demise of the stagecoach, the old men who congregated at Thetford's 'Bell Corner' would 'mardle' and reminisce about the 'good old coaching days' of their youth - perhaps after watching a new-fangled horseless carriage pass by.

This wonderful but rather fanciful drawing of the 'up and down coaches', captures something of the coaching era and Thetford's Bell Inn. The Bell was one of a number of important coaching inns on the route between Norwich and London. Ostlers, employed to take care of the patrons' horses, had to rely on 'tips' received from customers. The innkeepers, usually, only found their ostlers food and lodgings, probably no more than a straw bed in the stables. When Robert Drake died in 1850, it was reported that he was the head ostler at the Bell for between 30 & 40 years. Drake would have worked for two highly respected innkeepers, Elizabeth 'Betty' Radcliffe from 1792-1829 and Robert Edwards 1829-1886. Earlier innkeepers noted at the Bell are James Judd in 1740 and 1745, Thomas Feltwell in 1753, Richard Hovel in 1768 and 1777 and Alexander Radcliffe in 1792.

Turnpike Road

From Thetford to Newmarket

Notice is hereby given, that the next meeting of the Trustees of the said road will be held by adjournment at the George Inn, in Thetford, on Monday next, the 15th day of October inst. at 11 o'clock in the forenoon, when the tolls arising at the several Toll-gates and Bar upon the said road, called the Red Lodge Gate and Bar, & the Elden Gate, will be let by auction to the best bidders, and will be put up at the following sums respectively, (being the production of the said tolls for the last year, above the expendes of collecting them) viz. The Red Lodge Gate and Bar (therewith held) at £264 and the Elden Gate at £90.

Whoever happens to be the best bidder for either of the said tolls, will be required to give security with sufficient sureties to the satisfaction of the Trustees, for payment of the rent agreed for.

Source: *Bury & Norwich Post, 10 October 1804.*

It was here, in the yard of the Bell Inn that the daily coaches would stop on their journey between Norwich and London. In the late 1880s, Robert Nurse of Thetford recalled something of the coaching era in a letter to the editor of the Thetford & Watton Times.

...'In our old coaching days we had three stage coaches daily from Norwich to London and vice versa, passing through Thetford, named the Mail, the Magnet and the Expedition, the latter two were licensed to carry 12 passengers outside and 6 inside and the fare from Thetford to London outside was 17/6d. and inside 25/-.

Passengers had no want of fresh air as they would be poised on the top of the coach at considerable elevation, braving the element whatever the mood, whether it was rain or sunshine, snow storm or thunder storm, it must be taken as a man takes his wife - for better or worse. The inside passengers were stowed up like "Jack in the box". During the cold season they would be glad to shut up closely. These must be put up with the annoyance of sucking in their own breath, and that of their companions whose company they must keep from 10 to 12 hours. Besides this the practice of smoking and chewing tobacco was very common and generally adopted'...

Main River Crossing For Many Centuries *Thetford & Watton Times, 15 June 1990*

Many a bridge, old and new, has been built on or very close to the site of an ancient ford. Thetford's Town Bridge is probably one of these. It was for many centuries the main and most central of the town's river crossings, spanning the Little Ouse river. In earlier times the Town Bridge was known as the Great Bridge, also the Christopher Bridge.

Although it is not known when the first bridge was erected on the Town Bridge site, Alan Crosby in his *History of Thetford,* tells us that it must have been well before 1290, when a Thetford deed mentions Matthew de Bryggegate.

It is known that new bridges, all constructed of timber, were built in 1610, 1696 and 1794. The present cast-iron bridge was erected in 1829, exactly 50 years after the world's first iron bridge was built at Ironbridge, Shropshire.

...the Christopher Bridge requires reparation and is incapable of carrying heavy burdens.
Agreed the general proposal for rebuilding St Christopher's not to exceed £350... **Source:** *Corporation of Thetford Minute Book, 9 January 1794 and 11 April 1794.*

It is perhaps surprising that the present Town Bridge was not constructed by local iron founders, but by William Bough and George Smith of Middlesex, from designs by Francis Stone [1775-1835], who was for nearly 30 years architect of the city of Norwich and surveyor of Norfolk. That same year as Thetford's Town Bridge was built, Francis Stone designed and built of cast-iron, Fye Bridge, Norwich. This bridge has since been replaced by one of brick.

Bridges have been and, in some cases, still are a great source of income from tolls. The custom of tolls was usually in the possession of the manorial lord, as was the repair and maintenance of the bridge. The collection of the tolls was often leased or farmed out to an individual. A Bailiff's Roll of Thetford in 1403-04 records, *'£12 from the crossing of the Great Bridge of Thetford and Jusselford in the county of Norfolk and of the bridge of Euston and Honeweton [Honington] in the county of Suffolk; together with the toll of the town of Thetford, this year leased to John Sturmy...£12 0s. 0d.'.*

Thetford Bridge Tolls:- By an old charter, the Corporation have the right of levying tolls at these bridges, as boards fixed up there designate on "waggons 2d. and carts 1d. when laden with saleable things". These tolls are let to the highest bidder, and the lessee catches what he can. A poor old woman in her donkey and cart, who brings a cabbage or two or basket of apples as a present to her married daughter up the back lane is invariably pounced upon, and even drivers of empty gig carts, coming in for shop goods are bullied and abused into payment... **Source:** *Letter to the Bury & Norwich Post, 14 November 1855.*

Until 1880, carts and wagons carrying saleable goods and beasts being driven to market were subject to a toll when crossing the several bridges of Thetford and Brandon Bridge. Before the tolls were finally abolished by the Corporation, there were many disagreements between travellers and the toll keepers. One such incident occurred in 1878 when a cattle drover argued with the toll collector over the evasion of an old toll and caused nearly 200 impatient bullocks, restrained by the toll chain being drawn across the bridge, to create mayhem in Bridge Street.

As a busy river crossing, on the main road between London and Norwich, several substantial buildings have been built, at different times, very close to the Town Bridge. On the south-west bank was the medieval hospital known as Domus Dei. Another hospital, dedicated to St Mary and St Julian, stood on the north-east bank and seems to have been a hostelry for poor travellers and pilgrims. Its ruins were pulled down in 1777. The north-west bank is occupied by Bridge House, once the old George Inn. The Christopher Inn stood on the south-east bank and gave its name to the bridge between the early 17th century until the middle of the 19th century.

It is now 160 years since the Town Bridge, possibly one of the oldest bridges of its kind in the country, was built for the passage of horse and cart. It continues, nevertheless, to carry heavy motor vehicles over its narrow width - deserving an eminent place amongst the architectural remains of old Thetford.

Thetford: An Old Score:- On Monday afternoon, the 16th inst., some little excitement was caused in Bridge Street. A drover in charge of about 180 large bullocks, directed from the railway, and the property of Mr Makins [Essex], was proceeding to Woolpit Fair, but the toll keeper on the bridge, recognising the drover, put the chain across the bridge and demanded on old score, together with his present charge of 3s. 4d. This led to an angry discussion, the language used being very unparliamentary, and in the meantime the animals completely blockaded the street up from St Peter's Church, causing quite a stampede. The shopkeepers hastened to put their shutters up, and at a private house used as a school, a bullock most unceremoniously popped his head through a large square of glass, but on seeing the children it withdrew. The ornamental railings, with brick and stone coping, to Mr Colby's entrance was completely knocked out of shape. Ultimately, on the drover paying the present toll, and giving his employers name, he was allowed to depart, after which mops, pails and birch brooms were brought into speedy requisition. **Source:** *Bury & Norwich Post [Supplement], 24 September 1878.*

A drawing of the Town or Christopher Bridge, the main river crossing, by the Reverend Joseph Wilkinson in 1818. It was published the following year in Frederick Accum's 'Guide to the Chalybeate Spring of Thetford'. A stone tablet, on the outside of the tower of St Mary's Church, commemorates Joseph Wilkinson, Rector of East & West Wretham, who died in 1831 aged 67 years.

This drawing of the wooden, Town Bridge was also made by the Reverend Joseph Wilkinson, in 1822.
In 1794 it was agreed by the Town Council that the rebuilding of St Christopher's Bridge was not to exceed the sum of £350. A new wooden bridge was constructed, to be replaced thirty-five years later by the present cast-iron structure.

The present cast-iron, Town Bridge, built in 1829. It is probable that all previous bridges over this important river crossing were constructed of wood. The Town Bridge is now something of a local icon and, as such, it is unlikely ever to be replaced.

How The River Gangs Made The Long Haul
Thetford & Watton Times, 6 September 1991

Looking at the Little Ouse river from Thetford, through Brandon to where it joins the Great Ouse, it is difficult to imagine it was once part of an elaborate system of navigable inland waterways.

Thetford and Brandon were both important regional ports, where barges known as 'lighters', laden with coal, grain, timber, fertilisers, bricks, gravel and many other goods, were a familiar sight for several centuries.

Before the railway network was established, these waterways, some of them man-made, were vital for transporting raw materials and manufactured goods. They linked not only the major centres of industry and population with the seaports but also more rural regions such as ours.

The Little Ouse, or Brandon River as it was also called, has probably been used for transporting heavy goods from time immemorial - certainly from 1669 when an Act of Parliament empowered the Corporation of Thetford to make the river navigable.

The main import was coal, shipped by sea from the north-east coal fields to King's Lynn. There it was loaded on to lighters for such places as Ely and Cambridge by way of the Great Ouse; Mildenhall and Bury St Edmunds on the River Lark; and Brandon and Thetford on the Little Ouse.

The lighters were worked by lightermen or watermen, an occupation to which a boy or young man could be bound as an apprentice. Nine year old Robert Rampling was apprenticed in 1797 to Daniel Hammerway, a lighter owner and waterman of Brandon. William Murrell, after a three-year apprenticeship, served many of Thetford's lighter owners in the first quarter of the 19th century before settling in Brandon. His descendants continued as the owners of lighters and pleasure boats into the 20th century.

The 1851 Census reveals eight watermen at Brandon and seven at Thetford - there may have been others along the navigation. One boatwright lived at Brandon and three at Thetford, suggesting that a small amount of boat building and repair work was undertaken on the river. Furthermore, a small amount of casual labour was also used to load and unload the lighters.

Three to five lighters were usually coupled together, bow to stern, to form a 'gang'. Each gang was known by its owner's name. Godfrey's, Gill's and Pallant's gang were each well known in the 19th century. Two or three watermen manned each gang of lighters, while a towing horse was led or ridden by a boy along the haling or hauling path.

At times, voyages between King's Lynn or Wisbech and Thetford, the furthermost point on the navigation, must have been difficult. The hauling path used to deviate from one side of the river to the other, forcing the horse and boy to wade or swim across - dangerous when the river was swollen or flooded. Fences and other obstacles were often placed across the path by landowners and farmers.

The typical 'fen lighter' was about 42 feet long by 9 feet wide at bottom and 10 ft. at deck and drew when empty about 12 inches, and when loaded with 25 tons about 3 feet 6 inches. Lighters on the Little Ouse, however, could not take such loads; the draught from the Gt. Ouse to the Two Mile Bottom was only about 3 feet and the latter place to Thetford 2 feet.
Source: W. G. Clarke, *In Breckland Wilds*, Robert Scott, London [1925].

The navigation was financed through tolls paid by those using the waterway - originally a fixed charge of 6d [2.5p] per chaldron [53 cwt or 2692.4 kg]. Later, a more sophisticated scale of charges was introduced for different cargoes and distances.

A continual problem was the evasion of payment and the embezzlement of cash and goods. These matters caused the navigation to be described as *'mismanaged and neglected until 1827, when it was put into the hands of a superintendent'.* After this, things improved and the Corporation of Thetford was estimated to have received 90 per cent of its income from the navigation in 1833. In 1845, the highest tolls recorded in one year were received: £1,728 including the carriage of 15,000 tons of coal.

From then on, trade declined. The railway through Brandon and Thetford, opened in 1845, enabled heavy goods to be carried faster and more economically to and from a greatly extended market. However, the navigation continued in competition against the railway for another half-century before its final termination.

Recollections of the navigation, for those whose childhood spanned the 1880s and 90s, were not of coal, legal disputes or toil, but memories of annual Sunday school outings in decorated lighters loaned by Mr Fison, a local merchant. On the great day the lighters, fully laden with excited children, departed from the Town Bridge wharf destined for Two Mile Bottom Common or Santon Downham. There they disembarked with their teachers for an afternoon of games, stories and a picnic. The return journey home through the peaceful, open heathland of the Breckland landscape, passed with the singing of songs and hymns of praise. These memories endured a lifetime.

Brandon – Whereas we have for many years suffered great injuries by the embezzlement of corn going down to Lynn, also of goods brought from thence by water; and a discovery being lately made, some of the offenders are now in custody, and two more described as under, being absconded [John Field of Wilton Ferry, John Neve of Brandon, Waterman]; *We offer a reward of Half a Guinea for each man, all reasonable charges, for taking and securing either of them. Robert Denton, Robert Dade, John Brewster...* **Source:** *Ipswich Journal, 26 February 1757.*

Amongst the few surviving photographs of the Thetford Navigation before it became redundant in the early years of the 20th century: lighters at the Town Quay near the Town Bridge, circa 1887 [courtesy of Thetford Town Council]; the Little Ouse river and the Haling Path, circa 1905; the First Staunch, circa 1887 [courtesy of Thetford Town Council]; and perhaps the most poignant photograph, published on a picture postcard about 1905, that of two derelict and decaying lighters, abandoned and semi-submerged, near the old Brandon Bridge.

One of Thetford's greatest assets is its rivers. In bygone days they provided, among other things, a source of power for local industries, a watering place for livestock, a mode of transport, and a source of food.

Today the rivers' usage is mostly for leisure and recreation. What better place to spend a warm summer afternoon – boating, fishing, paddling, walking along the lush green banks or perhaps just sitting watching the dark waters slowly flow by?

As early as the year 1250, laws were made to control fishing within the limits of the Borough, when it was decreed that, *'all fishers who took pike or other fish in the common stream should not sell them to strangers, but expose them for sale in the town'*. Locally caught fish was sold at the 'Bell' corner until the custom died out in the early 17th century.

A number of fine fish have been taken from Thetford's rivers. The Reverend Francis Blomefield in his, *'History of Thetford'*, published in 1739, records a sturgeon taken from the Paper-Mill Pool, which weighed 13 stone 10 pounds and was over 7 feet long. In this another fisherman's yarn?

Fishing
For those who prefer fresh water fishing the Lesser Ouse presents a favourable opportunity. It abounds in eels, pike, perch roach, dace, barbel, and sometimes salmon is caught. Permission to angle is seldom refused on proper application to the proprietors.
The Lesser Ouse, or, as in some deeds it is denominated, Brandon river, rises in a swampy meadow, near the village of Lopham. It divides Suffolk from Norfolk. **Source:** Frederick Accum, *Guide to the Chalybeate Spring of Thetford*, London [1819].

As a boy, a favourite venue of mine during the summer months was the council swimming baths, situated on the Little Ouse river, close to the Nuns' Bridges. It consisted of a few wooden changing cubicles standing on a concrete bank. Bathing sheds were first erected here in the early 1890s. This was after the council had received complaints from indignant ladies of the town, who while walking along the Water Meadows were often confronted by the sight of naked boys bathing in the deep pool by the First Staunch. The council swimming baths became redundant when the indoor pool at the Breckland Sports Centre was opened in 1972.

One of a number of boats decorated as part of Thetford's coronation celebrations for King George VI in 1937.

The rivers have also been the scene of numerous celebrations and carnivals, such as Queen Victoria's Diamond Jubilee in 1897. Another event occurred in June 1913, when it was reported that 2,000 people lined the river bank between the Town Bridge and the First Staunch to watch a procession of illuminated boats. Also included were aquatic sports and the rescue of a mimic suffragette who *'accidentally'* fell overboard. The carnival was organised to raise funds to clear weeds from the river.

Messing about on the river has always been popular. A great attraction from 1893 until the early 1900s was the 'Pride of the Ouse', a former ship's longboat, converted into a paddle steamer and powered by a steam engine built at the Charles Burrell engineering works that abutted onto the river.

On certain days during the summer months, the 'Pride of the Ouse', with its owner, Mr Jimmy Arbon, at the helm, carried day-trippers to Brandon and on occasions longer excursions to Denver Sluice, Ely and even Cambridge.

RIVER CARNIVAL AT THETFORD
Upwards of £25 was cleared by a river carnival held on Thursday in last week, for the purpose of raising funds for clearing the river of weeds... Later on Messrs. Harrison and Crossland attracted a large crowd with a black and white boxing match in a boat in the middle of the river... The children were hugely delighted with a display of daylight fireworks discharged by Mr E. Bond, and up near the staunch there were said to be an exciting rescue of a mimic suffragette who "accidentally" fell overboard... The charming effect produced by the procession of decorated and illuminated boats, which were marshalled by Mr Woods, evoked general admiration. Excellent views were obtained from both sides of the river, and each boat was more or less cordially applauded... **Source:** *Thetford & Watton Times, 7 June 1913.*

At various times, attractive walks have been laid-out for those who prefer a leisurely stroll along the river bank. The Spring Walk was created in 1819 for visitors to the pump room and bathhouse at Thetford's Chalybeate Spa, situated in a meadow close by the Little Ouse.

The Haling Path, another popular riverside walk, was opened in 1887 to commemorate the Golden Jubilee of Queen Victoria's reign. A few years earlier it was the scene of an event that has become a local legend – the so-called 'Thetford Riots'.

Bathers and spectators at the Council Swimming Baths circa 1930. The gentleman standing at the rear is the Attendant, Mr W.J. Drake.
[Photograph courtesy of John and Marjorie Mayes]

1749 28th Feb. Burried Elizabeth wife of William Warner, & Mary his daughter of St Mary's parish who were both unfortunately drowned in the River near the Christopher Bridge in this town.
Source: Parish Register of Burials St Cuthbert's, Thetford 1737-1754.

This photograph was taken from Canterbury Way in 1972, the same year that Thetford could at last boast an indoor swimming pool, built on the Croxton Road.
Although bathing in the local rivers is generally less popular since the arrival of the indoor swimming pool, in the warm summer months children continue to paddle and swim at certain parts of the local rivers, or even jump from the Town Bridge into the slow-moving waters of the Little Ouse.
[Photograph courtesy of Eastern Daily Press 2003]

In a previous historical *Thetford Dateline* it was briefly mentioned that Thetford's rivers once provided the motive power for a number of local industries before the arrival of steam power and electricity. The Domesday Survey in 1086 recorded eight mills at Thetford. These mills would have been water-powered. The watermill is known to have been used in Roman Britain, preceding the introduction of the windmill by many centuries.

The mill was an important part of the local economy and the property of either the manorial lord, some other powerful individual or a religious house. Several of Thetford's former religious establishments had a mill in their possession.

Although the watermill was originally used only for grinding or milling grain, it was later used in the wool, papermaking, metal and mining industries.

Situated on the Little Ouse river, is the site of one of Thetford's ancient mills. Today it is referred to locally as the 'Pulp Mill'. In the 12th century it was in the possession of the Bishop of Ely and known as Bishop's of St Audrey's Mill.

The Bishop's Mill was, at one time, used as a fulling-mill for treating ready-woven cloth with fuller's earth. From the 1730s, possibly before, paper was manufactured on the site. The Paper Mill was Thetford's largest manufacturer and employer of labour until the middle of the 19th century, when it was surpassed by the agricultural engineering works of Charles Burrell.

In 1879 the Patent Pulp Manufacturing Co. Ltd., was established and began production of pulpware on the site. The patent pulp process involved the conversion of wood pulp or other vegetable fibres and rags, into a pulpy sludge. After treatment, it was formed into a wide range of light, durable and inexpensive products such as babies' baths, bowls, chamber pots, flower pots, jugs, trays and even spittoons.

In the 1930s, more than one hundred and fifty different articles were being made in an array of colours and designs. Examples of these can be seen in Thetford's Ancient House Museum.

After the Second World War, during which vulcanised fibre fuel tanks for aircraft, crash helmets for dispatch riders and fire buckets were produced at Thetford, pulpware gradually became obsolete as the demand for plastic products increased.

Thetford Moulded Products, the present name of the original company, is today one of the world's largest manufacturers of motor cycle crash helmets, now produced by plastic-injection moulding. Also manufactured by the same process and exported world wide are safety helmets for use in the mining, building and civil engineering industries. Ear defenders and eye protectors are also produced to complete the range of high quality personnel safety equipment.

Of the many household items once produced, only the manufacture of moulded tea and sandwich trays has continued. Now made of laminated plastic using a pulp core, these trays known as the 'Thetford Collection' are available in a variety of shapes, colours and designs.

It is probable that Thetford Moulded Products, the town's oldest industrial company, occupies a site where industrial activity has been carried out continuously for 1,000 years.

PROCESS OF MANUFACTURE
From Scandinavia comes the wood pulp in crude form, and the preliminary stages of treatment subject it to processes somewhat similar to those carried out in paper making. Conspicuous are:- The boiling vats, the paper mill or rag engine for grinding the pulp, the vats from which the pulp is moulded, and the stamping machine...the pulp is placed in large tanks in which the apparatus for crushing and tearing is at work, and when reduced to the required extent the water is strained off, and the residue is passed on to a series of hydraulic presses, each of which can take various shapes and sizes of moulds. Thus each press can turn out a great variety of shapes. As it is necessary that these shapes should be well dried large rooms are requisitioned for the purpose, constructed over or near the boilers, as they have sometimes to be heated by the steam pipes...In an adjoining building are the hydraulic stamping machines, whose mission it is to press the rough shapes into the densest form, and add a smooth surface, rendering the body of the ware hard and solid, and more correct and defined in shape...
From the stamping machines the goods, still known as blanks, go to another department to be cut and trimmed...The goods must next be indurated* and painted. Indurating is one of the most important of the processes, much of the life of the ware depending upon the thoroughness with which it is done...In the decorating room are employed a number of girls and women preparing and putting on the ornamentations, such as floral and geometrical designs. Much of the decoration is done entirely by hand. **Source:** East Anglian Industries - 5. The Patent Pulp Manufacturing Company, Ltd., Thetford, *Bury Free Press, 28 August 1907.* * Indurated – to make or become hard.

Mill Lane and part of the premises occupied by the Patent Pulp Manufacturing Company Limited about 1900.
The 'pulp works' covered an area of about 4 acres and several times during its history was badly damaged by fire, that often resulted in major rebuilding. Industrial activity finally ceased on the site when it was sold for residential development in 1989.
[Photograph courtesy of the Ancient House Museum, Thetford]

Many different articles were made at Thetford's 'pulp works'. In the late 1890s, the company advertised, washing basins, jugs, spittoons, square pans, chambers, bread trays, biscuit dishes, show bowls, mugs and plates, water cans, flower pots, ash and pin trays, decanter stands, card trays, crumb trays, trays and waiters, tobacco jars, helmets, plaques, finger plates, miners' hats, water bottles, cabmen's hats, life buoys, glass stands and bottle stands.
A display of pulpware can be seen at Thetford's Ancient House Museum.

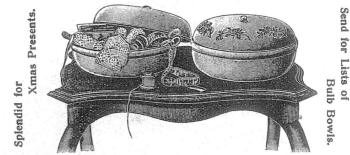

THETFORD PULP WARE.

Splendid for Xmas Presents.

Send for Lists of Bulb Bowls.

LADIES' WORKBOXES. Plain and Decorated.

Illustrated Lists of these and many other Articles will be sent post free on application to the

PULP CO., THETFORD, NORFOLK.

A view of the cutting and trimming room in the early years of the 20th century. In the foreground on the right are bowl blanks and behind them small chamber pots.
[Photograph courtesy of the Ancient House Museum, Thetford]

Last Reminder Of Town's Great Milling Days *Thetford & Watton Times, 14 August 1992*

In the 19th century Thetford could boast of at least three windmills for grinding grain or corn into flour. Flour milling was certainly a significant local industry from the earliest times. The Domesday Book recorded eight mills at Thetford and these are likely to have been water-powered because the windmill is believed to have been unknown in England at this time.

While all of Thetford's windmills have disappeared, a former watermill still survives. Known today as the Old Mill or sometimes the Coffee Mill, it straddles the River Thet in what has become an attractive and appealing part of Thetford. Although the present structure probably dates only from the early years of the 19th century, there has been a mill on this site from at least the time Domesday was completed 900 years ago. In the 15th century it was known as Pitt Mill, a name retained on George Bird Burrell's, *Plan of the Ancient Town of Thetford,* published in 1807.

The Domesday Book reveals the extent to which most of the Borough - as opposed to the defended town in the centre - was agricultural. It refers specifically to 34 acres of meadowland and pasture, and sufficient arable land to support 10 plough-teams, and this represents only a small proportion of the total, since a large area was not subject to tax. Reflecting the importance of agriculture the Survey refers to seven or eight mills, implying a thriving corn trade. Four of these were on sites known to have been occupied by later medieval mills: Melford Bridge (the name of which is a corruption of Mill Ford), the Bishops Mill (now the site of the moulded products factory), the Pit Mill, and the Castle Mill, upstream from Nuns Bridges on the River Thet. The other sites have been lost. **Source:** *Alan Crosby, A History of Thetford, Phillimore & Co Ltd [1986].* Reproduced by kind permission from A History of Thetford by Alan Crosby, published in 1986 by Phillimore & Co Ltd., Shopwyke Manor Barn, Chichester, West Sussex, PO20 2BG.

The mill stands at what was the furthermost point of the Thetford Navigation, adjacent to the Stone Quay or Wharf. Early in the 19th century it was occupied by the Gills, a prominent family of millers and merchants, who also owned a 'gang' of lighters or barges for transporting grain, flour and other merchandise along the Thetford Navigation towards King's Lynn and Wisbech. The Mill was known as Thetford Water Mill when John Withers Gill, miller and merchant, was declared bankrupt in the mid-1860s. The Gills' reign in local commercial and civic life [they were mayor on six occasions] then came to an end.

After the Gills' collapse, farmer William Jillings of the Nunnery Farm and James Cronshey, a maltster, miller and artificial manure manufacturer, formed a partnership and occupied the mill until about 1900. James Mayes and Sons then expanded their business interests by operating the Thetford Water Mill. James Mayes already occupied a windmill and farm, situated on the London Road [site of the Plover public house].

Water continued to drive the mill machinery until about 1924 when James Mayes and Sons ceased business there. This was a period of national economic and industrial depression when many of the numerous water and wind-powered mills scattered about the countryside ceased working, eventually to be replaced by modern roller mills situated close to sea-ports.

It must have been welcome news at Thetford in 1936 when the Ibex Coffee Company announced that it was to begin processing coffee and tea at the Old Mill. The flour miller's dusty environment was to be replaced by the rich aroma of raw coffee beans as they were roasted before being ground, blended and packaged for home and world-wide markets. In 1938,

the Ibex Co. was purchased by a rival company, R. Twinning and Co., as a war emergency factory in case its London premises were bombed. Twinnings traded from the Old Mill, providing much needed employment for about nine men and thirty women, until 1956 when industrial activity on the site finally ceased.

Valuable and Important Mercantile Property with Possession Thetford, Norfolk...to sell by Auction, on Monday the 28th November, at the Bell Hotel, at Three for Four O'clock in the Afternoon, in Lots:

Lot One

All that valuable FREEHOLD ESTATE, now in the Tenure of Mr J.W. Gill, driving four pairs of stones, with all the machinery and going gears complete, and with an old established connection attached.

A Counting House, Range of Stables, Harness House, and other Out buildings.

Extensive WINE VAULTS, Bottling house and Granaries over, and a very valuable Paddock at the back of the Mill, the whole contains about TWO ACRES. **Source:** *Bury & Norwich Post, 8 November, 1864.*

Despite new technology and a different process it is interesting to note that, for a time, mill machinery used for grinding the coffee beans was driven by water-powered turbines. Diesel turbines were maintained only for emergencies.

After the Old Mill's working days were over it was bought by a local businessman and Freemason. Recently renovated it now serves as a Masonic Lodge - forming an attractive landmark and a reminder of Thetford's industrial past.

The exterior of Thetford's last surviving water mill has changed very little since this photograph was taken over 100 years ago. The interior, however, has altered considerably, while being converted and adapted for different uses.

Before visiting the Ibex Coffee Co., Ltd, (at The Old Mill) I believed coffee to be one of those everyday commodities that are "just bought and sold". But I was soon disillusioned by Mr T.C. Doe (the manager), from whom I learned that the blending and roasting and preparation of coffee for various markets is a very intricate and interesting business.

The majority of the green (or raw) coffee arriving at the mill comes from Kenya in British East Africa (where the Ibex Company owns plantations) and from Jamaica in the British West Indies. In addition to these two main sources of supply coffee arrives from several other parts of the world - notably from Mysore (India), Costa Rica (Central America) and Arabia, these growths being used to give "point" or character to certain blends.

Coffee, when growing on the tree, is not unlike the English cherry, and after it is picked, the fruit or (pulp) is removed to reveal the coffee beans in a parchment covering. This covering is also removed, leaving the raw beans to undergo certain processes before dispatched to England for conversion into the roasted and ground coffee which we are familiar.

Samples of the raw coffee are received at the Old Mill before any consignments are delivered and these samples are carefully tested for their suitability as regards aroma, flavour and strength. This, of course, is a very important aspect of the business, as on it depends the maintenance of the high standard of the coffee sold by the Ibex Company.

The raw coffee arrives in sacks (each weighing about 190 lbs.) and is conveyed to the roasters as required by automatic elevators. The beans are roasted by gas and electric power, the gas being forced into the roasters at high pressure by special "Premix" arrangement. The time taken in roasting varies from 10 - 20 minutes - according to the type and quantity of coffee being dealt with. The four roasting machines at the Old Mill range in capacity from 3 c.w.t. to 3 lbs., and when the beans are roasted to the required degree (generally the colour of a ripe chestnut) they are automatically expelled from the roasters into the electrically - cooled trays, the rapid cooling process checking the heat and sealing the strength and aroma into the beans.

Suction elevators next convey the beans either to the patent granulator (which cuts them into small segments) or to the grinding mills - the beans being elevated by suction to make sure that all foreign matter is eliminated and only pure coffee reaches the mills.

When ground and ready for packaging the coffee is passed through automatic weighing machines into the various containers - some blends are packed into air-tight containers and in vacuum sealed tins - thus ensuring that the coffee remains fresh for several weeks...

The machinery at the Old Mill is driven by modern turbines the power being derived from the river Thet. There is also a power-house containing an emergency 20 horse-power oil engine and plant. **Source:** 'Industries of Thetford No 3 The Ibex Coffee Factory', *Bury Free Press 16 July 1938.*

Norfolk's first railway, between Norwich and Yarmouth, was opened in May 1844, at the height of the '*railway mania*', when Parliament was inundated with proposals to build more and more railways throughout the country.

About the same time the Norwich and Brandon Railway Company received the Royal Assent to build its line. This was soon followed by assent to plans by the Eastern Counties Railway to extend its line through Cambridge and Ely and on to Brandon. Construction began in June 1844.

On the 29th July, the following year, the completed part of the Brandon and Norwich Railway was opened at the same time as the Eastern Counties Railway extension to Brandon. Thus, for the first time, Norwich and London were linked by rail.

Thetford - The 30th of July was an eventful day in this ancient borough, and never was there so much interest excited as was created by the opening of the Norfolk Railway, on which occasion the Hon. W. B. Baring gave and honoured with his presidency, a sumptuous entertainment to the Directors, Engineers and élite of the town, provided by the worthy landlord of the Bell Inn, Mr Edwards in a style surpassing even his usual excellent taste and liberality. Thanks to railway expedition, at a few hours notice, Covent Garden Market supplied an abundance of every luxury the eye and taste could desire in the shape of fruit and vegetables...On the following day a large number of railway labourers were entertained with a substantial dinner served by Mr Golding of the Fleece Inn, others having previously regaled in the same manner at the Kings Head Inn. **Source:** *Bury & Norwich Post, 6 August 1845.*

The line terminated at Trowse, on the outskirts of Norwich because of difficulties building a swing-bridge over the river Wensum. Once the bridge was completed, in December 1845, London was linked to Yarmouth by rail by way of Norwich Thorpe station. An alternative route from London to Norwich via Ipswich and Colchester was opened in 1849.

A print of the station soon after it was built.

Although the journey time from Thetford to London was less than four hours, much quicker than by stagecoach, the euphoria that greeted the opening of the railway soon evaporated. Within days, serious accidents began to occur and continued with alarming frequency, resulting in loss of life and appalling injuries to passengers and railway employees until the late 1850s. The length of track between Harling Road and Brandon appears to have been particularly prone to accidents, perhaps as a consequence of the speed in which the railway was constructed.

Thetford's railway station was built on the main line, although it had first been planned to serve the town by a branch line. The station building was originally a small, flint structure with only one platform - it is still visible today beside the red-brick extension added in 1889. When first built, there were no sidings to the east or west of the station but it is probable that one was laid before the end of

1845, when a local newspaper advertised a freight service from Thetford.

A level-crossing, just west of the station platform, once carried the busy Mundford Road, now Station Road, across the railway. This busy crossing was the scene of many near-accidents between rail and road traffic until the 1880s, when it was removed and the road to Mundford closed at this point. A new road had been constructed linking the Croxton Road, just north of the railway bridge, with the Mundford Road north of the station - the road that now passes the Recreation Ground. At the same time the present footbridge was built over the railway, to give passengers access to the station platforms.

The arrival of the railway had a profound effect upon many aspects of local life. Not everyone welcomed railways and despite the economic and social advantages, some tradesmen in the town considered the line '*to injure materially the business of the town*'. Some of the local tradesmen to have suffered the most were hand-craft workers, who now had to compete with mass-produced factory goods brought in by rail from industrial regions. One rope maker openly declared that his trade was ruined by the railway.

But local opinion must have soon changed. Grain and coal merchants, maltsters, farmers and others were soon dispatching their products and receiving goods by rail. In 1846, more than thirty tons of poultry and game were sent by rail from Thetford to the London markets for Christmas.

For many people of different social backgrounds the railways opened up new employment and travel opportunities. The day trip to new and distant places was now a reality.

This rare glimpse of Thetford's railway station from the Croxton Road Bridge dates from about 1880, before the station was extended in 1889. Level crossing gates just west of the station platform and an engine or goods shed on the east side of the station can also be seen.

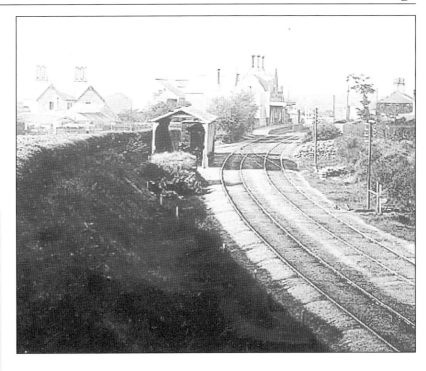

Thetford...The Norwich & Brandon railway passes through the Northern side of the town, under a new and tasteful bridge constructed of brick and passing under the Croxton Rd by a small cutting; the station is a light and pretty building; yet with the great accommodation afforded to the town and passengers by this speedy transit, it is considered by the inhabitants in trade here to injure materially the business of the town. **Source:** *Kelly's Directory of Norfolk 1846.*

This photograph, taken in 2002, clearly shows both the original Thetford station, constructed of flint with ornate gables in 1845, and to the right, the red-brick extension added in 1889.
The platform serving trains to Norwich, with its waiting rooms and boundary wall, is of a similar construction as the 1889 building on the opposite platform.

The days of steam locomotives, regularly hauling goods and passenger trains through Thetford, ended in the 1960s.
This photograph, taken in 1952, captures 0-6-0 locomotive 67293 about to depart for Watton and Swaffham.
The canopy over the platform, supported with decorative pillars, was probably added when the station was extended in 1889.

Before the 1930s, Thetford's Minstergate was full of the sights, sounds and smells of industrial activity. It was the site of the famous St Nicholas Works of Charles Burrell & Co., Ltd, manufacturers of steam traction engines, marine engines, threshing and seed dressing machines, straw elevators, saw benches and corn mills.

It has often been quoted, *'in the year 1770 Joseph Burrell commenced business with a forge in St Nicholas Street, Thetford'.* Researching the origins of this statement and the history of the Burrell family, I discovered amongst the parish records of St Cuthbert and St Peter, evidence which suggests a different beginning.

Joseph Burrell [*circa* 1759-1831], was in business as a whitesmith by the late-1780s. In the mid-1790s he was paying parish rates on a foundry and shop, not in St Nicholas Street but near the old Market Place, in the parish of St Cuthbert. It was not until the early 1800s that he moved into the parish of St Peter, presumably close to the ruined church of St Nicholas. As a whitesmith in a small, rural community, Joseph Burrell's livelihood depended initially upon the general repair and manufacture of a wide range of articles.

From the early 1800s, Joseph, William [1766-1822] and James Burrell [1769-1837], were jointly manufacturing a variety of agricultural implements and machines. After Joseph's death in 1831, the business passed successively to James, and in 1837 to James' second and youngest son, Charles [1817-1906]. It was Charles Burrell who began the production of a portable steam engine in 1848, followed in 1856 by the manufacture and development of a self-propelled road locomotive, using James

Boydell's 'Endless Railway'.

Charles Burrell 1817-1906.

Three of Charles Burrell's sons, Charles [1847-1929], Robert [1849-1904] and Frederick [1855-1927], became directors of the business - a limited company from 1884.

From a small foundry and workshop, the 'works' eventually covered an area from the river, northwards to St Nicholas Street. In 1851 Charles Burrell employed 52 men and 9 boys, about 200 men in 1860 and at the turn of the century over 300 people in the various works departments.

Thetford: Celebration of the Marriage of the Prince of Wales. Never within the recollection of the oldest inhabitants has this ancient borough presented so gay and festive appearance as on the present occasion. In all parts of the town were to be seen triumphal arches, illuminated with devices in gas and coloured lamps, and decorated with every variety of flags and banners, which were also plentifully displayed on the houses and public buildings. The poorer inhabitants and their wives, to the number of 1174, were entertained with a substantial dinner of roast beef and plum-pudding, in the spacious workshops kindly lent for the occasion by C. Burrell, Esq., of St Nicholas Foundry...Pipes, tobacco and ale were provided for the men, and all enjoyed themselves from about 2 to 4 o'clock when the bell rang and the company dispersed... **Source:** *Bury & Norwich Post, 17 March 1863.*

The closure of the 'works' was not a sudden event but a gradual decline which had begun in the years before the 1914-18 War. However, during the war, the workforce was increased with the employment of female labour engaged in the production of Government munitions. Traction engine manufacture continued, though at a reduced level.

The post-war period began optimistically. In 1920 Charles Burrell and Co., Ltd., joined the Agricultural and General Engineers Ltd, a group of engineering companies that had amalgamated in an effort to increase production and sales.

St Nicholas Works - Messers Charles Burrell and Sons have been very successful exhibitors of traction engines during the past season, having taken the special silver medal at the Worcestershire Society's show, held at Stourbridge, the special silver medal at the Staffordshire show, held at Stafford; and the special silver medal at the Long Sutton show. We are glad to learn that the firm has of late considerably increased the number of their hands, owing to the considerable influx of trade. **Source:** *Bury & Norwich Post, 27 September 1881.*

After some initial success, it was eventually destined to failure. AGE Ltd, in a streamlining effort, closed the St Nicholas Works in February 1929. Now 61 years later, the Charles Burrell Museum is soon to be opened in the former paint shop in Minstergate. On display there will be photographs, drawings, documents, tools, machinery and some of the numerous products manufactured at the St Nicholas Works.

Not only has this once important firm influenced Thetford's past, it also has a place in the history of agriculture and transport.

Benjamin Burrell son of Thomas and Elizabeth Burrell of St Peter's Parish, Thetford
Bapt. St Peter's, Thetford 1725- Buried St Mary's, Thetford 1793
1757 [m] Mary Bull *c.1732-1807* of Bury St Edmunds

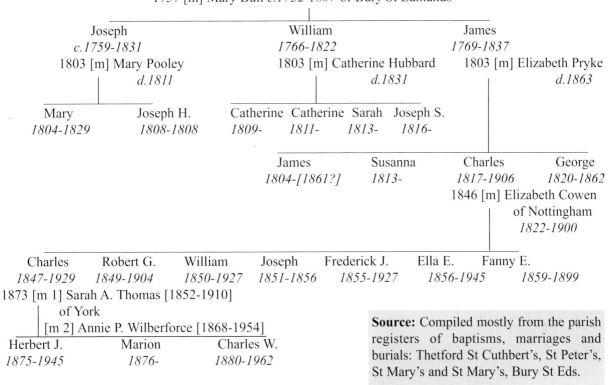

Joseph	William	James
c.1759-1831	*1766-1822*	*1769-1837*
1803 [m] Mary Pooley	1803 [m] Catherine Hubbard	1803 [m] Elizabeth Pryke
d.1811	*d.1831*	*d.1863*

Mary	Joseph H.	Catherine	Catherine	Sarah	Joseph S.
1804-1829	*1808-1808*	*1809-*	*1811-*	*1813-*	*1816-*

James	Susanna	Charles	George
1804-[1861?]	*1813-*	*1817-1906*	*1820-1862*
		1846 [m] Elizabeth Cowen	
		of Nottingham	
		1822-1900	

Charles	Robert G.	William	Joseph	Frederick J.	Ella E.	Fanny E.
1847-1929	*1849-1904*	*1850-1927*	*1851-1856*	*1855-1927*	*1856-1945*	*1859-1899*

1873 [m 1] Sarah A. Thomas [1852-1910]
of York
[m 2] Annie P. Wilberforce [1868-1954]

Herbert J.	Marion	Charles W.
1875-1945	*1876-*	*1880-1962*

Source: Compiled mostly from the parish registers of baptisms, marriages and burials: Thetford St Cuthbert's, St Peter's, St Mary's and St Mary's, Bury St Eds.

While the traction engines and other machinery produced at the St Nicholas Works were renowned for their reliability and craftsmanship, working conditions in the various workshops reflected little of these commendable values. Perhaps this is not surprising, when one considers the general standards of health and safety found in the workplace in the 19th and early years of the 20th century. Moreover, there are numerous accounts of Burrell employees being seriously injured by such things as falling objects, moving machinery and molten metal. Some accidents were even fatal.

At different periods, during the history of the works, there is also evidence of open conflict between certain sections of the workforce and the management. Trade union activity was probably at its strongest, however, in the immediate post-Great War years, when boilermakers participated in strike action for several weeks. This photograph of the fitting shop was taken in the early 1920s. [Photograph courtesy of the Ancient House Museum, Thetford]

By the mid-1850s, railway locomotives were already becoming a fairly common sight, puffing smoke and steam as they passed through many parts of the English countryside. Road locomotives at this time, however, were still in their infancy, even though portable steam engines could frequently be seen, working in the farmyards and fields. The development of the road locomotive created a great deal of interest amongst the general public and a few individuals who could foresee something of their potential.

When describing the history and development of the traction engine and road locomotive, two names frequently appear, those of James Boydell of Camden, London, and Charles Burrell of Thetford, Norfolk.

Many years before road locomotives became a reality, James Boydell must have envisaged a 'road train' - a road locomotive capable of hauling a number of wagons along the highway. From sometime in the 1840s, he had been involved in designing and manufacturing a device, fitted to the wheels of a steam-powered road vehicle, which would overcome the loss of traction from smooth, rigid wheels carrying a heavy payload and able to support the very heavy weight of a locomotive over soft ground. He called this device, an 'endless railway'.

James Boydell exhibited his 'Endless Railway' at the Royal Agricultural Society Show at Carlisle in 1855. It was described in the catalogue of agricultural implements as follows:
'Stand No. 85. - James Boydell, of Camden Works, Camden Town, London, Middlesex.
Article No. 1. - A portable Steam Engine, fitted with an Endless Railway; invented and improved by the exhibitor; the engine manufactured by R. Bach & Co., Birmingham; and the endless railway by Boydell and Glasier, of Camden Town. This engine, being fitted with the exhibitor's patent apparatus or endless railway attached to the wheels, is intended to do the work of horses, by drawing ploughs through the ground, or any loads over fields or along common roads. Price, including patent-right £500'.

Also exhibited was a wagon designed to be drawn by the engine and fitted with Boydell's 'Endless Railway'. Price £70.

The following year, one of the earliest references I have found of the term 'traction engine', appeared when the enterprising agriculturalist, J. J. Mechi, wrote an account of Boydell's *'Traction Steam Engine'.*

'I devoted two days last week to the examination of the operation of this machine as a locomotive and tractive power, and have come to the conclusion that it is a "great success". This success is owing to the endless and wide railway attached to the circumference of the wheels, which gives a fulcrum for the lever, and a bearing sufficiently wide to carry a great weight on soft ground without imbedding in the ground. Although it weighed nine tons, its impress was scarcely perceptible where a horse's foot left a deep indentation. Mr Boydell's machine walked from Camden Town to Acton, taking in-tow its four wheeled wagon with coals, and four heavy iron ploughs, and water enough for four hours work.

When on the soft turnip field [after a nights rain] it drew after it ploughs, scarifier &c., with perfect ease, and then walked home again to Camden Town. It can ascend an acclivity of one-in-three, which is nearly walking up-stairs one-in-two. It can back, advance or stop instantaneously the pinion being shifted from the cogs of the driving wheel, and the power thus suddenly released is carried off by a separate fly-wheel, which may be used for driving threshing machines, mill-stones and other purposes. In fact, instead of a farmer sending for and sending back a six-horse power engine & threshing machine, requiring each trip six horse, this machine will move itself anywhere - draw the corn to the market, bring home manure and do all the cultivation and work on the farm. I hope a company will be formed for its development, Mr Boydell having expended nearly £10,000 in accomplishing his object'.*
Source: *Bury & Norwich Post, 30 April 1856.*

Two years after Mechi's comments, *The Illustrated News Of The World*, published a fascinating drawing of Boydell's engine, accompanied by a detailed description which began, *'THE TRACTION ENGINE. The engine exhibited at East Acton on Thursday, Friday, and Saturday in last week, of which we give an engraving, was the first built at Mr Burrell's establishment at Thetford. It has been shown ploughing publicly near Thetford; at Wimbush-hall, Essex; at Farningham, in Kent; at Louth, in Lincolnshire; gained the prize of £30 given for steam ploughing at York; and has since been employed by the owner of it, Francis Hamilton, Esq., of Friar's - Place, Acton, in scarifying his land and other work. It is composed of two 7-inch cylinders, with 12 inches stroke, and the highest pressure of steam used, 70lbs, per square inch'...* Indeed, Charles Burrell was one who appreciated the possibilities of Boydell's enterprise and sought to capitalise on the knowledge gained and to develop the engine further.

Thetford - Mr C. Burrell's Machine Works:- We visited these works last week, and were a good deal surprised at their increased extent, and the number of men employed in the construction of a great variety of machines. We found many men employed in building Boydell's large engines with the endless railway, these engines having been ordered by firms in America, Russia, Prussia, Sweden and other countries. The working and the power of the traction engine, with the endless railway, on the common roads have been fully and satisfactorily tested at Woolwich, before a committee appointed by the Government, and also before many agriculturists on the fields in the neighbourhood of this town, but since then great improvements have been made by Mr Burrell in the steerage part of the engine. By its use we have seen the heaviest loads can be drawn with greater economy than by horse power, and in ascending and descending the steepest hills, or in passing over soft or marshy ground where no road exist, this engine and railway have been found to overcome difficulties which no amount of horse power could accomplish... **Source:** *Bury & Norwich Post, 13 July 1858.*

*'This Memorial Commemorates The Firm Of Charles Burrell & Sons Limited
Who Carried On Business In These Premises From 1770 To 1930
They produced The World's First Heavy Duty Steam Road Haulage Engine In 1856
Followed By A Great Variety Of Traction & Other Engines & Agricultural Machines
Erected by Public Subscription In 1957, Being The Hundred And
First Anniversary Of The Above Engine Leaving These Works'.*

The plaque was unveiled in Minstergate in 1958. More recent research has revealed that the inscription on the plaque is not completely accurate as it appears that Charles Burrell's ancestors did not open a forge on this site in 1770 and the 'first heavy duty steam road haulage engine' was most probably that made for James Boydell by R. Bach & Co., of Birmingham. When traction engines first appeared they were frequently referred to as 'steam horses'.

Thetford Wool Fair:- ...After the Fair, Lord Walsingham and other gentlemen inspected the new engines, with the endless railway attached, at Mr Burrell's works. Two new engines were exhibited which were ordered by the Pacha of Egypt and by the Indian Government...This new engine is a great improvement in many respects on Boydell's patent. The driving wheel is made of wrought iron instead of wood, and reduced in size, while at the same time it is increased in strength. The guiding or steering apparatus is much simplified and reduced in size, and the shoes for the endless railway are improved in form. Indeed, the engine, for the Indian Government, is of much larger size and both are intended to drag heavy guns or heavy weights. **Source:** *Bury & Norwich Post, 12 July 1859.*

Thetford:- On Thursday last an immense traction engine of 40 h.p. with many improvements introduced by Mr Charles Burrell, of St Nicholas Works, was exhibited in our streets, attracting great attention. It presented a very beautiful appearance compared with former ones, and is capable of drawing 50 tons on a common road, turning corners with ease, and making but little noise. It is intended for the Brazilian Islands, with break van, a train of waggons etc., etc., for the transmission of heavy loads. **Source:** *Bury & Norwich Post, 24 July 1860.*

A great amount of publicity was given to the development of the traction engine during the 1850s. Engineering and agricultural journals of the day carried lengthy reports, as did non-specialist publications, magazines and newspapers.

Engineering historians, such as R. H. Clark and Michael Lane, have used some of these accounts to good effect in describing this important period in the development of steam as a source of power in the great industry of agriculture and on the roads.

Boydell's engine was reported to have given an unsuccessful demonstration of direct ploughing with Colman's plough.

Certainly within a few months of the Chelmsford show, Charles Burrell had completed his first traction engine, based on Boydell's design and fitted with the famous 'Endless Railway'. Early in March 1857, it was reported that Mr Burrell's engine had been seen on trials about Thetford and in a field belonging to a local farmer. Not long after this, Charles Burrell felt confident enough to put publicly his engine to the test and a

Thetford Ploughing By Steam
Amongst all the operations of the agriculturalist performed by machinery, none has puzzled scientific men more than the invention of an implement calculated to supersede the ordinary system of ploughing by horse power; and while all believed steam ploughing to be within the bounds of possibility, none were able, until recently, to hit upon the exact mode of performing the operation. The large premiums offered by the Royal Agricultural Society for the invention of a suitable machine acted as an incentive to the

This wonderful illustration, a Burrell-Boydell engine at work, is reproduced from a hand engraved wood block, circa 1857. It is believed to be of the steam ploughing demonstration at Croxton in 1857. [Print courtesy of the Amberley Working Museum, West Sussex].

Nonetheless, the following includes some additional information that is worthy of publication, both for its technical detail and social value.

After Mechi's examination of Boydell's traction engine, the engine was next seen at the Royal Agricultural Society show at Chelmsford in July 1856. It was described in the official catalogue as, *'A Locomotive Traction or Stationary-portable Engine invented and improved by the exhibitor, and manufactured by Boydell and Glasier, of Camden Works, Camden Town, (the component parts being purchased from several parties).* At this event,

demonstration of ploughing in the neighbouring parish of Croxton was arranged.

Since then, this important event has gained a great deal of interest, particularly a poster advertising this event, which has been reprinted several times in different publications. Yet, as far as I know, a surviving contemporary account of this interesting event has not reappeared. The following, makes fascinating reading.

exertions of the ingenious, and at the last meeting of the Society the plan propounded by Mr Boydell pronounced to be the one approaching nearest to perfection.

An enterprising manufacturer of agricultural implements in this neighbourhood, - Mr Charles Burrell of Thetford, - has lately turned his attention to the subject of steam ploughing, and also to the not less important matter of making steam engines available for drawing heavy weights on common roads; and Thursday and yesterday were fixed as the days for trying a series of experiments,

A 19th century print of the Burrell-Boydell engine, at a ploughing demonstration at Louth, Lincolnshire, just a few weeks after the demonstration that took place at Croxton in 1857.
[Print courtesy of the Ancient House Museum, Thetford]

with implements worked by Boydell's traction engine.

The proceedings were looked forward to with great interest by almost all classes of the community, and it was anticipated that a very large number of persons would be present to witness the experiments. This anticipation was fully realised, upwards of 6,000 spectators being upon the ground.

This being probably the commencement of a new era in mechanical farming, perhaps it will not be out of place if we give a brief description of the several experiments, by which Mr Burrell has shown that all field work can be accomplished by the use of the traction engine.

The first operation of the day was that of giving the public an illustration of the amount of weight that can be drawn along the common road by simple traction. Mr Burrell exhibited two traction engines of 10-horse power, and one small portable engine of 6-horse power. The two traction engines were powered by Boydell's patent endless-railway, and the small engine was a common portable fitted with a new apparatus called a chain propeller, patented by Mr Burrell,

for the purpose of converting all portable farm engines into traction power, combined with two wheels fitted with Boydell's patented endless-railway. One of the 10-horse power engines drew 13 tons up an incline of 1 in 17 to the great satisfaction of all spectators. The other engine of similar power and construction was engaged in surface ploughing by six of Mr Burrell's ploughs of a very novel construction, by which one man is able to work two ploughs. It was very satisfactorily shown that ploughing can be accomplished in a manner equal, or even superior, to that performed by horses, for about 4s. per acre, being about half the cost of horse ploughing. The next operation was a trial of sub-soil and drain ploughs by Cotgreave of York; and although the district is not suitable to these ploughs, the advantage of working them by traction engine was clearly demonstrated.

A most important experiment was tried with the small engine constructed with Mr Burrell's and Mr Boydell's patent combined. The object of the machine is to convert all portable steam engines into self-propellers, and the way it is accomplished is by an endless chain simply connecting the engine shaft to the driving

wheel. The endless chain is a great desideration, as it is a very simple and effective application, and is the great novelty to this class of engine. The six-horse engine with which the experiment was tried, performed the great feat of drawing from Mr Burrell's foundry to the plough field a thrashing machine of 2 tons weight, with no less than 40 men and boys riding inside. By this means a great point is gained, as the number of horses required in the transportation of thrashing machines is a great draw-back to their general use.

All the experiments were attended to with the most complete success, and gave entire satisfaction to the whole of the numerous company attracted to witness these novelties.

Every accommodation was afforded to visitors by omnibus and coaches constantly running to and from the town to the ploughing fields; and refreshments were well supplied by Mr Tyler of the Red Lion Inn, though the immense concourse of persons assembled, access to the booths was no easy matter. The days proceedings terminated with a dinner at the Bell Inn'. **Source:** *Bury Free Press, 9th May 1857.*

Smallpox [variola], so named to distinguish it from the greatpox [syphilis], was once a persistent cause of death and suffering. For many centuries it terrified all classes of society, from the Royal Court to street beggars.

The first symptom of this highly infectious disease was a fever lasting 3-6 days. This may have been the initial symptom for any number of illnesses but for those who survived the fever, a more telling sign was the appearance of skin eruptions, chiefly on the face, forearms and hands. Large pustules formed from the skin eruptions, and as they aged, their tops became covered in scabs. After two or three weeks the scabs dropped off leaving deep, disfiguring scars. Many of those who contracted smallpox, yet escaped death [the mortality rate of smallpox was about 25%] were either blinded or bore the characteristic and ugly pock-mark scars on face and limbs as a testimony to their suffering.

The early history of smallpox is obscure but it appears to have been a common disease in 16th century Britain. There was a smallpox epidemic in 1561-62 when Queen Elizabeth I suffered from a severe attack and was near to death. Major outbreaks of smallpox are known to have occurred in the following century. The inhabitants of Norfolk and Norwich suffered in 1669-70 and 1681-82. In January 1670 the Recorder of Norwich wrote in a letter to Joseph Williamson, MP for Thetford, that the disease *'rageth still amongst us, and poverty daily invades us like an armed man'*.

Evidence of smallpox is strongest throughout the 18th century when it was never absent from England. Probably the growth of provincial newspapers and other sources during this period has increased our awareness of smallpox during this time, rather than the fact that smallpox was then more widespread than in previous centuries. Eighteenth century newspapers certainly provide telling evidence of smallpox in Thetford during this period. In March 1748/49 a notice appeared in the Ipswich Journal signed by Thetford's Borough Justices of the Peace, ministers, doctors, surgeons and apothecaries, the parish churchwardens and overseers, and the Master and Usher of the free school.

Burgh of Thetford, in the Counties of Norfolk and Suffolk, March 3, 1748. Whereas the SMALL-POX, with which several inhabitants of this Burgh have been lately visited, is at length entirely ceased. We whose Names are hereunto subscribed, having first made a full Examination of, and Enquiry into the Fact, take this Method of informing the Publick thereof.

And do certify to all it may concern, that not a single Person has fallen down of the said Distemper, in any Part of our Town, within the Space of three Weeks and five Days last past; and that all the Parishes thereof do now remain entirely free from the same.

Tho. Sanders, Mayor, Geo. Clark, Coroner, Justices of the Peace for the Burgh.

T. Vaughan, John Wright, Ministers.

M. Manning, Doctor of Physick.

Alex. Falconer, James Mingay, Surgeons and Apothecaries.

William Rolfe, Wood Bidwell, James Judd, Robert Dade, John Bensted, John Rolfe, William Miles, Jos. Gill, Churchwardens and Overseers of the three Parishes.

J. Collman, LL.B, William Knowles, Master and Usher of the free School.

Source: *Ipswich Journal, 4 March 1748/49.*

A smallpox epidemic would certainly disrupt trade and commerce, whilst the frequent appearance of statements of this kind from the officers of cities, towns and parishes was obviously an attempt to reassure both inhabitants and travellers that all was well.

Despite the numerous outbreaks of smallpox in 18th century England, some form of prevention was being practised from the early 1720s after inoculation was first introduced into Britain by Lady Mary Wortley Montagu [1690-1762]. Lady Mary, wife of the British ambassador to the Ottoman Empire, had observed variolation or inoculation being practised by old women in Turkey, long before medical practitioners recognised and understood micro-organisms or germs. Ritual practices had developed in a number of Asian countries which involved breaking the skin, either between thumb and forefinger or in the nose, and implanting or inoculating infected matter from a smallpox pustule. The resulting infection brought about the desired immunity, though there was always the danger that it might develop into a full-scale case. A memorial to Lady Mary was erected in Litchfield cathedral towards the end of the 18th century, *'Sacred to the memory of the Right Honourable Lady Mary Wortley Montagu, who happily introduced from Turkey, into this country, the salutary art of inoculating the small-pox. Convinced of its efficacy, she first tried it with success on her own children, and then recommended the practice of it to her fellow citizens'.*

In its early years inoculation had its opponents and critics amongst the medical profession and clergy. Amongst them was the Norfolk historian, Francis Blomefield [1705-1752], rector of the Norfolk parish of Fersfield. Francis Blomefield had been educated at Thetford Grammar School, and in 1739 published a history of Thetford. Ironically, Blomefield died from smallpox at the age of 47 years.

Despite the impact made on the spread of smallpox during the 18th century - inoculation produced a death rate 1/10th that of a natural smallpox infection - epidemics continued to appear from time-to-time. Not everyone was able to afford inoculation and, because there was little understanding of bacteriology, there was little provision for isolating victims of the disease.

Smallpox was again prevalent at Thetford in 1768/69 and in 1778 when the usual list of officials informed, ... *'whom it may concern, That the small-pox, which has long infested this town, is by the help of inoculation, entirely got through, and that, at this time, there is not one person in the town with that distemper'*.

Towards the end of the 18th century, however, another great advance in the prevention of smallpox took place. Country folk had known for a long time that those who caught cowpox, a mild disease, would never catch smallpox. Edward Jenner [1749-1823] a country doctor of Berkeley, Gloucestershire, was intrigued by this and inoculated a local boy, James Phipps, with cowpox taken from a milkmaid. He was soon able to show that the boy was then immune from smallpox. This new form of inoculation was called vaccination ['vacca' Latin for cow]. The idea of infecting a human body with the disease of an animal brought criticism, not unnaturally, from many at the time. Nonetheless, vaccination gained recognition to become generally adopted, even though the old method of inoculation continued to be practised by many until 1840 when it was finally banned by law. Anthony Batty Shaw in his recently published *Norfolk & Norwich Medicine* writes, *'In Norfolk members of the upper classes were quick to take advantage of vaccination but vaccination of the poor was more slowly introduced'*.

Edward Jenner was born in 1749, the youngest son of the vicar of Berkeley. He began his medical studies at the age of 14 and later went to London to study at St George's Hospital. He was 23 when he returned to Berkeley and settled into his life as a country doctor. Over the next 25 years, he made detailed observations of local birds and mammals, performed various scientific experiments, wrote medical papers and tended his patients. **Source:** *The Jenner Museum, Berkeley, Gloucestershire.*

No wonder that smallpox epidemics continued almost unabated for at least the first quarter of the 19th century. Norwich had a major outbreak in 1819, *'attributed to neglect of vaccination and many families moving into Norwich from the country over the previous three years during a period of rural poverty'*. Although vaccination gave protection against smallpox, it was many years later before the French scientist, Louis Pasteur, and the German pathologist, Robert Koch, established that infectious diseases were due to micro-organisms and not causes such as 'unhealthy air'.

Smallpox epidemics were frequent throughout Britain in the period 1840-70. In 1864/65, Thetford suffered a serious outbreak. According to one source, twelve people died from about two hundred reported cases in the Borough during the winter. Most were adults who had not been vaccinated. Very few children contracted the disease owing to vaccination. At some date about that time it was made compulsory for children to be vaccinated and parents or guardians who failed to have this done appeared before the local magistrates at the Petty Sessions. Punishment in such cases resulted in a fine with costs.

The next serious smallpox epidemic in England was 1900-05. By then, however, health authorities were better able to deal with such an emergency. Mass vaccination had obviously reduced the number of potential victims and local authorities were compelled to establish smallpox isolation hospitals to prevent the spread of infection. A smallpox isolation hospital was built at Thetford in 1902, on land south of the town, close to where the Fulmerston Road Christian Fellowship Hall stands today. There is no evidence, however, that any smallpox victims were ever confined there. Thankfully, a World Health Organisation [WHO] vaccination programme has recently eradicated smallpox from the world.

Thetford Small - Pox. There are no less than eighteen cases of small-pox reported this week to exist in St Mary's parish alone, many of which are believed to be owing to the bad state of the drainage and neglect of the commonest precautions against the spread of this frightful disease. On the 1st instant a special meeting of the Sanitary Committee was held in the Guildhall to take into consideration the sanitary conditions of that parish. Inspector Newland reported that it was very desirable that measures should be taken to remove the accumulation of filth and other 'debris' from the south-west side of the church, where small-pox has been most rampant. The sanitary arrangements in this particular locality are said to be very bad, and there has been, hitherto, no common sewer to carry off the filth. It was revealed that immediate steps should be taken to make a drain from thence to the river. **Source:** *Bury & Norwich Post, 9 August 1864.*

Workhouse Cast Its Shadow Over The Town's Poor
Thetford & Watton Times, 5 January 1990

On the outskirts of Thetford, at the edge of Barnham Cross Common, stands a new and attractive groups of dwellings called St Barnabas Close. Today it is difficult to visualise the grim, prison-like features of the building which previously occupied that same site. Through most of the 19th century and the first quarter of the 20th century, it brought fear and foreboding into the minds of local people at the mere mention of its name, the 'Union Workhouse'.

Thetford Union – Supplies: All persons desirous of Contracting with the Guardians of this Union for the supply of Seconds Flour, Bread made at the same, for the three divisions in this Union and for the Workhouse at Thetford, and Beef, Mutton, Pork, Bacon, Butter, Cheese, Tea, Sugar, Oatmeal, Rice, Peas, Potatoes, Soap, Soda, Pearl-ash, Candles, Starch, Indigo, Coals, Beer, Blankets, Rugs, Scotch Sheeting, unbleached Calico, Striped Cotton for shirts, Grey Cloth for men and boys Clothes, Shoeas and other articles at the Workhouse in Thetford... Sealed tenders with samples of such Articles as require the same, free of expense. Wm. Clarke, Clerk of the Union. **Source:** *Bury & Norwich Post, 8 March 1837.*

The Poor Law Amendment Act of 1834 [the new Poor Law] created a number of Union Workhouses. The Thetford Union Workhouse was built in 1836 for 300 pauper inmates, replacing the Borough Workhouse situated in Magdalen Street. Whereas the Borough Workhouse maintained only paupers from Thetford's three parishes, the new Union Workhouse maintained these paupers as well as those from 29 neighbouring parishes. It is these 32 parishes which initially formed the Thetford Union.

Each parish was compelled to maintain its poor within the new workhouse. This resulted in many poor families and individuals not only being removed from their kin and homesteads into unfamiliar and regulatory conditions of the workhouse but also at a distance, miles from their own parish.

An elected body of officers, known as the Board of Guardians, was partly responsible for the administration of the workhouse. Their duties included the appointment of the workhouse officials: clerk, master, matron, medical officer, chaplain, porter, schoolmaster and mistress.

The 1834 Act created a strict discipline in the workhouse, principally to discourage the able-bodied poor from seeking relief on the parish rates. Others caught in the system were the genuine poor - orphaned children, the sick, aged and feeble-minded.

Although, at times, life in the workhouse was harsh and unjust, arguably, it was no worse than for those labouring classes struggling to exist outside the workhouse, very often below the 'breadline'. Perhaps the most inhumane rule enforced in the workhouse was the segregation of the sexes, whereby a married male pauper was separated within the workhouse from his wife and children, except perhaps for one hour each week.

Surprisingly, for some time a policy of non-employment for the inmates existed at Thetford. However, this changed in 1849 with the introduction of oakum picking [plucking twisted, tarred lengths of rope into fibres for caulking boats]. Six able-bodied paupers refused to do this work and were gaoled for 14 days with hard labour. There are many other instances of punishment being administered to those who broke the workhouse regulations. As late as 1910 four women were locked up four days on a diet of bread and water, after singing vulgar songs and disobeying the matron's orders.

Towards the late 19th century there was an increase in the numbers of mobile poor, better known as tramps or 'roadsters'. The strict enforcement of regulations to deter vagrancy did little to solve the problem.

The workhouse became a popular over-night refuge for tramps. Many of them were men tramping from town to town, seeking employment. Each tramp slept over-night in a vagrant's cell and was given supper and a breakfast. Before being released they were required to do a menial task, such as breaking granite for the roads.

Thetford: On Tuesday, Charles Tilney, an incorrigible able-bodied inmate of the workhouse was taken before Mr A. G. Cronshey, and committed for seven days hard labour for not breaking 7 c.w.t. of granite as ordered by the Guardians. He only broke 1 c.w.t. and said he could do the other if they gave him time to do so. **Source:** *Bury Free Press, 27 August 1904.*

Thankfully the 'workhouse' has little use in our language of today. In Thetford there are only a few surviving, isolated pieces of evidence from that cheerless institution. The flint wall that surrounds St Barnabas Close is the same wall built in 1837 to enclose the Union Workhouse, and in St Mary's Churchyard there is a headstone inscribed:

Sacred to the memory of John Lucas
Who departed this life
August 23rd 1854
Aged 56 years
For 16 years Governor of
Thetford Union Workhouse
and much respected by all who knew him

These cottages, now 16 & 20 Magdalen Street, originally formed one house. It was purchased by the Corporation in the mid-1760s and converted into a workhouse. It served as the Thetford Borough Workhouse, for the parishes of St Cuthbert's, St Mary's and St Peter's, until the Thetford Union Workhouse was built in 1836. The old Borough Workhouse was then purchased by local brewer and merchant, J.W. Branford and converted into cottages.

Below:- The former Thetford Union Workhouse built on the edge of Barnham Cross Common in 1836 at a cost of about £5,000 and demolished in the mid-1970s.
The union workhouses built in the 19th century have often been referred to as 'Pauper Palaces'.

Inmates	Male	Female
0-12 years	32	17
13-20	13	8
21-30	6	5
31-40	3	5
41-50	3	2
51-60	10	1
61-70	16	2
71+	14	2
Total	97	42

Source: Analysis of the 1851 Census, Thetford Union Workhouse.

The interior of the workhouse chapel with seating for 150. This photograph captures the chapel decorated for the Harvest Festival in 1909.

The Thetford Union Workhouse Chapel, erected by voluntary subscriptions in 1863 and dedicated to St Barnabas [the name means 'son of consolation'], is in the process of being demolished.

The interior, furniture, and decorations are Early English, and comprise a communion table, reading desks, open seats and an organ, the later of which, with the illuminated windows, was presented by the Rev. Augustus Sutton, Rector of West Tofts, who officiated at the laying of the foundation-stone and at the opening ceremony. **Source:** A. Leigh Hunt, *The Capital of the Ancient Kingdom of East Anglia*, A. G. Dennant [1870].

A Hospital For The 'Working Classes' *Thetford & Watton Times, 14 October 1988*

To commemorate the 40th anniversary of the National Health Service Act which created for the first time a free medical service for all, a small exhibition was held at the Day Hospital in Earls Street. Displayed was the history of the building and the part it has performed within the community.

Another milestone in the hospital's history is soon to be reached. On 29th October, it will be exactly 90 years since being opened as the Thetford Cottage Hospital. The building of the hospital was made possible by local brewer, Mr Thomas Shelford Bidwell, who wanted a hospital to be built in the town to commemorate Queen Victoria's Diamond Jubilee in 1897 and *'for the benefit of the poor and working classes in times of sickness and affliction'.* He gave the Earls Street site and £400 towards the building costs. Another £800 was raised by public subscription.

Before the Cottage Hospital was opened, Thetfordians and local villagers had to travel to hospitals at Bury St Edmunds or Norwich. It must also be remembered that at the time there was no such organisation as an ambulance service to provide transport. The prospect for most people seeking medical care was to pay for the visit of a local doctor or a person who possessed some medical knowledge.

On Tuesday last a lad about 10, named Archer, son of poor parents, had the misfortune to fracture his arm. His father took him to a medical man, who, it is said, refused to set the limb unless a payment was made at a price named. The money not being forthcoming, father and son took the earliest train to Bury St Edmunds, where the surgeons of the West Suffolk Hospital pronounced it a bad fracture, and at once attended to it. Our long talked-of Cottage Hospital would be of service in such a case. **Source:** *Thetford & Watton Times, 1 January 1883.*

The opening ceremony of the Cottage Hospital was held in the adjacent Oddfellows Hall. It was the members of the Oddfellows Lodge and other local benefit societies who had played a major part in raising subscriptions for the Hospital fund. Valuable monetary contributions were also made by the Duke of Grafton of Euston Hall and Lord Iveagh of Elveden Hall.

To the credit of those responsible for the administration of the hospital, two valuable concessions had been made from the time of the opening. Firstly, patients were to be admitted free-of-charge, once a letter of admission had been obtained, signed by a local doctor and one of the hospital's trustees; secondly, the doctors had agreed to give their services, while at the hospital, free-of-charge.

Nevertheless, it was estimated that each year, voluntary contributions amounting to £200 would be needed to pay for the upkeep of the hospital. In the 1920s and 30s, funds were raised at an annual event known as Hospital Sunday, held in the Castle Park. Schemes were also put forward, whereby, workmen could have one or two pence deducted from their weekly wages, towards the Hospital Fund.

Since surviving closure of the wards and a threat of permanent closure in the 1960s, Thetford's Hospital has expanded in size and the services provided. Today, a staff of about twenty-five people provide blood tests, chiropody, community health care, a mental health resource centre, geriatric day-care, out-patients, speech therapy and X-ray; and it is still free-of-charge!

New Cottage Hospital at Thetford:- Thetford was 'en fête' on Saturday week on the occasion of the new cottage hospital. The proceedings commenced with an imposing demonstration of the Friendly Societies and Trade Unions of the town, who paraded the town, headed with the Volunteer Band and the Salvation Army band. Collections were made along the route to the Oddfellows Hall, which was densely crowded. The hall was adorned with choice ferns and flowers from the conservatories of Mr Sutton and Mr Burrell...the idea of erecting this hospital originated solely with Mr T.S. Bidwell, as the most fitting memorial of her Majesty's Diamond Jubilee. Its sole object was to benefit the poor and working classes. **Source:** *Bury & Norwich Post, 8 November 1898.*

The Cottage Hospital in Earles Street erected in 1898 on land presented by the late T. S. Bidwell Esq. is a structure of red brick with stone dressings erected from designs by Mr H. J. Green, at a total cost of £1,200. In 1901 a mortuary was added & in 1907-1908 a balcony and further additions made by J. Vavasseur Esq. C.B. of Kilverstone Hall. There are six beds and one cot. In 1907 49 patients were treated. The hospital is supported entirely by voluntary subscriptions. **Source:** *Kelly's Directory of Norfolk 1908.*

The Cottage Hospital photographed soon after opening in 1898. When first built, it boasted six beds and one cot.

The Cottage Hospital as it appeared about 1925. Improvements continued when a new wing was built and opened in 1924. Comprising two bedrooms, dining room for the staff and an X-ray department, it was built as a memorial to those who suffered and perished in the Great War.
Thetford had a number of medieval hospitals but it is unlikely they were all hospitals in the modern sense of the word. However, they had all ceased to function before the end of the 16th century. Until fairly modern times, hospitals were mostly used by the very poor - those unable to afford the visit of a doctor or other medical practitioner.

Today the exterior of the hospital is barely recognisable from that erected over a century ago as the Thetford Cottage Hospital. Whilst there have been no in-patients since the wards closed in 1964, the scope of the services provided by the Hospital has advanced enormously.

A Brief Account Of Thetford's Common Rights

The Newsletter of Barnham Cross Common Conservation Volunteers, Summer 1994

Most of us, along with countless generations of past Thetfordians, have taken advantage of the open space of Barnham Cross Common, an ancient remnant of the local countryside that pre-dates even the time when the feudal manor was the central institution of medieval life.

From the Conquest and into the 20th century, Thetford's manorial lords have held a major portion of the land that formed the Borough of Thetford, including Barnham Cross Common. The lord's tenants and others were granted, through the manor court, certain communal rights over well-defined and designated pieces of land - the commons or commoners' land. The most customary privileges granted to the commoners were the right of common pasture and that of taking wood and furze for fuel.

Whereas several Persons for some years-past, have presumed to make divers Incroachments upon the Rights of Common Pasture, and other Liberties belonging to the Inhabitants of the Town of Thetford, by Ditching, Fencing and Plowing up Part of the same; and whereas, many of the principle Inhabitants of the said Town are come to a Resolution to recover back, maintain and support their ancient Rights and Privileges against all such arbitrary invaders. This is therefore to give Notice to all Persons who have offenced herein, that unless such Rights are restored by throwing down the said Fences or Setling an equivalent upon the Poor of the said Town, in lieu thereof, before the First Day of December next, such Fences will be destroy'd, or such Persons prosecuted as the Law directs.
Source: *Ipswich Journal, 8 November 1746.*

Even after the erosion of the manor and all it entailed, Thetfordians continued to enjoy their ancient rights and customs over Barnham Cross Common. Moreover, human nature being what it is, the inhabitants of Thetford, and elsewhere, also enjoyed more than their customary rights. There is ample evidence that people took advantage of the lord's failure to exert his authority over the commons. Without the lord's consent, they literally helped themselves to land, turf, wood and anything else that grew there, including game. Mineral deposits, such as stone, gravel, chalk and sand were also plundered. It wasn't all take, however, as some local people used Barnham Cross Common as a dumping ground for their rubbish and if that weren't enough, a persistent cause of concern, more to the annoyance of Thetford's inhabitants rather than that of the manorial lord, was the frequent presence of gypsies and travellers, squatting on the common for long periods.

Things might have changed once Edward Mackenzie of [Santon] Downham Hall became Thetford's new manorial lord in 1869. As he tried to exert more control over his estate, Thetford's 'common rights' and those of Barnham Cross Common in particular, frequently became the subject of dispute and litigation. The main difficulty for Mr Mackenzie was that people had become so accustomed to doing what they liked on Barnham Cross Common, they assumed it was their 'ancient right'. Whereas, the Lord of the Manor contested that their only common right was that of pasture. This put even the Corporation of Thetford in a difficult position, having extracted gravel and stone for the repair of roads, over many years, without the lord's permission.

Notwithstanding all the apparent abuses of common rights, the one that appears to have troubled Mr Mackenzie most of all, however, was that of shooting game on the common. But even in this matter, after taking a few alleged game trespassers to court, he failed to stop what had become a well established practice and assumed 'right'.

Thetford Town Council - Common Rights
The question of carting an unlimited number of loads of stone and sand off Barnham Cross Common by the contractor of the new railway station was discussed, and it was suggested that he should, as a stranger, pay for this, as it compelled the borough to go elsewhere for such when required, and there was not an unlimited quantity of good road material to be found at this spot. - Mr Houchen [Town Clerk] said he did not see how they could interfere as the soil belonged to the lord of the manor, and on a previous occasion the contractor was prevented carting the common away in this manner. - Mr Shaw again raised the question of gypsies camping on the Common, but it was found that the Council had no power in this matter either.
Source: *Bury Free Press, 11 May 1889.*

After many years of apparent abuse and neglect, things began to change once Barnham Cross Common became the responsibility of Thetford Town Council in 1923. Bye-laws were passed making Thetford Town Council responsible for many of the former responsibilities of the manorial lord. Moreover, the chief police officer at Thetford was ordered to act as an officer of the Council in the enforcement of the bye-laws.

Since then, many of the earlier customs appear to have ceased, as much through social changes rather than regard for the law. Barnham Cross Common is now classified as a Site of Special Scientific Interest [SSSI] and is carefully managed to preserve and protect its unique, ancient habitat and landscape.

On Barnham Cross Common which adjoins Thetford on the south is the stone socket of the ancient Franchise Cross which divided the Liberty of Thetford from the Liberty of St Edmund. Botanically, the common occupies a position unique in the British Isles, for on no other does the typical Breckland flora occur. There are flourishing colonies of six of the restricted "Breck" species, the Spanish catchfly, sickle medick, least medick, field wormwood, perennial knawel, and wall bedstraw. The spring speedwell was formerly found, but is apparently extinct. With the exception of the bedstraw, these occur on heath pastures, chiefly on banks and tracks where the competition from the furze is less keen. It would seem that the area of the original steppe flora has been greatly reduced by the encroachments of the furze and sandsedge, which have also acted detrimentally to the heather. In the spring the whole of the pasture area is covered with a white sheet of vernal whitlow grass. In addition to the ordinary plants of heath pasture, hounds-tongue, sheeps-bit, purple mountain milk-vetch, rough clover, fine-leaved sand wort, naked-stalked candytuft, hairy bitter-cress and smooth bitter-cress are not uncommon. Few area in East Anglia yield the botanist from outside its borders so many uncommon species of plants. Its bird life is that of an ordinary furze-clad common, with the addition of the stone-curlew and occasionally of the ringed plover. Linnets and meadow-pipits are probably the most abundant nesting birds, the former in the furze and the latter in the long grass around it which is protected from grazing animals by the sharp spines. Sand-martins nest in the sand-pits, and wheatears occasionally occupy their disused tunnels. Other nesting birds include the lapwing, nightjar, whinchat, stonechat, bullfinch, whitethroat, willow warbler, and yellow bunting, while the marshy portion of the common is frequented by the common snipe. Among its bird visitors are almost all those found in the district, for river, marsh, pasture, furze, sandpits, whitethorn hedges, and the bordering pine belts provide diverse attractions.
Source: W. G. Clarke, *In Breckland Wilds*, Robert Scott, London [1925].

Barnham Cross Common covers an area of 72 hectares [180 acres] and parts of the ancient boundary are marked by a line of Scots Pine. This photograph was taken on the south eastern edge of the common, towards the Little Ouse River but a part known locally as 'The Barnham River'. For many centuries, a battle has been waged between those who have sought to preserve and protect the common and those who have endeavoured to exploit and misuse it for all sorts of reasons.

A little over forty years ago, when cattle were still regularly grazed on the common, it was almost a treeless landscape. Now, there are numerous young trees, including oak, creating wooded areas.

Although many species of plants are to be found on the Common, perhaps the most conspicuous with its bright yellow flower and prickly leaf is gorse. Almost every year, particularly in hot summer months, fire has destroyed and damaged different areas of the common, leaving the affected vegetation black and charred. Even so, new growth soon appears through the blackened landscape and within a year or two the landscape has usually recovered.

The cause of the Thetford riots is one that seldom fails to arouse strong emotions, rhetoric or even violent actions - the attempted enclosure of a public 'right of way'. The 'right of way' in question was a piece of ground beside the Town Bridge, on the south side of the river that was used on occasions as a quay and a public pathway. It now forms the Haling Path, but in 1885 the Haling Path that we know did not exist. In fact the haling or hauling way on the south side of the river, from the Town Bridge towards Brandon, used primarily by horses towing barges along the river, extended only for a few hundred yards as thick undergrowth and a boathouse made any further progress impossible on this side of the river bank. At this furthermost point, near a place called 'The Chalk Hole', horses towing the barges along the haling way had to wade across to the other side of the river in order to continue their journey, a pattern that was followed as far as King's Lynn.

The ownership of this small piece of ground by the Town Bridge had been in dispute for several years. A Miss Laura B. Cooke, who lived at Alexandra House [now called Losinga] beside the Grammar School, claimed that part of the quayside at the end of her garden belonged to her property. In 1882 she wrote to the Borough Council informing them, ... *'I am about to put up a fence for the purpose of marking-out the boundary between my land and the Haling Path'.* Even though the Corporation disagreed and managed to delay Miss Cooke's intentions for a few years, a process that involved a great deal of correspondence through her solicitors, she finally defied the Corporation by taking the law into her own hands in May 1885. This was when the troubles began.

In the mid-1880s the Town Bridge was a favourite rendezvous for the town's unemployed. Undoubtedly, they were aware of the dispute between the Corporation and Miss Cooke's claim, and when local builder Mr Sam Holden and his workmen arrived early in the morning of Friday 8th May, with timber and nails and began erecting a fence to enclose part of the quayside, a recognised 'right of way', it created great interest and indignation from the large band of jobless spectators who viewed the proceedings as an encroachment upon their ancient rights.

As word of what was happening spread through the town, the crowd on the Town Bridge gradually increased. By late evening when Mr Holden and his men finally completed the task of erecting a fence, six feet high and about fifty feet in length, there must have been several hundred jeering spectators. Their anger reached new heights when Miss Cooke, along with a gentleman friend, a Mr Boby, walked from Alexandra House outside into the garden in order to view the newly erected fence. Their entrance, into an already excited arena, was the spark that turned the angry crowd into a violent mob. As Miss Cooke and her companion hastily retreated to the safety of their house, the action began.

This is how a local newspaper described what followed: ... *'The excitement was then at its height when a few boys endeavoured to pull down the boards, soon hundreds of men commenced in earnest, and in less than half an hour the boarding was all down, and thrown into the river. The mob then commenced singing "Rule Britannia", but the proceedings did not end here. The cry then went up, "To the Spring Walks", whither hundreds flocked - even women, girls and children. The Patent Pulp Company some time ago enclosed what the people imagined a right of way, and here the fencing was soon demolished and thrown into the river, in spite of the protests of the manager (Mr Millington), who was threatened. At one time fears were entertained for the large drying shed, but happily that was not wrecked. The rioters then dispersed for the night after breaking some of Mr Cronshey's windows'.*

No special precautions appear to have been taken for policing the Borough the following day. Perhaps the small, local police force and authorities believed the worst of the troubles was over. Events, however, were to prove their optimism to have been mistaken. By 8 o'clock in the evening, a large crowd gathered once more on the Town Bridge, having planned to right a few more wrongs and perhaps settle a few old scores.

From the Town Bridge they proceeded along the haling path to the boat house, which was soon demolished and thrown into the river along with some fencing that stood in the nearby vicinity. At this point Police Inspector Culley and a constable appeared upon the scene and attempted to stop the mob, despite being assaulted and threatened with being thrown into the river. From there the mob charged back towards the Town Bridge and onwards to the area by the Small Bridges, near the Pulp Works. Here they began in earnest to demolish a wall recently erected by Mr Charles Burrell, enclosing his land.

By now, Mr Sowells the Mayor, Major Marsham a much-hated local magistrate, Mr Houchen the Town Clerk, Mr Read the Clerk of the Peace, and three police officers had caught up with the mob. Taking up a position under the gas lamp on the Small Bridges, the Mayor read out the Riot Act, warning the crowd that by taking part in such an assembly they were liable to two years' imprisonment. A few stones, thrown towards the Mayor and his officers, put out the gas lamp and one hit the Mayor in the face. This

The Haling Path in 2002. The land disputed in 1885 is easily recognisable today. The flint wall marks Miss Cooke's legal boundary, while the seat and strip of grass in the centre marks the point or line where Miss Cooke attempted to encroach with her fence.

was the final act, for rather than inciting the mob to further violence, it had the effect of bringing them to their senses. The once angry and excited crowd gradually dispersed. Order had been restored and the so-called Thetford Riots were over.

Normality was maintained during the next few days by over one hundred police constables, including fifty men from the Burrell works [specially sworn-in as Special Constables] and extra police drafted from other parts of the county.

Thetford: The town is now in a quite state, only about three extra policemen remaining and the special constables are dispersed with. Some tasteful rural seats have been erected on the hauling way, where the fencing demolished in the recent disturbances stood. **Source:** *Bury & Norwich Post, 19 May 1885.*

William Baker, William Mann, Robert Nichols, William Platfoot, Haves Ruddock and William Tuck

were subsequently arrested for their part in the riots. At the local Petty Sessions they were sentenced to be bound over in the sum of £5. In default of finding surety, the first five named were each sentenced to one month's imprisonment at Norwich Castle. They were cheered off to Norwich by hundreds of supporters, and when they returned to Thetford one month later, hundreds of Thetfordians greeted them on their arrival at the railway station. From there they marched, cheering and singing on a parade of the town; the cheering changed to groans and jeers as they passed the Mayor's house and that of Miss Cooke. Eventually, they made their way to the Market Place where a reported crowd of one thousand people gathered to hear a number of stirring speeches, including a resolution, copies of which were sent to the Mayor and Town Clerk: *'We the inhabitants of Thetford, in the Market Place assembled, tender our thanks to the five men for their gallant conduct in suffering imprisonment in Norwich Castle for one month in defence of common rights, and we call upon*

the Town Council to insist upon the maintenance of our rights, and to prevent any encroachments in the future by instituting proceedings against any persons who may endeavour to enclose land in dispute'.

If the same circumstances were to arise again, I wonder if we might do the same?

Thetford - The Encroachments Miss Cooke having begun a new four-strand wire fence outside the trees bordering her meadows on the towing path, in the place of the fence lately pulled down, a large concourse of people assembled on the Town Bridge on Friday evening at dusk, and made an onslaught of the wire fence. In less than half an hour the whole wire for about 100 yards were wrenched off and thrown into the river, leaving the holdfasts in the trees. The crowd then dispersed with shouts of rejoicing. Many of the 3/4" screw spikes driven 4" into the trees had been drawn out. **Source:** *Bury Free Press, 13 June 1885.*

Success To The Fleece And Plough - Agricultural Life In Nineteenth Century Thetford

Part I: Farms and Farmers *Thetford and Breckland Magazine, Magazine of The Thetford Society, Spring 1995*

Although farming is no longer a significant part of local life, it was, until fairly recent times, an important local industry, providing many of life's basic necessities and numerous employment opportunities. Moreover, well into the 20th century, local industries such as malting, milling and tanning all processed agricultural and farming produce, while others supplied the farms with a wide range of goods and services.

Capital Flock of Norfolk Stock Ewes, Dairy of fine poll'd Cows and young stock, 3 Teams of Horses, Swines Etc.
To be Sold by Auction by Noah Baker & Son
On Monday, Sept. 29th 1806, and Three following days,
on the premises called the PLACE FARM,
in THETFORD, Norfolk.
All the truly valuable Live and Dead farming Stock, Implements in Farming, Dairy Utensils, part of the household furniture and other effects of Mr Garner Wright, quitting his farm; consisting of upwards of 40 score of Capital Norfolk stock ewes; and about 70 tods of fine fleece wool; 15 strong and useful draft horsesss, and mares, and 1 riding ditto; 22 beautiful poll'd cows, well timed for calfing, and a poll'd bull; 22 handsome spring heifers, two or three years old; 17 home-bred steers (chiefly poll'd) and a bull of the same age; 30 small shoats; and 2 remarkable fine fat hogs; 5 waggons; 4 tumbrills; ploughs, harrows and rolls; drill machine and chaff engine; cart and plow harness, with many useful implements; a full-size barrel churn, nearly new; lead and deal milk trays, butter and milk keelers, tubs and beer casks in good condition; several good bedsteads, and bedding and hangings, table and chairs, kitchen, backhouse and pantry requisites, with a variety of other articles... **Source:** *Bury & Norwich Post, 10 September 1806.*

Throughout the 19th century, a period that saw great changes in the way farming was carried out, there were three large farms in the Borough of Thetford. All three occupied land that once belonged to local religious houses before they were dissolved in the 16th century. Known appropriately as the Abbey Farm, Canons' Farm and the Nunnery or Place Farm, between them they occupied over 6,000 acres of land. The largest was the 4,000-acre Canons' Farm but much of this, about 3,000 acres, was heath or waste land, some of which was rented to warreners for the cultivation of wild rabbits.

Both the Abbey and Canons' Farm belonged to the Manor of Thetford, purchased in 1868 by Edward Mackenzie of Buckinghamshire; both farms remained with the Mackenzies into the 20th century. The 1,750-acre Nunnery Farm belonged to Sir Robert Buxton and his heirs of Shadwell, near Thetford. The Buxtons had settled at Shadwell in the middle of the 18th century and remained there until the estate was purchased by John Musker at the end of the 19th century.

As might be expected, the tenants of these large farms were substantial businessmen. Undoubtedly, one of the wealthiest of these tenant farmers was Henry Bartlett, who occupied the Canons' Farm from *c.*1840-*c.*1873. He was described in 1846 as, ... *'an opulent farmer, who has a beautiful residence at this spot'.* He was Mayor that year and on two later occasions.

Tenant of the Abbey Farm from circa 1853 - circa 1873 was William Salter, who was also a Mayor of the Borough of Thetford on five occasions between 1860-68.

The longest of three tenants at the Buxton's Nunnery or Place Farm during the 19th century was William Jillings, from *circa* 1850 - *circa* 1900. Jillings also farmed at Santon Downham and before the end of the century was also involved in steam milling and merchandising seed-cake, corn, flour, offal and coal. Jillings was also an Alderman of the Borough and, like his fellow gentlemen farmers, no doubt helped to protect the interests of his landlord.

It is when the tenancies changed hands that we can sometimes find details of the farm from sale advertisements in local newspapers. When Daniel Sewell quit the Abbey Farm in 1826, his livestock included over one thousand sheep. There were also twenty-two carthorses, six red-polled Suffolk cows, some with calves, five sows and a boar. The implements included two double-breasted and eight wheeled-ploughs, six harvest wagons, four tumbrils, harrows, rolls, drills and a variety of useful utensils.

Sheep were also the principle livestock at the Nunnery or Place Farm when Edward Palmer quit in 1842. Over six hundred Down and half-bred Down & Norfolk ewes were offered for sale, besides twenty-two bullocks and an unspecified number of pigs. Sheep-corn farming was an ancient custom in the Breckland, the sheep manuring the light, sandy soils.

Edward Palmer's farming implements were either manual or horse-powered as there was no mention of a steam engine on his farm. New types of horse and manually-powered machines were increasingly being introduced, on the large farms in particular, from the early years of the 19th century.

J.S. Cotman's impression of the Abbey Farm dated 1818. Several buildings that once formed the old Abbey Farm still survive, surrounded by the Abbey House, more recent residential developments and the ruined Cluniac Priory.

It wasn't until the mid-1840s that steam power, in the shape of portable engines, first began to make their appearance on the large farms and estates in the district. Twenty years later, however, steam engines were a common sight, driving an array of newly-designed machines, especially the threshing drum.

A Sample of Thetford Farmers
Henry A. Bartlett of the Cannons, farmer employing 39 out-door men and 5 indoor servants.
Thomas Featherstone of Abbey Farm, farmer of 1,000 acres employing 20 labourers.
Noah Howe of Norwich Road, farmer & dealer.
Joseph Howard of King Street, farmer & smith employing 2 men.
W. H. Jillings of Place Farm, farmer of 1,700 acres employing 19 labourers.
Stephen Oldman of Oldman's Lane, miller, baker and farmer of 24 acres employing 1 miller, 1 baker & 2 labourers.
Edward Palmer of King Street, farmer of 14 acres of land.
John Reed of Croxton Road, farmer of 45 acres employing 3 men.
Harrison Turner of Pike Lane, farmer of 64 acres employing 2 men.
Source: The National Census 1851.

Besides the three large farms of 1,000 acres or more, there were at least six much smaller ones and an unidentified number of smallholdings, containing just a few acres scattered about the borough. For example, when Noah Baker died in 1814 he held a 4 acre field at the bottom of the Croxton Road, near the Fleece Inn; another 4 acres called the Abbey Close, presumably near the Abbey Farm; 10 acres called Burrells at the top of Croxton Road; and 14 acres abutting the Norwich turnpike. Most, if not all, of this land would have been rented.

Farming was often a precarious business, even for the large farmers and, as small farms were generally not economical enough to produce a good return, most small farmers had another occupation, supplementing their incomes as bakers, blacksmiths, carriers, dealers and other work where they could retain some form of independence, something that was very much in their nature. It was because of their economic circumstances that small farmers were generally reluctant to modernise their holdings and change to modern practices. As a result, they often continued out-dated methods into the 20th century.

While the large farmers lived on their farms in substantial farmhouses, employing a retinue of house servants, the very small farmers were to be found residing in small, unfashionable houses close to their land on the outskirts of the town, or in similar dwellings much nearer the town centre. Small farmers could be found living in such places as Grove Lane, King Street, Painter Street, Pike Lane, Mill Lane and St Mary's Row; and rarely did they employ a house servant, except some member of the family.

The Kimms were not only small farmers but also millers. In the middle of the 19th century they farmed 20 acres of land just off the London Road, close to where their windmill and farmhouse stood. The Plover public house now stands on the site of their old farmhouse. Although not easily recognisable, there is still some evidence of these small, almost forgotten, farmhouses in the town today. The Ark public house was once a farm house, as was a small, detached, flint house in Vicarage Road: number 1. Redgate House in Green Lane was once a farm house, as was number 57 Bury Road.

The farmhouses occupied by the large farmers are much easier to recognise, and two have survived. The Abbey Farm House and some of the farm buildings were, until a few years ago, used as a works depot by the District Council. The Place Farm is now partly occupied by the British Trust for Ornithology, and private residences.

Success To The Fleece And Plough - Agricultural Life In Nineteenth Century Thetford
Part II: The Farm Workers
Thetford and Breckland Magazine, Magazine of The Thetford Society, Summer 1995

Of all the different occupations found in 19th century Thetford, agricultural or farm workers were the most numerous, at least for the first six decades, before engineering became a much more important local industry. In the middle of the 19th century, twenty per cent of Thetford's male workforce consisted of agricultural workers. At the same time, agricultural labourers formed 25 per cent of the nation's male workforce, the largest occupational group.

By analysing the 19th century population censuses it is possible, at ten-yearly intervals from 1841-91, to identify many of Thetford's farm workers, not only the numerous labourers but also shepherds, carters, dairy maids and herdsmen. They could be found living with their families in most parts of the town. Only a few workers actually lived on the farm, whereas, in the previous century when there was less social difference between farmer and his farm servants, many more farm workers shared the farmer's table.

Workmen...In respect of Day labourers, two remarkable circumstances are united; namely, hard work and low wages! A Norfolk farm labourer will do as much work for one shilling, as two men in other places, will do for eighteen pence each. There is an honesty...about them, when working by the day, which I have not found in any other country. **Source:** William Marshall, *The Rural Economy of Norfolk* [1795].

The 19th century farm worker and his family were much more mobile than is often supposed. Many of the agricultural labourers and their spouses living in Thetford in the middle of the 19th century, were born in parishes outside the Borough. Undoubtedly, many had drifted into the town, believing that conditions and opportunities in a market town like Thetford offered greater and more favourable opportunities than the rural village, where squire and parson often had a powerful influence and control.

While Thetford's small farmers engaged no more than two or three men, except at harvest time when extra labour may have been recruited, the more substantial farmers employed a much larger workforce. At the time of the 1851 Census [30/31 March] the Canon's Farm employed 39 men, the Abbey Farm 20 labourers and the Place or Nunnery Farm 19 labourers; a total of 78 men. Altogether, Thetford's farmers reckoned they employed a total of 85 men and boys in 1851, yet 190 individuals gave their *'Rank, Profession or Status'* as 'agricultural labourer'. Some of this apparent difference can be explained by the fact that some agricultural labourers living in Thetford actually worked on farms in the neighbouring parishes, setting off early each morning to the distant fields. How numerous this daily migration of labour was is not entirely known. Considering that several of the estates surrounding Thetford contained many thousands of acres, the numbers may have been considerable. Another plausible reason, however, is that at the time of the Census, many of Thetford's agricultural labourers were actually unemployed.

The term 'agricultural labourer' fails to discern between the many different tasks this occupation could involve: caring for the farm animals and livestock, ploughing and preparing the soil, sowing the seeds, hoeing, harvesting the crops, maintaining ditches, hedgerows, farm machinery, buildings and other jobs. Some of this work required skills that were only perfected after many years of experience.

Besides the great army of male agricultural workers, women and children were also found working on the farms and in the fields. Although child and female agricultural workers fail to appear in any great numbers in the 19th century censuses for Thetford, it is known from other sources that both groups were at least occasionally employed in considerable numbers. This was particularly so at harvest time, when the corn was gathered in. Women also found work hoeing, dibbling and stone picking but not, it would seem, in the notorious 'labour gangs' used in some parts of the country. However, the most likely reason why so few female agricultural workers appear in the local censuses is that it was considered unnecessary to record their occupation, especially if it was just seasonal or part-time. Moreover, for those females who sought employment, there were other opportunities in the town besides fieldwork.

Historians have described at length the miserable, poverty-stricken plight and conditions experienced by many of East Anglia's 19th century agricultural workers. It is arguable, however, that agricultural workers conditions were no worse than many other sections of the labouring poor. Certainly by the 1850s East Anglia's farm workers appear to have been much more contented than in the previous four decades when they frequently rioted, broke farm machinery and set fire to crops and farm buildings. Although such incidents were reported in many parishes surrounding Thetford, the borough appears to have escaped the worst of the labourers' protests. Rather than resort to acts of violence in order to improve their conditions, large numbers of Thetford's farm workers joined the newly formed National Agricultural Labourers' Union in 1872. They held one of their first meetings at the Temperance Hall, *'for an advance* of wages and shorter hours'. Between 1872-74 many labourers went on strike, only to be 'locked out' by the farmers in 1874. It was during the 'Great Lock Out' that union leaders addressed large crowds of farm workers on the Market Place and in the surrounding parishes.

Certainly, from the middle of the 19th century, as mechanisation on the farms began to reduce the need for manual labour, there was an increasing movement of workers from the fields as they sought employment opportunities elsewhere, or faced unemployment. By the 1880s the number had shrunk of individuals living in Thetford who were described as 'agricultural labourer'. Many more were now termed 'general labourer', a worker who sought employment in any industry, when and where it could be found. The 1851 Census had revealed just 76 'general labourers' living in the town. Thirty years later they numbered over 200, while there was less than half the agricultural labourers found three decades earlier.

As the farm workers in the Borough of Thetford gradually disappeared, along with the harvest 'horkey' and other old farming customs, the town had changed from a small, predominantly agricultural town into a more populous, industrial centre. Somewhere, at the heart of this progression, must have been the growth of Charles Burrell's agricultural engineering works.

A 19th century print of haymaking, the oldest and most common method of conserving grass for winter feed. The grass is usually cut between May and June before the grass flowers and becomes stemmy.

Harvest time is one of the busiest periods of the farming calendar. At this time of the year, farm labourers could always reckon to increase their wages and even put some of it aside for leaner times. This photograph was taken on the Nunnery Farm in the late 1890s. [Photograph courtesy of Brian Jermy]

A pastoral scene captured towards the end of the 19th century. Bertie Crook, a shepherd of the Nunnery Farm, with his dog and a flock of his master's sheep. Although sheep had grazed the ancient heathland surrounding the town for centuries, their numbers were in decline when this photograph was taken. The 1851 Census recorded twenty-two shepherds living in the Borough of Thetford. Thirty years later, there were just six. [Photograph courtesy of Brian Jermy]

Success To The Fleece And Plough - Agricultural Life In Nineteenth Century Thetford
Part III: Fairs And Markets *Thetford & Breckland Magazine, Magazine of The Thetford Society, Autumn 1995*

It was at the numerous fairs and markets that farmers, dealers and merchants bought and sold animals, crops, seeds, implements, tools, and even hired labour. Many of these fairs and markets were ancient institutions dedicated to some revered saint. However, a few of these important commercial centres, either specialising in certain goods or serving as general markets, were relatively new and reflected both economic and demographic changes.

Fairs:- The grant of a weekly market usually contained similar permission for an annual fair. Such events were another important part of commercial life, and at least 115 are known to have been established in Norfolk between 1227 and 1475. Normally a fair lasted two or three days, and was centred on a particular feast day, which can often be tied to the dedication of the local parish church. **Source:** David Dymond, *The Norfolk Landscape,* Hodder & Stoughton [1985]. Reproduced by permission of Hodder & Stoughton Limited.

In the early years of the 19th century, Thetford had a mixture of both old and new fairs and markets. Two of the most important fairs to be held in 19th century Thetford were newly established, specialising in sheep and the fleece or wool they produced. Sheep and wool had been important local commodities for many centuries. Much of the great expanse of heathland that surrounded the town was ancient sheep pasture and rabbit warren, and until quite recent times, sheep and rabbits easily out-numbered people in the Borough of Thetford.

The first of the newly-established fairs in 19th century Thetford was the annual Thetford Wool Fair. It was instituted in 1793 by Norfolk's most famous agriculturalist, Thomas William Coke, Earl of Leicester [1754-1842] of Holkham Hall in the north of the county. As Thetford was situated geographically in the centre of Norfolk and Suffolk, and with a generous network of turnpikes and other roads reaching out in all directions, Coke saw Thetford as an ideal centre for attracting not only East Anglia's largest landowners and wool growers, but also wool merchants or factors from as far away as the western counties and Yorkshire. It is said the Thetford Wool Fair was the first institution of its kind to be established in England.

Thetford Wool Fair...the greatest number of persons seen on the like occasion, upwards of 120 gentlemen sitting down to dinner in the room at which Mr Coke presided, besides many other rooms of that and other inns in the town being filled. Among the company present were the Duke of Bedford, Lord Clermont, Sir Charles Davers, S. Bevan Esq... the conversation was almost entirely agricultural. **Source:** *Bury & Norwich Post, 17 July 1799.*

Coke chose the George Inn, beside the Town or Christopher Bridge, as a suitable hostelry for such a meeting of gentlemen farmers and wool merchants. Here they conducted their business selling and buying wool from selected samples, before sitting down to a sumptuous dinner provided by the host. Very often, as many as one hundred and twenty of these wealthy individuals dined at the Thetford Wool Fair, their formal dinner speeches, conversations and numerous toasts revolving around the great business and industry of agriculture and farming. One can only imagine the interest that such a gathering of gentlemen in the town attracted. In some respects it must have resembled Assize Week when the town was full of visitors.

The former George Inn.

Although Thetford was at the centre of a considerable sheep and wool growing district at the beginning of the 19th century, when it came to the business of selling sheep and lambs, local shepherds had to drive their flocks as far away as Ipswich Fair. Concern over the problems this caused, particularly reducing the value of the lambs after such a long journey, prompted local farmers to meet in 1806 to establish an annual Thetford Lamb Fair, to be held on the Abbey Farm. From an uncertain future, within a few years Thetford Lamb Fair had become a recognised event in the local agricultural calendar, attracting flock masters from a wide area of the Breckland. In 1833, for example, it was reported that 10,000 sheep and lambs were penned at Thetford Fair. By this time, however, the indigenous black-faced Norfolk Sheep had been replaced by the new breeds with superior wool, such as New Leicesters and Southdowns.

Besides the two newly-established fairs there were at least three ancient ones held on different fairsteads in the town, Thetford May Fair on the Grammar School Plain, Magdalen Fair on the Market Place and surrounding streets, and Holyrood Fair on the Abbey Farm. Even though Thetford's Fairs continued to be a part of local life into the last three decades of the 19th century, progress and change had reduced their earlier value. Certainly by the 1890s most, if not all, had disappeared. One of the first to go was Thetford May Fair, abolished by the Fairs Act in 1871. By then Magdalen Fair had evolved into an amusement or funfair, and from the number of complaints arising from 'steam rides' on the Market Place, it was certainly thriving into the 1880s. Holyrood Fair, however, probably disappeared soon after 1875 when it was described as being 'poorly attended'.

The newly-established fairs also suffered a similar fate as the ancient institutions. After the Thetford Lamb Fair in 1880 it was reported, 'The annual Lamb Fair is now a thing of the past, not a single lamb or sheep was seen there yesterday'. And by 1880 very little business was transacted at the Thetford Wool Fair. By then it had virtually become just a farmers' social, centred around a dining table at the Bell Inn.

Thetford Fair, for the sale of lambs, &C., held last Friday, was considerably larger than last year; the day proved very unfavourable, there being so much rain, notwithstanding which a great part of the lambs and sheep sold. The half-bred Leicester and Norfolk, and Down, seemed to have the preference...altogether the sale was tolerably brisk, and this newly-established fair firmly supported by the numerous growers of lambs in the neighbourhood. **Source:** *Bury & Norwich Post, 21 August 1816.*

After the prosperous 1850s and 60s, the period after 1870 was generally one of falling agricultural prices and values. Locally, sheep were no longer the important and valued commodity they once were, and local farmers had clearly lost an interest in supporting the local fairs. However, the reason for the decline of Thetford's lamb and wool fairs is unclear, especially as at nearby Barnham, a successful lamb sale had been established in 1871 and a similar event was held at Harling.

Thetford Magdalen Fair: This rapidly expanding fair was held as usual on the 2nd & 3rd of August. The attendance of shows and booths was not so numerous as last year; but the proprietors of those present expressed themselves more satisfied with the state of their finance at the close of the fair.
The attendance of visitors from the surrounding country villages on Saturday evening was good.
The usual rustic sports were celebrated with éclat. The spacious dancing saloon of the lessee Mr C. D. Taylor was thronged both evenings; it was well lighted with gas.
The refreshments were good, the attendance also. On Saturday evening at one time 530 were present, the greater part engaged in dancing.
By the judicious arrangements of the magistrates, all the police were in attendance at the fair, to prevent any gaming booths or boards being erected, to which, in great measure, may be attributed the exceeding good order which prevailed, not one riot of any description occurring to disturb the hilarity which reigned on the occasion. **Source:** *Bury & Norwich Post, 14 August 1850.*

As the 19th century progressed, besides the fairs and markets, a new kind of event had evolved. This was the agricultural show, promoted by the many agricultural associations that had blossomed from the early years of the 19th century. The agricultural show had its roots in the annual agricultural gatherings pioneered by T. W. Coke and other like-minded agriculturists in the later part of the 18th century. The agricultural show soon became a rich and valuable part of Victorian agricultural life and, like the ancient fairs and markets, they acted as an important 'shop window' for agriculturists and manufacturers of agricultural implements, machinery and other products. Likewise, they were an important catalyst for the dissemination of new ideas and information.

The School Green or Plain and the ruined priory of the Canon's.

The Royal Agricultural Society founded in 1838 as the English Agricultural Society held an annual show in different parts of the country. These were hugely popular events and in 1849 the RAS show was held at Norwich, attracting thousands of visitors, many arriving in special trains. Another agricultural organisation was the Norfolk Agricultural Association. It held its annual show at different venues in the county and in June 1873, it was the turn of Thetford to host this prestigious event. It was held on fields adjoining the Nunnery or Place farm. As the Place Farm was on the Suffolk side of the town, this is probably the only time that the Norfolk Show has ever been held in Suffolk. During the two-day event, over ten thousand visitors paid to enter the show ground and view the great variety of cattle, horses, sheep, swine and implements amongst the exhibits. By then, however, Thetford's agricultural ties had already been loosened. Later, as we all know, they were to become well and truly undone.

One mile to the west of Thetford, standing on high ground just off the Brandon Road, are the remains of a small, 15th century house called Thetford Warren Lodge. Substantially built of flint and dressed stone, it is one of the few reminders of the rabbit industry that once formed an important part of the local economy.

The sandy soil surrounding much of Thetford and Brandon, although unsuitable for growing grain or crops, was an ideal environment for medieval landowners to experiment with the husbandry of the rabbit or coney, much valued for its meat and fur and introduced into Britain from France or its native western Mediterranean by the 13th century.

The hunting of game was then carefully controlled and restricted by the Crown, which sold exclusive hunting rights to landlords by means of a charter of 'free warren' - allowing the breeding and hunting of small game such as pheasants, hares and rabbits within a specified area. Today we use the term 'warren' to describe any piece of waste ground inhabited by wild rabbits.

Many of the warrens established in this region were created by ecclesiastical landlords. Brandon and Mildenhall Warrens were created by the Bishopric of Ely and the Abbot of St Edmundsbury respectively. Thetford Warren, however, was granted to a lay-landlord, the De Warennes, Earls of Surrey. It later came into the possession of Thetford's Cluniac Priory. The size of the warren may have varied greatly but those in the Breckland were usually very large, sometimes covering 1,000 acres or more.

A big burrow is very complicated in layout and may descend for several feet. The tunnels are not constructed to any specific plan and have been made by many generations of inhabitants. Each rabbit has from time to time taken a turn in improving the system, in an unorganised way. In some cases, the ground becomes so undermined with tunnels that the surface collapses under the weight of a horse, cow or man moving over it. This was specially common on old rabbit warrens or in game preserves. Rabbits appear to sleep on the bare soil of their burrows and it is likely they huddle together for warmth, especially in cold weather. On the other hand, a doe rabbit about to give birth to a litter, will make a nest, consisting of fur plucked from her breast mixed with a few leaves, grass and chips of bracken...

Many writers have been fascinated by the breeding rates of the rabbit and tried to estimate the size of a family of rabbits after one, two or more years. Most of the estimates were wild guesses and greatly exaggerated its reproductive powers. Bewick, for example, thought that one pair of rabbits could have 7 litters, each containing 8 young, in a year and in 4 years the family would grow to over 1,274,840. Copeland in the nineteenth century arrived at a different answer...

The fecundity of the colony reflects to a large extent the living conditions of the rabbits. Where there is enough food, the does are able to rear several litters each year, but under adverse conditions they have the ability to halt pregnancy. The process, called resorption, was not known to warreners and early naturalists...

Source: John Sheail, *Rabbits and their history,* David & Charles Ltd [1971]. Reprinted by permission of David & Charles Ltd.

Certainly in the 19th century, rabbits were farmed inside earthen-banked enclosures, topped with gorse to deter predators. The warrens were maintained by the aptly named warreners, whose job was to ensure that there was a sufficient supply of food for the rabbits, particularly during the breading season and to protect them from natural predators and poachers.

The warreners' busiest time, however, was between September and the following February, the so-called 'killing season', when extra help was often employed to cull the rabbits. Nets, ferrets, long-handled shovels called 'digging staffs' and lurcher dogs [a cross between a collie and a greyhound] were all used in a variety of ways to trap and catch rabbits at this busy period, when the rabbit's fur was at its thickest.

Thetford Warren Lodge, 1995.

Once captured, the rabbits were swiftly killed by the warreners' skilled hands. By careful management, a skilled warrener could greatly increase his own earnings and the landlord's profits, although by the 15th century most landlords had abandoned direct control by leasing or renting out the warren.

Until quite recent times, local warreners supplied Brandon's furriers with vast numbers of rabbit carcasses and skins which were processed for the felt-hat making industry. In the 1840s the processing of rabbit skins gave employment to about 200 women and girls in Brandon; the numbers employed there had increased to nearly 400 by the end of the century. Furthermore, local game dealers flourished, supplying rabbit meat to near-by and distant markets.

Not everyone, however, profited from the rabbit. Farmers suffered greatly from damage to their crops and soil erosion, as a result of rabbits that had established wild colonies well away from the confines of the warren.

Besides the warrener and the farmer protecting his crops, the rabbit's life was continually threatened by the poacher, certainly its most incessant hunter. A good poacher was as cunning as any predatory animal and almost as effective in capturing the wild rabbit as the warrener. Armed gangs of poachers are known to have been operating from Thetford, certainly by the middle of the 15th century. For this reason it is probable that the Warren Lodge was built as a residence for a gamekeeper or warrener and as a look-out to deter the threat of poachers.

The illegal taking of rabbits certainly continued as a frequent activity until the introduction of myxomatosis in the early 1950s, which virtually wiped out the local rabbit population and ended many old traditions.

Warreners, dressed in their traditional smocks, photographed on a local estate in the early years of the 20th century. Note the long handled shovels, ferret cages, Lurcher dogs and dead rabbits.

Elveden Estate Game Register
1894/5-1951/2 Rabbits killed by shooting parties and warreners

1894/5 - 6,778	1913/14 - 36,720	1935/36 - 52,606
1895/6 - 4,152	1914/15 - 23,698	1936/37 - 51,163
1896/7 - 56,569	1915/16 - 48,708	1937/38 - 48,870
1897/8 - 61,571	1916/17 - 38,609	1938/39 - 43,416
1898/9 - 56,089	1917/18 - 44,801	1939/40 - 42,294
1899/1900 - 83,319	1918/19 - 78,884	1940/41 - 31,706
1900/01 - 58,627	1919/20 - 81,130	1941/42 - 20,348
1901/02 - 45,286	1920/21 - 99,195	1942/43 - 15,765
1902/03 - 58,524	1921/22 - 128,856	1943/44 - 13,218
1903/04 - 47,745	1922/23 - 102,656	1944/45 - 22,744
1904/05 - 61,570	1923/24 -123,928	1945/46 - 40,376
1905/06 - 65,236	1924/25 -104,708	1946/47 - 47,742
1906/07 - 54,845	1925/26 - 89,406	1947/48 - 50,009
1907/08 - 63,336	1926/27 - 60,006	1948/49 - 53,793
1908/09 - 43,764	1927/28 - 51,563	1949/50 - 47,645
1909/10 - 42,009	1928/29 - 61,571	1950/51 - 27,381
1910/11 - 52,762	1929/30 - 55,986	1951/52 - 23,535
1911/12 - 50,962	1930/31 - 51,777	
1912/13 - 45,619	1931/32 - 57,240	
	1932/33 - 48,602	
	1933/34 - 58,561	
	1934/35 - 54,169	

Source: T.W. Turner, *Memoirs Of A Gamekeeper Elveden 1868-1953*, Geoffrey Bles, London [1954].

Three miles south of Thetford, in the neighbouring parish of Elveden, stands a huge mansion known as Elveden Hall. Now stripped of its former grandeur and wealth, it is an empty and hollow memorial to a past era, a period enjoyed by an elite class of game preserving landowners.

In 1813, William Newton, a rich West Indian merchant, purchased Elveden Hall and the huge Elveden Estate from the Earl of Albermarle and set himself up as a country squire. Like his predecessor and many other country squires, Newton was an enthusiastic game preserver, enjoying the pleasures of shooting on his country estate.

During Newton's occupation of Elveden Hall, parts of the local landscape were transformed to provide cover and feed for partridge, pheasant and other game. Farming continued because it was essential to the well-being of the game, even though crops were damaged.

Gamekeepers and other staff were employed to oversee the game and protect it from natural predators and poachers. The game-preserving landowners and their servant keepers, fought a long, bitter and often bloody war against poaching gangs and individuals. In 1850 during one of many affrays between gamekeepers and night poachers, William Napthan, an estate gamekeeper, was killed.

Elveden Hall was then a modest, brick-built, Georgian house. However, after Elveden was bought by the Maharajah Duleep Singh in 1863, the Hall was completely rebuilt so that little of the Georgian mansion survived. In its place stood a splendid and opulent palace, greatly influenced by its new oriental owner. At the same time the estate, then about 17,000 acres, was turned into one of the richest game preserves in the land and a venue for some of the wealthiest and, arguably, the greatest shots.

Elveden Hall photographed circa 1885, was one of several country houses that once surrounded Thetford. These large mansions were at the centre of extensive estates, very often rich with game.

The Maharajah, reputed to have been an excellent marksman, is recorded in 1876 as having shot in one day, 780 partridge for one thousand cartridges expended - rated as the largest bag ever made in England from one gun.

In his *Memoirs of a Gamekeeper*, Mr T. W. Turner, a former head gamekeeper at Elveden, recalls seeing the Maharajah using three, double-barrelled, muzzle-loading guns, assisted by two liveried loaders who were constantly supplying the necessary powder and shot.

As the more efficient breech-loading gun gradually came into use from the middle of the 19th century, the favoured method of shooting on large, game estates was the Continental 'battue', a system whereby gangs of men, acting as beaters, drove the game towards and over the waiting guns. This later method increased the rate of slaughter, and brought about a greater demand for birds as the 'bags' increased. This led to thousands of pheasants being hand-reared in purpose-built hatcheries or pens, sited on the shooting estates. The old tradition of 'walking-up', shooting at game as it took flight from the field or specially designed coverts, became less common.

Nonetheless, despite the Maharajah's great sporting achievements, it was the year following his death that Elveden began its greatest era as a sporting estate. In 1894 the Elveden estate was purchased by the 1st Earl of Iveagh, the former Sir Edward Guinness, who immediately began rebuilding the hall, transforming it into a mansion of such lavish style and magnitude that it even surpassed the splendour created by its previous owner. At the same time, the estate farms and game preserves were improved. The game department alone was increased to seventy men, including twenty-four liveried gamekeepers.

In the first season at Elveden, Lord Iveagh and his guests shot 15,100 pheasants, 1,978 partridges, 679 hares and a smaller number of other game. At times as many as 20,000 pheasants were reared in a season. As a shooting estate it had few equals.

From the late 1920s, as agriculture began to take a more prominent role on the estate, its importance as a game preserve gradually declined. As the 2nd Lord Iveagh, who was determined to make the poor soils of Elveden into profitable farm land, later explained, *'I had a shrewd idea that the sporting estate would shortly become an anachronism - because the mode of life into what it fitted was passing beyond recall'.*

A shooting party at Elveden Hall, December 1876.
Back row, left-right: Lord de Grey, Lord Holmesdale, Lord Amherst.
Centre: Lord Powerscourt, Lord Beaumont, Prince of Wales, Lord Stradbroke, Lord Ripon.
Front: Duke of Athol, Maharajah Duleep Singh.
[Photograph courtesy of the Ancient House Museum]

Elveden Estate Gamekeepers, 1885. Left-right: C. Howlett, J. Cross, T. Trayes, J. Mayes, W. Gathercole and Bessie the dog.
[Photograph courtesy of the Ancient House Museum]

The preserves of Maharajah Duleep Singh, near Thetford, were recently shot over by a party of six guns. They were at it a week, and 8,312 head of game were killed.
Source: *Thetford & Watton Times, 17 November 1883.*

The estate game staff had a busy and well-ordered life. Towards the end of the shooting season, hen birds were caught alive for the rearing pens. Warm and hot eggs, found in the wild, were placed under broody hen birds. Thousands of young pheasants were hand reared in pens.
[Photograph courtesy of the Ancient House Museum]

Unknown to me at the time I began my school life, 36 years ago, at the Thetford County School, Norwich Road, I was following in the footsteps of some of my grandparents and great-grandparents. They also went to school in the same buildings, then known as the Thetford Board School.

It was our ancestors born in the 1860s and 70s who were among the first generation of children to benefit from the establishment of the non-denominational board schools.

The 1870 Education Act provided that England should be divided into districts, and that elementary schools be set up in areas where school provision was insufficient.

Elected Boards were established to manage each district. These were the first local authority-run schools. The school board for the united district of Thetford and the parishes of Little and Great Snarehill, and Kilverstone was formed in 1876.

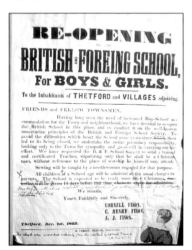

A poster announcing the re-opening of the British & Foreign [note the spelling] School in 1863.

Thetford's Board School was first established in two of the redundant school buildings of the various religious sects. The boys were in the former British and Foreign School of the dissenting sects. This building was originally a Wesleyan Methodist Chapel and school, built in 1805-06. It is now Nether Hall in Nether Row. The road behind the hall is called School Lane today.

The girls and infants were located in the former National School of the Established Church, erected in Croxton Road in 1825. This site is now occupied by the Ambulance Station.

These school buildings soon became overcrowded and inadequate and in order to provide a school large enough to accommodate 750 pupils, a new board school was planned and built on the outskirts of the town, beside the road leading to Norwich.

The newly-completed school was formally handed over to Mr Cornell H. Fison, Chairman of the Thetford School Board, on the 1st May 1879. The following week, Mr Whiteley, Head Master of the Boys' School, Miss Cleghorn, Headmistress of the Girls' School and Miss May, Headmistress of the Infants' School, received their first intake of pupils.

Thetford School Board. Attendance: 198 girls, 199 infants, 262 boys. It was stated that the present teaching staff of the girls' school was one head teacher, an assistant misstress, three pupil teachers and one monitor...Ultimately it was found according to the Code, a headmisstress should teach 60 children, and that for every 40 children beyond that number a pupil teacher must be engaged. As an assistant misstress was expected to do the work of two pupil teachers, and the average attendance in the girls' school was 196, it was clear there was a greater teaching staff than that stated by the Code... **Source:** *Bury & Norwich Post, 7 October 1879.*

The board schools were financed by a combination of Government grants, local rates and attendance fees. Each child attending school paid 2d. per week; families who were penniless or in distress could seek exemption by applying to the Board. Fees for elementary education were abolished in 1891.

*The School Board for the united district of Thetford, comprising the borough of Thetford and the parishes of Great and Little Snarehill, and Kilverstone, was formed in January 1876...New schools have been built on the Norwich road, on the outskirt of the town; site, 1? acre; cost, £6484 10s 6d., including master's house...***Source:** *William White, Directory of Norfolk [1883].*

Most parents and guardians ensured that their children attended school regularly. Those who failed to do so, received a visit from the school attendance officer. Persistent non-attendance resulted in parents appearing before the local magistrates at the Petty Sessions.

Since the Thetford Board School first opened its doors, there have been, very briefly, several important Acts which have affected children's education and development. In 1880 school attendance was made compulsory for all children aged 5-13 years, except if a certain standard was attained. In 1902 the County and County Boroughs became responsible for both elementary and secondary education. In 1907 a school medical service with compulsory medical examinations was introduced. In 1918 the school leaving age was raised to 14 years. In 1944 the principle of a secondary education for all children was established; the 11-plus arrived and the school leaving age was raised to 15 years. In 1973 the school leaving age was raised to 16 years. This month, school governors take on management of schools' finances and other responsibilities.

Children of the Norwich Road School at play in the early years of the 20th century. Although general conditions, standards of education and discipline at the school have changed enormously from that a century or more ago, many of the original school buildings have survived and the class rooms have retained much of their original Victorian architecture and other features.

The Norwich Road School photographed from the air at the end of the 20th century – about 120 years after the school was built. At least some of the bricks for building the school were transported to the town from St. Ives, by 'lighters' on the Thetford Navigation. The building work began in April 1878 and was completed by May the following year when the school was opened.
[Photograph courtesy of Studio Five, Thetford]

Sitting upright, with their pens in readiness, most of the fifty-seven girls in this delightful classroom scene appear to be participating in the well practiced discipline of 'pen-drill'. Although this photograph was taken about 1917, when there were restrictions of many basic necessities because of the European war, these girls appear to be well turned-out.
[Photograph courtesy of Michael Burton]

School One Of First In Region *Thetford & Watton Times, 8 January 1988*

One hundred years ago the provision of a technical or grammar school for girls was virtually unknown. Thetford became one of the earliest places in East Anglia to provide this form of education when Mrs Amherst, of Didlington Hall, near Northwold, opened Thetford's Grammar School for Girls on the 31st January 1888.

The school was built in London Road, almost opposite the Boys' Grammar School. This was despite protests over its siting made by the Reverend Benjamin Reed, Headmaster of the Boys' School.

Mr J. Osborne Smith, the architect responsible for the school's design, was a former pupil at Thetford's Grammar School for Boys.

Built for forty-six pupils, the new buildings consisted of an assembly room, one classroom and cloakroom. Adjacent, a house was built to accommodate the headmistress. The cost was paid out of funds granted from the Fulmerston and Williamson bequests. The will of Sir Richard Fulmerston, proved in 1566, provided for the establishment of the Grammar School for boys. Sir Joseph Williamson [1633-1701] was a former Recorder and Member of Parliament for the Borough of Thetford.

The Girls' Grammar School, in the London Road, was erected in 1887, at a cost of £3,500 defrayed out of the funds of Sir Joseph Williamson Charity, & is at present available for 50 girls, with a boarding house for 5 boarders. **Source:** *Kelly's Directory of Norfolk 1892.*

The curriculum under the Headmistress, Miss M. E. Hailey, included mathematics, algebra, Euclid, English grammar and literature, Latin, French, history, geography, drawing and singing.

There were eight pupils during the first term. At the end of the first year the number of pupils had increased to thirty-five. Many of these girls were the privileged daughters of local businessmen, 'white collar' workers and traders.

The school continued to be a success. So much so that by the early 1930s, with as many as one hundred and forty-six pupils, overcrowding had become a

The Girl's Grammar School published on a picture postcard, postally used in 1904.

problem. In order to accommodate the increasing number of pupils, further improvements and extensions to the school buildings were made in 1932. The new buildings contained a hall and gymnasium, laboratory, kitchen and dining room and a new classroom. The fee for pupils was then £8 per year for girls whose parents lived in Thetford. For those who lived outside the town the fee was higher.

After the 1944 Education Act, the school ceased to be fee-paying. Under this Act the school governors, the same governing body as the Boys' Grammar School, handed both schools to the County Council to maintain.

From 1974 the two schools became known respectively as Thetford Fulmerston School for Boys and Girls. The following year the two schools became co-educational. On the school roll were three hundred and ninety girls and three hundred boys. In 1981, after over thirty years of local authority control, the school reverted to its former independence, as the Thetford Grammar School.

Today, the school provides a wide-range of courses to GCSE and GCE A-level for boys and girls aged 8 to 18 years.

Many of the present pupils will be familiar with the often-mentioned *'notable old boys'* of the Grammar School. But who are the *'notable old girls'*? One who immediately comes to my mind is Mrs Marjorie Sutherland [née Boughton] who attended the Girls' School 1911-1922. During the 1950s when Thetford's proposed expansion was under discussion, Mrs Sutherland, as either Mayor, an Alderman or Borough Councillor, had an influence on the town's future. Later, as Chairman of the school governors, her influence and guidance helped to steer the school to its present position, a totally independent fee-paying school.

Opening of a Ladies' Higher Grade School...Candidates over seven years of age are to be admitted, after the preliminary examination by Miss Hailey. The school is divided into three terms of 13 weeks each, there will be an annual examination, and pupils are prepared for the University, Locals, and Foundation Scholarships will be annually awarded. A report of each pupil's progress will be sent to her parents at the end of each term. The buildings are lofty and well warmed and ventilated, with ample playgrounds... **Source:** *Thetford & Watton Times, 28 January, 1888.*

A classroom at the Girls' Grammar School, published on a picture postcard in the early years of the 20th century. At the time, a number of pupils at the school were boarders.
A message on the postcard printed on the previous page reads, 'This is my present abode, except on Saturday & Sunday which I spend in my parental establishment'.

Girls at study in the early 1930s. In 1931 the Girls' School annual tuition fees were advertised at £8 per for Thetford pupils, £10 10s. for Norfolk pupils and £21 for pupils from outside Norfolk. Pupils aged 7-18 years were admitted, while there was a preparatory department for girls under 7 years.
Fees were abolished in 1945, following the 1944 Education Act.

A domestic science room was added in 1912 at a cost of £1,500. It is just one of many improvements carried out since the school first opened.
At different times in the 18th & 19th centuries, several schools were established in the town for the education of young ladies. A Miss Warriker ran such a school in the 1790s, a Miss Dade opened a boarding & day school for young ladies in 1808, Mrs R. Edwards advertised a ladies' school on the Bury Road in the 1850s and the Misses Wilkinson advertised a school for young ladies at the Shrublands in the 1860s.

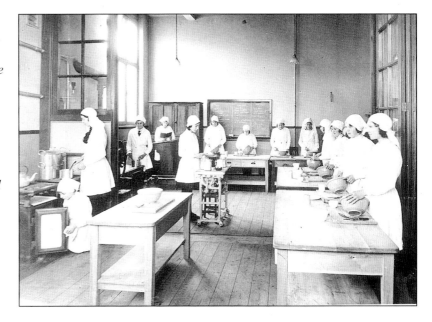

Footing The Bill For Firefighting 100 Years Ago *Thetford & Watton Times, 16 October 1992*

Since the publication in 1988 of *A History of the Borough of Thetford Fire Brigade* some exciting discoveries have come my way, throwing new light on the local fire service as it was before national legislation created the modern fire service.

Firstly, the *Ipswich Journal* newspaper of December 1776 provided an account of a fire engine being used to extinguish a fire at Thetford's Paper Mill, more recently the Mill Lane premises of Thetford Moulded Products, but now demolished and waiting development. This report is particularly interesting because it is by far the earliest reference to a fire engine in Thetford. As this was more than a century before the Borough Fire Brigade was formed, it is probable that Borough Constables manned the engine and procured volunteer helpers at the scene of the fire, to assist with 'pumping' and other duties.

Thetford Town Council:- The Watch & Bye-Law Committee recommended the furnishing of buckets and fire cromes for the use of the fire engine and that the management of the engine be in the future part of the duty of the police. **Source:** *Bury & Norwich Post, 18 February 1846.*

Two of the other discoveries were kindly given to me, after being found among the personal effects of the late Miss E. Kerridge of East Harling. They are two unique and hitherto undiscovered documents. The older is a small booklet bearing the Borough 'coat of arms' and the title, *Rules & Regulations of the Thetford Fire Brigade*. It was published in February 1883, two years and three months after the Borough Brigade was formed. The rules, which were probably drawn-up by the Fire Brigade Committee, stipulate the number of firemen, *'a Captain, two Lieutenants, one Superintendent of Engines and sixteen men, who shall be appointed by the Town Council'*. They further laid down that the brigade's uniform *'shall be a brass helmet, blue tunic with red facings, blue trousers with red stripe, Wellington boots, belt, axe and life line'*. Other rules detail such essentials as the chain of command for the giving and receiving of orders; individual responsibilities and duties; police and special constables' duties *'upon an alarm of fire'*; the system of issuing payment 'tickets' to additional volunteers, who were always recruited when fighting large fires, and the area in which the Fire Brigade was to provide assistance... *'all fires within the Borough and in the adjoining district if summoned, should the Captain or Officer in Command consider it expedient'*.

Thetford Town Council: A letter was read that the two present fire engines were almost worthless, and it was moved by Dr. Minns, and seconded by Mr Frost that a new one be bought at once...Mr Bidwell said the insurance company had been very liberal with him towards his new private engine which he would place at anyone's disposal in the event of a fire. The Rev. J. Allison thought we were better off now than hitherto, and that it was an unnecessary expense. **Source:** *Bury & Norwich Post, 6 February 1877.*

Following the list of rules is a scale of *'approved charges'* for the service of the fire brigade. After a large fire, property owners were likely to face a hefty bill if uninsured. For example, a charge of 2 guineas [£2.10p.] for up to 10 hours was made for the Borough engine and other fire fighting equipment. In addition, there was the Captain's fee of 13s. 6d. [67.5p.] for the first hour and 4 shillings [20p.] thereafter. For each fireman in attendance, a charge of 3 shillings [15p.] was made for the first hour. Moreover, on top of all of these expenses there was the cost of such items as horse hire [for pulling the engine], refreshments and damage to equipment.

However, if the property owner was of a provident nature and subscribed annually to the Borough Fire Brigade Fund, some charges were reduced by 25 per cent.

The second document clearly shows how these charges were made. It is a bill sent by Robert Hall, Captain of the Borough of Thetford Fire Brigade, to the Norwich Union Fire Insurance Society detailing the *'expenses incurred'* by Mr B. Golding after a fire at his College Farm, Rushford, on the 1st June, 1896. Two large haystacks were destroyed, while near-by farm buildings and the thatch-roof of the parish church were seriously threatened.

The bill to the Norwich Union, Mr Golding's insurers, totalled £26 5s. [£26.25p.]. One of the largest single items, £4 was for the hire of four horses including rider and driver. Another payment of £4 8s. [£4.40p.] was made to twenty-two men, who were probably farm labourers employed at the College Farm, for assisting all day 'pumping' the manual fire engine. Each man received 4 shillings, a good day's pay when Norfolk's agricultural labourers were only receiving about 10 to 13 shillings [50-65p.] a week.

Thetford: On Tuesday severe snow storms were prevalent...Skating is now thoroughly enjoyed as Mr J. Houchen, Captain of the Fire Brigade, had the engine out during the week and flooded large portions of the [Melford] common. **Source:** *Bury & Norwich Post, 18 January 1881.*

Finally, thanks to Ben Culey's 16mm cine-film of local events in the late 1930s and recently published on a home video by the East Anglian Film Archive, we now have visual evidence of the motor vehicle, converted into a fire tender, for towing the steam fire engine until 1938. It was given to the town in 1930 by Earl Iveagh of Elveden Hall.

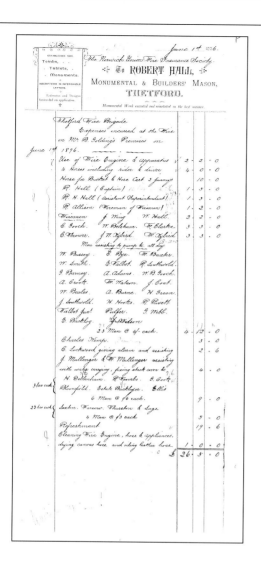

The Borough of Thetford Fire Brigade, the year of the Rushford fire. Front row, left-right: F. Dickerson, W. Hall, C. Kimm, J. Kybird. Middle row: R. Hall (Captain), W. Belsham, C. Thrower, B. Liddimore, J. Wing, B. Duffield, R. Allison, R.H. Hall.
On the manual engine: J. Baker, F. Kybird, E. Clarke, F. Clarke, G. Flack, F. Lister, H. Castle, W. Reeve.
The manual fire engine was replaced by a brand-new Merryweather steam fire engine in 1905. At the same time, the Borough of Thetford Fire Brigade was re-organised.

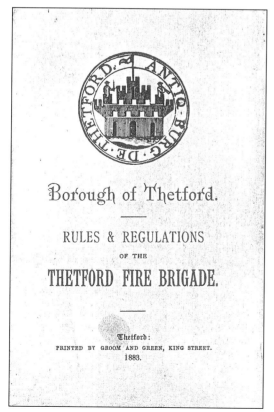

The Borough of Thetford Fire Brigade photographed in Mill Lane, circa, 1935. The fire engine is the 1910 Mercedes loaned by Lord Iveagh of Elveden Hall and converted to tow the steam fire engine.
[Photograph courtesy of East Anglian Film Archive]

The Abbey Farm Camp where Lt. General Sir Douglas Haig set up his HQ in 1912.

Not a day passes without a modern jet aircraft flying over Thetford. As we go about our business, very few of us even raise our eyes skywards to observe this common occurrence.

Seventy-five years ago it was a different story. Then, many Thetfordians witnessed a memorable event in the history of British aviation. At Snarehill, 1½ miles to the south-east of Thetford, just off the road to Euston, heavier-than-air flying machines took part for the very first time in a military exercise.

Troops arriving at Thetford Bridge station.

In August 1912, the aviator B.C. Hucks made the first recorded aeroplane flight over Norwich. On August 31, 1912, a section of aircraft belonging to the newly formed Royal Flying Corps began their journey from the government aircraft factory at Hatfield to their pre-assembled camp at Snarehill.

The rumour that the first of the aircraft would be arriving had spread through the town. Large crowds had gathered in Thetford and the surrounding countryside to witness this exciting spectacle. They were not disappointed.

At about 9 o'clock in the morning, approaching from the south-west, biplane number 201, piloted by Major Burke and accompanied by Lt. James, flew over the town before making a graceful descent on the airfield at Snarehill. Number 201 had flown from Hatfield to Thetford in just 1¼ hours at an average speed of 60 mph.

Over the next few days thousands of people, eager to get a view of the newly-arrived aircraft, jammed the surrounding roads and lanes with their motor cars, carts and bicycles. What great excitement to distract from the everyday chores!

A week after the arrival at Snarehill of the RFC, another great feat in transportation took place. Between nightfall on Saturday, 7th September and dawn the following day, 30,000 troops, 120 guns, thousands of horses and tons of munitions were transported by rail from Aldershot into the exercise area. This was done without interfering with the ordinary traffic on the railway system.

The manoeuvres were now ready to begin. The exercise area extended from Hertford and Dunmow in the south, Bedford and St Neots in the west, Diss and Stowmarket in the east with King's Lynn, Fakenham and Wymondham at the northern perimeter. In the middle was Thetford, where Lt. General Sir Douglas Haig set up his HQ.

Army aeroplane, Thetford, 1912.

For the next six days with all the activity of marching troops, motor lorries and mounted troops passing to and fro through the towns and villages, aircraft and airships passing overhead, it must have appeared to the local population as if the nation were at war.

One Thetford business was quick to spot the commercial advantages of the manoeuvres as the following advert which appeared in the local press shows: *Souvenir and Official Programmes of the Autumn Manoeuvres, also view postcards, maps of Thetford and District; agent for Goss China, Henry Green, Stationer, Thetford.*

On September 14th the manoeuvres ceased. The troops, no doubt tired after their week of activity, returned to their garrisons. The countryside of East Anglia, the towns and villages returned to peace and normality - for two short years at least.

A Breguet biplane at Snarehill, September, 1912, photographed by Thetford photographer R.J. Bantock and published on a picture postcard. Only two other postcards of this event are known to exist.
The following report was printed in the Bury Free Press early in September, 1912: 'On Monday morning and evening another series of flights were given by Captain Longcroft [Welsh Regiment] on the biplane No. 201 which arrived on Saturday in connection with the forth-coming manoeuvres. Flights will take place each day, and are in so much similarity that little can be said of them beyond remarking that the pilot has exhibited remarkable skill in the manipulation of the machine. The corps were busily engaged on Monday removing one of the large tents in which the machines are held,...The biplanes which will be stationed at Thetford will be of two types of engine. One type is the Farman which has the engine and propeller behind, and the other is the Breguet, a French type, which has the engine and propeller well forward'...

Another very rare photograph of the 1912 manoeuvres, again published on a picture postcard. Bearing a Thetford postmark dated September 25th 1912, the message on the reverse reads, "Dear Auntie What do you think this for a visitor in the Park for a week they came over the houses 2 mornings Maggie". The Bury Free Press, 21 September 1912 reported that the airship Gamma was observed over Thetford while the airship Beta arrived at Euston Park, where this photograph was probably taken. Note the 'ship' structure suspended under the balloon and spectators around the perimeter fence.

Ready for Duty

My story really starts in 1938. I had not been married very long when Thetford's Mobile Police Officer, Leonard Woods, called round my house and asked if I would be interested in signing on for the Police War Reserves. He informed me very little training would be required; there would be no lectures to attend, with the exception of a physical, no examinations to be undertaken. He added that I should gain sufficient knowledge of police work by accompanying policemen on the beat, at times suitable to myself. Moreover, he also informed me that I should only be called up for duty during times of war. I did not know then and thinking war was a very long way away, I promised I would call and see the Inspector.

The next day I visited Thetford Police Station and was interviewed by Inspector, George Dye, a big, fresh-faced man who looked every inch a police inspector. He asked me very few questions prior to bringing out the necessary documents for me to sign. I remember asking the Inspector why Police War Reserve Constables would be required and he told me so many policemen in the county were Territorial Army reservists, they would be the first men to be enlisted and people like me would have to replace them. It appears from what he told me, later to be confirmed, that I was the only man in Thetford who complied with their requirements! At that time Thetford's population was only about 4,000. They were looking for married men, six feet tall, of good character and a fair degree of schooling. I signed on the dotted line, much to the relief of the Inspector, for he had received orders to enlist four men similar to me and I was his first and only recruit.

About a month passed and I was requested to attend Thetford police station and from there to be taken to East Harling Police Station for the purpose of being given a physical examination and, at the same time, measured for my police uniform. When I arrived I made the acquaintance of two men in the same position as myself, one from East Harling and one from Attleborough. We were told our uniforms would be ready in about five weeks.

Police War Reservists 111 C. [Jack] Whalebelly, photographed in Painter Street, c.1943. [Photograph courtesy of Doris Whalebelly]

The day arrived when I was again requested to visit the police station – this time to try on my new uniform. I changed in one of the cells and paraded in front of the Inspector. He decided it was a good fit, to which I readily agreed, and I was amazed when he told me to take it home. That night I hung it in my wardrobe – one plain uniform, one plain cape and one peaked cap – with never a thought that war was less than twelve months away.

During the latter part of December 1938 and the early months of 1939, I accompanied three different policemen on the beat various dates and times. On one particular night I was in the company of Police Constable Tom Bowering, when he stopped an old man riding a cycle without lights. He told this man he would report him and put down what particulars he required for his note-book. When we got back to the police station he made out his report to be forwarded to the Superintendent's Office at Wymondham, the Divisional Headquarters. I was invited to attend the Petty Sessions when the defendant was brought before the local magistrates. He was fined five shillings, but I am quite sure now that my view of thinking this was an utter waste of time was wrong. I personally had taken no part in the proceedings, but I had gained valuable experience.

Nothing more of note took place until September 1939 when war was declared. I received a second uniform, a duplicate of my first issue, and during the first week of September I received various chevrons, badges and numerals with which to decorate my uniforms, cape and hats. I also received a truncheon, pair of handcuffs, leather wallet, note-book and pencil. Following instructions, my number was Police War Reserve 111. I inserted the various insignia and decorations to my uniform and, sartorially speaking, I was ready for duty.

With the declaration of war in September, I knew it would not be very long before my way of living was going to take a considerable change of direction. Sure enough, during November 1939 I received notification that I should be required to start duties as a Police War Reservist at Thetford on the 2nd of December. On the Tuesday before the 2nd of December, I was taken to East Harling Petty Sessions and formally sworn in as a Police Constable after taking the oath before the local magistrates.

As detailed, I reported for duty at Thetford Police Station on 2nd

December, 1939. When I arrived there someone else was already on duty. He was PC Arthur Youngs, a young man with less than 12 months' service who had transferred to the Norfolk Constabulary from being a postman at Swaffham. Amongst other things that morning, I was told to accompany PC Youngs on foot patrol in some of the main streets in the town. Perhaps a little apprehensive at the thought of this, I was surprised to find I did not feel at all embarrassed at showing myself to the local population, nearly all of whom I knew or were known to me. PC Youngs was not as tall as me and this may have given me added confidence.

My hours of duty on that first day were from 9 a.m. until 1pm and 2 p.m. until 6 p.m. When I returned for duty at 2 p.m. there was a different policeman in the office. He was Acting Police Sergeant John Emblem, a man of my own height but he had a far better physique. I later learned that he had once held a professional boxing licence at London's Blackfriars Ring. I wondered why he had given up his boxing career, for he was a wonderfully proportioned man only to learn that at some time he had damaged the upper knuckles in his left hand and this had been the sole reason for handing in his licence and hanging up his boxing gloves. Those very knuckles were going to be the subject of some concern at a later date. His rank of Acting Police Sergeant was awarded to him for his summer duties, being in charge of a police boat on the Norfolk Broads. At the close of each season on the Broads, he would be loaned to a Division in the county and then return to the Broads again the

following season. He was allowed to keep his rank during the close season but other than that, it did not mean much to him financially. I found Sergeant Emblem to be a studious type of man and very knowledgeable in his work. He could recite the Judge's opening speech used at all Assize Courts

The Bell Corner on the busy main road through the town in the summer of 1939. Within a few months and for the duration of the war, armored tanks and numerous types of other military vehicles were frequently passing through the town.

and he could repeat, word for word, any one of one hundred and six police definitions.

This, then, was our total strength at Thetford in that December, 1939. Two constables, one war reserve, one mobile policeman and one inspector. With the telephone having to be manned 24 hours and each man being entitled to one day off each week, you will appreciate we were not exactly overstaffed. During those first few months, I often found myself to be the only man on duty and there were times when the Inspector would tell me to put the telephone extension through to his house and do a short, sharp, foot patrol through the town, just to show there was a policeman about. However, in the July of 1940, our strength was improved with the coming of a new recruit to the regular police force in the person of Leslie Lovell. Although he was a young man, he must have weighed 16 stone. We christened him, 'Porky' and he turned out to be a good colleague. As the war

progressed, three more Police War Reserve Constables were enlisted and life became less hectic.

Motor Accidents

It was during my very first duty, alone in the police office, that I received information of a road accident not 200 yards from the Police Station. I informed the Inspector, who was at home at the time, and he told me I could go down and take the necessary particulars. No one had been hurt but damage had been caused to one set of the traffic bollards at the top of White Hart Street. The main reason for reporting accidents to the police is to allow the police to ascertain if the law has been broken. First to be scrutinized is the driver's licence and insurance, followed by the road fund licence, after which the vehicle should be examined to make sure it complies with the law. This particular accident came under the term 'simple' as road conditions were bad at the time. It was my opinion that no accident would have occurred had not the bollard been there. The bollard, one of two on a raised concrete base, had been smashed. It was the raised base which had caused the accident. I noted all the details I required and returned to the Police Station to make out my first report to my Superintendent. Damage had been occasioned to Norfolk County Council property and one bollard costing near on £30 had been demolished. I was inexperienced at that time but this was to be the first of six accidents I was going to handle that winter, as a result of those bollards. Further than that, I was going to be instrumental in having them removed.

We had more than our fair share of snow during that first winter of the war. Croxton Road was very busy with military motor traffic, it being the best way to the Battle Area and the fact that the Command Supply Depot was situated where the Breckland Sports Center now stands. The Middlesex Searchlight Regiment also had headquarters at Lodge Farm, Croxton. If you take into consideration that quite a few of the soldiers driving heavy motor vehicles during the first few months of the war were inexperienced on the road, some of them had probably never driven at all prior to being enlisted, you can imagine why the particular bollard in a direct line with Croxton Road was smashed three times in as many months. Heavy vehicles would come down Croxton Road, the brakes would be applied in order to stop at the Halt sign at the bottom, the wheels would lock on the snow covered road surface and the vehicle would simply slide in to the bollards.

After I had my fill concerning these bollards, I asked the Inspector if I could forward a report to Norfolk County Council relating my experiences, and pointing out that the bollards were really a hazardous obstruction because they could not be illuminated during the hours of darkness because of the Lighting Restrictions Order and the road junction would be safer without them. Within a very short time of my report being received by Norfolk County Council, through my Superintendent's office, the bollards were removed.

Talking of inexperienced drivers, I was called to a simple accident on the Croxton Road, just beyond the railway bridge, during my very early days. No one had been hurt but certain amount of damage had been done. My first request to the driver, who happened to be a Private in the Middlesex Searchlight Regiment, was to have a look at his driving licence. When he informed me he did not have a driving licence and had never held one, I told him I should have to report him for breaking the law. The next day I visited the Headquarters of the Middlesex Searchlight Regiment and was escorted to the Commanding Officer. I politely informed him I would have to report him for employing an unlicensed driver. He laughed aloud at this and asked his Adjutant to pass him an Army Driving Licence. The Adjutant passed him a license in the form of a small piece of card. He at once filled in the particulars, including the driver's name, whereupon I pointed out this did not permit him to drive on the day in question. He again had a little laugh to himself and back-dated the licence one week – and what could I do about that? I was beaten to a frazzle but the C.O. was a perfect gentleman, he insisted I sampled his John Haig whisky before I departed.

> *Only two of the "Keep Left" signs at the bottom of Croxton Road remain standing... The bollards, always a bugbear to motorists, have under recent conditions become a positive danger.*
> **Source:** *Thetford & Watton Times, 3 February 1940.*

On another occasion, I was standing at the top of White Hart Street, when I saw a lorry come roaring down Norwich Road at about 60 miles an hour and, without slowing down, go straight across the crossroad and into Station Road. I had my cycle with me at the time and immediately cycled after it along Station Road. As I approached the railway station I saw the lorry parked there. I waited by the lorry for the driver and, when he returned, I told him I was reporting him for dangerous driving. There were three types of charge for this particular driving offence: Careless, Reckless and Dangerous, in that order. I thought this was the worst driving I had ever seen. Well, it turned out that the reason for the dangerous driving was that the driver's brother, who had been on leave and was returning to his unit by train, had inadvertently left some equipment at East Harling station. The lorry driver, having noticed this, directly after the train departed with his brother, made the dash to Thetford. He had actually beaten the train from East Harling to Thetford.

Everybody was issued with a National Registration Identity Card. It was required to be produced on demand by a Police Officer in uniform or member of H.M. Armed Forces in uniform on duty.

About a year later, the same corner at the top of White Hart Street gave me an unpleasant experience one afternoon. I was called to an accident there in which an Army dispatch rider had collided with the wall of a house that stood there. When I arrived at the scene he was in a very bad way and I did not give him much hope of surviving. He was taken to Thetford Cottage Hospital and later moved to Newmarket where he died 5 days later. My enquiries proved that a military car had driven out of Station Road and forced the dispatch rider to collide with the wall. I took a statement from the driver of the military car, who happened to be the Regimental Sergeant Major of the Middlesex Searchlight Regiment. I later took two statements from witnesses.

From the evidence I had obtained, it appeared that the RSM was to blame. He had come out of Station Road with out stopping, ignoring the Halt sign at the junction there.

Later, everybody concerned with the accident was subpoenaed to attend the inquest that was held at Newmarket. I was amazed to find that the RSM was not there in person but his Adjutant was standing in for him. The Adjutant informed the Coroner that, 'the RSM was a very busy man – they only had one such man in their regiment and his duties did not permit him to attend the inquest'. The Coroner took a very dim view of this and threatened to adjourn the inquest, demanding the RSM's attendance. However, the inquest was completed that day and resulted in a verdict of 'Accidental Death'. After I had completed my report, in triplicate, I asked the Inspector for his personal view. He gave me to understand that no charges would be forthcoming as the result of this accident; we were at war and funny things happened during times of war. It was quite probable that this man's death would be recorded as having been killed while on Active Service.

I was also called to the scene of another fatal accident on the Diss Road. An accident had occurred, one beautiful summer day, after a shackle pin in the steering gear of a open lorry had come adrift, causing the vehicle to crash, head on into a tree. Two Indian soldiers standing in the back of the lorry had been thrown out, one collided head–first into the tree, breaking his neck and killing him. He had a gaping hole in his neck and his spine was clearly visible. The other soldier had landed over on the other side of a hedge and, I am told, had sprinted to the place where I had found him, at least one hundred yards away from where the crash had happened. Considering he had a very bad laceration to his right leg, it seems incredible that he was able

to run with such a bad leg wound. There is little doubt that fear can add to a man's energies and motivate all sorts of actions.

4
SIMPLE RULES
*for getting
home safely in
the black – out*

1 When you first come out into the black-out, stand still for a minute to get your eyes used to the darkness.

2 Look *both* ways before stepping off the pavement. Make sure there's nothing coming.

3 Where there are traffic lights, always cross by them. It is worth going out of your way to do this.

4 Throw the light of your torch down on to the ground.

LOOK OUT
IN THE BLACK-OUT !

The Indian soldiers were camped near by in Snarehill Woods and my course of action seemed quite clear. I would first have to get the injured soldier to hospital and then find an Indian doctor to certify the death of the other soldier. After making the injured man comfortable and covering the dead man with a waterproof sheet from off the lorry, I started to cycle the mile to the Indian regiment's headquarters in the woods at Snarehill. I was just about 200 yards from the camp entrance, when I came across another accident in which a soldier had been hurt. This man had been lying on the top of a stack of ammunition boxes being transported on the back of a lorry, when the lorry veered off the road, causing the soldier to hit his back very severely with a round metal bar that supported the roof. When I arrived, the injured soldier was laying on the grass verge beside the road, covered in an American airman's flying jacket to keep him warm. He was obviously quite

badly hurt and his whole body was shaking violently. After I had made a few enquiries with his colleagues, I departed to the Indian headquarters to phone the American headquarters at Elveden for an ambulance for the injured soldier I had just seen and to get a doctor for the Indian soldier. This only took a few minutes and when I returned to the scene of the second accident, an American ambulance was already coming up the road at high speed. A young, American doctor jumped out of the ambulance and examined the injured man. The ambulance driver opened the back of the vehicle and opened the drawers of a large medical chest. The injured soldier was still shaking uncontrollably from head-to-foot. The doctor took a pair of scissors and cut a slit in the upper arm of the soldiers shirt, injected him with morphine, immediately the shaking stopped. To me, seeing this rapid change was marvelous and a little uncanny. I then discovered the injured soldier was not an American, but English. I had been misled by the American flying jacket draped over him. I apologized to the American doctor for calling him out to deal with a British serviceman but he quickly dismissed my concern and said he had seen another accident down the road. When I told him there was another injured man there, he insisted on picking him up on his way back and taking him to the American Headquarters at Elveden. In both of my reports of the accidents I commented on the wonderful co-operation I had received from the American forces.

There were to be two more fatal accidents on the Diss road. The first one involved a lorry loaded with bags of cement, crashing into a tree. The impact had crushed the near-side door and the passenger's legs had been trapped. Unfortunately, before the passenger could be rescued the lorry caught fire and the passenger burnt to death. All the men involved with this accident

Thetford's Market Place and Castle Street photographed by an American serviceman during the War. Soon after the outbreak of war in 1939, the town and surrounding district was soon alive with allied military activity. This was further increased from the middle of 1943, when thousands of American servicemen arrived and were stationed at aerodromes and camps within twenty miles of Thetford.
[Photograph courtesy of 389th Bomb Group Collection, Hethel]

were Irish, some had been riding on the load. They asked me if a Roman Catholic priest could be found. This was done and I find it hard to describe the little memorial service I witnessed that day that was held over the body of the dead man at the crash scene in the beautiful woods at Snarehill.

The other fatal accident was the result of the blackout. A car had driven head-on into a large artillery gun, being towed by the last vehicle in a small Army convoy. The Commander of the convoy had heard bombs being dropped and exploding in the area, so he ordered all the vehicles in his convoy to halt and extinguish all lights. The car had driven straight into the rear of the convoy, pulled up in the road. The two people in the car never had a chance. I have never seen a car so badly damaged; the driver and his passenger must have been killed instantly.

This accident also reminds me of another I attended, just on the outskirts of Thetford, on the A11 going towards Elveden. This was also caused by the blackout conditions. A large lorry had parked on the nearside of the road, when a

RAF utility car, the sort with glass windows right round the body, collided with the stationary lorry. Both occupants of the car had been cut by flying glass, but they were still very much alive. The driver of the car happened to be Wing Commander Guy Gibson and his passenger a high ranking Czech officer. This was one night I shall never forget, for all the time we were attending to the injured officers, German bombers were continuously passing overhead. We had to have a small amount of light and I was desperately afraid that we should receive a load of bombs at any moment. Next morning, however, we learned that Coventry had been heavily bombed and it was our good fortune that the German pilots passing overhead were well-disciplined. Both men were taken to hospital where a local doctor spent some time picking little pieces of glass from the faces of both men. We were surprised when we put the Czech officer into bed, to find that he had an artificial leg.

Amongst many other motor accidents I attended, I think the one in which a driver was run over by his own lorry is also worth

mentioning. This happened on the A11 at Roudham Heath. The vehicle concerned was an unladen, articulated lorry. The driver had stopped and was inspecting the underside of the trailer when it was struck by another vehicle, causing the trailer to run over him. He sustained a broken pelvis and other injuries. The injured driver later claimed compensation and I was subpoenaed to attend the hearing. His Honour Judge Rowlands officiated and, prior to giving my evidence, I took the Oath, after which I gave my name and number. The Judge asked me to repeat my name and after I had again said, 'Clifford Jack Whalebelly, Police War Reserve Constable, number 111, stationed at Thetford', he made some remark, which I must confess I did not fully hear but was something about me having a relationship with the biblical Jonah. To say I was surprised is putting it mildly but I was not embarrassed for I had given evidence in court many times prior to this. Thinking very quickly about the situation, I decided to withhold giving my evidence for a full minute. The silence I created more than told His Honour that he had done wrong.

Roadblocks were occasionally placed to check vehicle road fund licences. These checks were held immediately after the expiry date and during the period in which a vehicle was allowed to be used, providing an application for a licence renewal had been made. In those days, the County Councils were responsible for road fund licences; if you did not renewed your licence, you committed an offence and the County Council would set its own fine to meet each individual case.

On one occasion after I stopped a man who was displaying a recently expired licence, I filled in the usual questionnaire which had to be forwarded to County Council Licensing Authorities. Eventually he received a mitigated penalty of nine shillings which was not paid. The County Council then requested the Police to take further proceedings against him and he was then summonsed to appear at Thetford Petty Sessions, which he failed to attend. After I had given my evidence, the Chairman of the Magistrates announced that he was fined ten shillings for not displaying a valid road fund licence. Inspector Dye immediately rose to his feet and told the Magistrate he had not asked if there were any previous convictions. The Inspector then told the Magistrate that besides being a habitual criminal, this was the defendant's fourth offence appertaining to the non-payment of a road fund licence. On hearing this information, the magistrates retired and, when they returned, announced that the defendant was fined £20. The law demanded this, for with each offence, the fine had to be increased – what an absolute fool this man had been – he could have got away with a nine shilling fine. In the end, the police had to levy for distress to collect the £20 fine.

Flying Casualties

It was the duty of the police to report to Divisional Headquarters all incidents of aircraft crashes, giving details and map references, within our area. With seventeen airfields within a 25-mile radius of Thetford, aircraft crashes were fairly common, particularly as the war progressed. Naturally, I did not attend all of them but I remember the first one we had in the very early days of the war. It was a Whitley bomber carrying a crew of three. Two men had baled out and we picked these up alright. I remember one of them was very distressed and constantly crying. When he eventually gained control of himself, he told us he had tried so hard, but could not get the pilot to leave the plane. This man had left it until the very last moment before jumping out, loosing one of his flying boots in the process. When we searched the crashed aircraft we were able to recover the body of the pilot. It was most unusual, having regard to later experiences that the aircraft did not catch fire. The missing, wool-lined, flying boot, however, was never found.

There is little doubt that the worst crash we ever had on our 'beat' happened at about 10 o'clock one morning. A plane from Honington, carrying a crew of seven, crashed near some houses on the Croxton Road. The aircraft had immediately caught fire on impact, creating a terrible scene of devastation. Recovery of the bodies, some of which had been decapitated, was carried out by a unit from RAF Honington. Identification of the bodies was impossible and I remember I could not eat my dinner that day. It was a horrific experience for everyone concerned.

One night, I was on telephone duty at the Police Station, from midnight until 8 a.m. At about 4 a.m. the doorbell rang and I went to the door

and opened it. There stood an airman holding, what I took to be a large bundle of cloth. This bundle was actually an opened parachute. I asked him to come inside and he then told me he had just baled out from a bomber aircraft. It was a very foggy morning and the pilot had been unable to find his base and fuel was getting low. The airman told me his pilot had ordered the crew to bale out while he continued to fly the plane round in a circle. Whilst he was telling me this, the telephone rang. It was another member of the same crew who had baled out. I asked him where he was speaking from but he could not tell me. I told him to stay where he was and I would ring him back. I enquired at the telephone exchange where the call had come from and they soon told me it was from the kiosk at Great Hockham. I immediately dialed the Hockham number and was relieved to hear the airman's voice. I told him that he would be picked up by our patrol car. PC Woods was roused and quickly made his collection from Hockham. I then telephoned the base at Mildenhall from where the aircraft had come. I was told that the pilot was missing but the missing crew members had landed in Suffolk. The plane had crashed in Green Lane and was completely destroyed by fire. When dawn broke and a search made of the crash site, there was no sign of the pilot. A search party from the Middlesex Searchlight Regiment was organized to search the area for the pilot, in case he had been injured and was still alive. The search party was still out, when at about 10.30 a.m., young Mr Hepburn, whose father was the agent for Sir John Musker of the Shadwell Estate, called in at the Police Station to report that there was a dead airman in a field at Brettenham. He was unable to tell me very much, as he had been too frightened to view the body fully. I asked him to take me to the body and, sure enough, there was the body of the missing pilot. He must have delayed his exit from the aircraft too late. His parachute must have just been opening when he hit the ground, breaking his neck. When I telephoned the pilot's base at Mildenhall to report the discovery at Brettenham, it was received with much sadness. The Commanding Officer told me that Pilot Officer Youngs, the dead pilot, although just 21 years old was a highly proficient and respected pilot.* Incidents such as these meant we had to work very long hours. Every available policeman was ordered to join the search parties. This particular crash gave me 17 hours continuous duty – without overtime pay may I add!

* Pilot Officer Youngs was probably 1292391 Sergeant Stephen Youngs, a pilot of the Royal Air Force Volunteer Reserve, who died on Monday 23 March 1942. Age 20 years. **Source:** *Commonwealth War Graves Commission, Debt of Honour Register.*

Later on in the war, a few German pilots tried to perfect a system of following the bombers home and shooting them down over their own airfields. This actually happened at Wretham, when a Stirling bomber was shot down just off the runway. The rear gunner was killed by cannon fire. I was there in attendance with the Inspector and PC Woods when the gunner's mutilated body was removed from the gun-turret. He body was in such a terrible condition that it had to be placed in a 'ground sheet'. The Americans were then stationed at Wretham and, as Inspector Dye and three other men carried the body away from the wreckage, there was one particular American serviceman who kept pestering the Inspector to let him have a look at the dead gunner's body. He was curtly told it was not a pretty sight but, as he was so persistent, the Inspector stopped and undid the 'ground sheet' for the American to

have a look. I doubt very much if the inquisitive American ever made another similar request. Seeing the mutilated corpse, he at once began to vomit and, apparently, was a very ill man for the remainder of the day.

I also remember the airfield at Wretham being the scene of another strange aeroplane crash. A plane was coming into land when one of the wings struck a steam road roller carrying out repairs to the runway. The wing snapped in two, instantly killing the 63 year old steam roller driver. The aircraft, apart from the wing, was only slightly damaged. I was told that it was flying again three days later.

Joe Blunt's Bridge was the scene of yet another plane crash. This involved a Mustang fighter plane which came down for no known reason. The pilot had not used his parachute and was killed in the crash. The aeroplane's camera, which automatically switched on when the guns were fired, was missing. The Americans were very concerned about this missing piece of equipment, until it was eventually found, some 400 yards from the wreck and still housed in part of the wing. After the film was developed, it was clear that the aircraft had been in combat and the crash had been a result of damage it had sustained.

I also clearly remember another incident that happened after I had completed some enquiries at the petrol depot on the Mundford Road. When looking up to the sky, I could see a Flying Fortress flying around at about 2,000 feet with one of its engines on fire. From the ground it looked as if the pilot was flying round in a circle to keep the flames away from the fuselage of the aircraft. It was a very bright and clear day and, as I stood watching, I saw a parachute coming down at a rate that was obviously too fast to be healthy. In the few seconds I stood watching the parachute

descend, I also noticed that a panel on the plane was missing. The airman hanging on the end of the parachute was doing his best to make it revolve, to create more air resistance. He was not having much success, however, as he was merely swinging from side-to-side. He landed no more than half-a-mile from where I was standing and I knew he must be hurt from the speed he had been descending. I immediately returned to the petrol depot and telephoned Inspector Dye. I could only have been back on the Mundford Road for 2 minutes when the Inspector arrived in the patrol car driven by PC Woods. It only took us a few minutes to locate the airman, for we could get the car within 100 yards of where he lay, in terrible pain. His main injury appeared to be a compact fracture of the right leg and he kept imploring the Inspector, dressed in plain clothes – whom he thought was a doctor - to give him a shot of morphine. It later transpired that the airman was USAAF doctor who had been taken up for a 'flip round' when the aircraft caught fire. He had been ordered to bale out but his parachute had caught some part of the aircraft on his immediate descent. Fortunately there was a happy sequel to this incident, as the surgeons were able, after about six months treatment, to save his damaged leg. Apparently he was discharged from the USAAF and presented with the parachute before returning home to the United States where, I guess, it adorns a wall somewhere in his house to this day.

That same day as the USAAF doctor was injured, another member of that same crew from the Flying Fortress was brought into the Thetford Police Station after he had parachuted out. He didn't look more than 19 years old and had landed alright but his body had been in the wrong body position when his parachute opened – the cords between the parachute and his body had caught him under his armpits. The sudden and abrupt movement had badly injured his shoulders, for they were both very swollen when he arrived at the station. He wasn't distressed, however, in fact he kept laughing so relieved as he was and still alive to tell the tale.

Gloomy nights!

There were many other incidents in a policeman's life during the war other than road accidents and aircraft crashes. I remember one or two interesting 'black-out' offences. I had occasion to report to Mr Sebbings, who kept a butcher's shop at the bottom of St Giles Lane. He had a glass panel over the top of his front door which was not blacked-out in any way and allowed light to be seen. I had previously warned him about this matter and, when I saw the light a second time, I told him I was reporting him for infringing the black-out regulations. Well, you might well understand, as far as he was concerned, my name was 'MUD'. He was summonsed to appear at Court and was fined £2. Well, it so happened, not long after this case, I was on duty in Castle Street at about half past eleven one night, when I stopped a soldier riding a cycle without lights. I was not so concerned about the fact that he had no lights, but I suspected that the cycle had been stolen. I took him back to the Police Station, telephoned his unit and, of course, it transpired that he had in fact stolen the cycle. By chance, I happened to be on duty at the Police Station the next day when Mr Sebbings, my black-out offender, called at the station to report the theft of his son's cycle the previous evening. When the case came to the Petty Sessions, Mr Sebbings was called to prove the identity of his son's cycle and, after the completion of the proceedings, I had the pleasure of delivering to Mr Sebbings, 5 shillings for his expenses in attending Court. My pleasure was two-fold when I was

able to refuse 5 shillings proffered to me by Mr Sebbings.

Another black-out offence occurred one night at the Red Lion and I had to report the landlord, Mr Mills. It was not long after he had been summonsed and fined £2 for the blackout offence that I had occasion to visit him whilst I was on duty. The previous night I had

been up most of the night as my wife was giving birth to our daughter, so I had not had the chance to shave before going on duty. I happened to mention this to Mr Mills and that I felt a bit scruffy in my appearance. He immediately insisted that I went to his bathroom and used his facilities. It was the first time I had used a Rolls razor and I departed the Red Lion with the impression that reporting Mr Mills for showing a light, had cemented our friendship.

During the war, the Central Hotel, opposite the Red Lion in the Market Place, was used as an ARP [Air Raid Precautions] meeting point and, when the air-raid siren sounded, ARP personnel assembled there to receive their orders. Well, it

so happened that PC Lovell and I were standing on the front steps of the hotel one night, when the air raid siren, situated across the road behind the Guildhall, began to wail. I have little doubt that the proprietor of the hotel went through his usual ritual of switching on the dimmed light in his entrance hall, ready to receive the air raid wardens as they arrived. On this occasion, however, he appears to have pulled the wrong switch, for the front of the hotel suddenly became flooded in light from a large, round, glass globe the size of a football. This light was fitted on a bracket immediately over the front entrance of the hotel. PC Lovell had a wonderful presence of mind – he drew his truncheon and, almost as soon as the light came on, he smashed the globe to smithereens with his truncheon. That was one light which did not show again during the war.

During my short career as a policeman, only twice did we seek the assistance of Scotland Yard. The first occasion was after Inspector Dye had been approached by an Army Major

A rare image of the Thetford Police Station and Inspector's House that was built on the Norwich Road in the mid-1930s. It served solely as the Police Station until a new extension was completed and opened, adjoining the old Police Station, in 1964.

who had befriended a lady in the bar of the Bell Hotel. The Major thought the lady was a Fifth Columnist and he must have convinced the Inspector for he immediately contacted MI5 for further information. The following night I was told to go to the railway station and meet, off the late night mail train, a detective from London and escort him to the Police Station. He was very smartly attired in a blue pin-stripe suit, black Homburg and light raincoat. He carried a rolled umbrella and I thought he looked more like a gentleman from the world of banking rather than a detective. The following night he went to the Bell and soon made his acquaintance with the lady in question. The next day he returned to London and I was allowed to read his report. It stated that he was satisfied that the suspect was no more than a high-class prostitute. He had even had the chance, which he had refused, to go to bed with this lady on the one and only evening he had been in her company. I am confident to this day, that she is unaware that she was once the subject of a MI5 investigation.

The second time that Scotland Yard was called in, was for a murder case. A 12 year old girl, an evacuee, had been found stabbed to death at Riddlesworth, just the other side of Rushford. She had received eleven stab wounds around her neck. Inspector Dye, in company with the chief Norfolk CID men, spent several days on enquiries before calling in Scotland Yard. Statements had already been taken from everyone in the village, including a unit of twenty-nine men of the Pioneer Corps. Suspicion fell on this small group of young men. The investigation was now led by Chief Superintendent Tom Barrett, at that time one of the top CID men. As soon as he arrived, one of the first things he did was to have an extra telephone placed in the Inspector's house which adjoined the Thetford Police Station. This was a direct line to Scotland Yard and after a lengthy discussion with Inspector Dye, he spent over an hour on his telephone, asking Scotland Yard for the previous records, if any, of the twenty-nine men attached to the Pioneer Corps unit at Riddlesworth. He was told that seven had previous convictions, three of them had

convictions against females. One of these three turned out to be the murderer.

Several more days were spent investigating the crime scene, including a massive search to find the murder weapon, thought to be a knife. It was never found. No conclusive evidence had been found by the time Superintendent Barrett decided to bring in for further questioning, a Private Howarth of the Pioneer Corps, the main suspect. He was not arrested but brought to Thetford Police Station and placed in PC Woods' front room. During that afternoon, a CID man was always in the room with him and no conversation was allowed. Four different officers took it in turn to be on duty in the room with the suspect. At 6 o'clock, the suspect asked to see the Superintendent and confessed to the murder. A statement was taken from him and made out in triplicate. After they had been signed, one copy was sent to Police Headquarters at Norwich, one to Scotland Yard and one was kept at Thetford. Private Howarth was then formally cautioned and

Essex County Constabulary.

Head Quarters,
CHELMSFORD.

5th July, 1943.

This is to certify that PWR-111 Whalebelly.

of Norfolk County Police

has completed a Course of Anti-Gas Training held under the auspices of the Chief Constable of Essex, and has acquired sufficient knowledge of Anti-Gas Measures to enable him to carry out his duties as a Police War Reserve.

Nature of course attended   Full Course.

Name and qualification of Instructor   Inspector R. B. Hagger, A.R.P.S.

Date   5 - JUL 1943   Captain.
                                                Chief Constable of Essex.

This certificate does NOT qualify the holder to act as an instructor under any circumstances.

Gas masks were issued to everyone before the start of the war; children were given a Mickey Mouse-faced mask and babies a special suit. Gas was a real threat to all for the duration of the war.

arrested. His braces and boot-laces were removed and he was taken away to one of the custody cells. Dirt from under his fingernails was carefully removed and his clothes thoroughly searched for hairs from the dead girl. Even a cotton thread from her clothing would have been conclusive evidence. Grass seeds and other small particles were also removed from the suspects clothing for forensic analysis, to establish a link between the prisoner and the spot where the girl's body was found. Private Howarth eventually stood trial at Norwich Assizes. He was convicted of murder and sentenced to be detained at His Majesty's pleasure.

Another interesting incident but one that did not require the help of Scotland Yard, happened one Sunday after a man had flashed his money in the bar of the Anchor Hotel. After closing time, he was taken along the London Road in a car and robbed of a £100. Three men had been involved, a soldier, a sailor and a civilian. The Inspector, knowing that uniformed sailors in Thetford were something of a rarity, telephoned the CID in Portsmouth and asked them to make enquiries at Naval headquarters to see if they could help him. He was in luck. They could even name the sailor who

was likely to have been involved. He was soon arrested at Portsmouth by the CID there and brought back to Thetford Police Station.

Inspector Dye, with his questioning, was soon able to break the sailor. The sailor happened to be a religious man, obviously with a guilty conscience. He soon confessed to his involvement in the robbery and named his two accomplices. The civilian involved was his brother-in-law and the soldier was a member of the Middlesex Searchlight Regiment stationed nearby. When the case came to court, it was obvious that the civilian was the ringleader. It had been his car that was used and he had previous convictions. The civilian was given 6 months imprisonment while the two servicemen were severely reprimanded and to be further dealt with by the military authorities. After the trial, I escorted the civilian prisoner on the train to Norwich, where he was to serve his sentence. I swear he cried all the way there, saying he had a raw deal seeing he was the only one to have to do time. At the conclusion of this case, Inspector Dye received a commendation for his police work.

Thetford Police Court Thursday. – Before the Mayor (Mr G.E. Lambert) in the chair, Mr H.J. Burrell, Mr S.G. Brown, Dr. A. Oliver, Mrs A.S. Law, and Mrs L. Clarke.
Two soldiers, John William Bull and Joseph Garvey, were charged with taking and driving away a motor car without the driver's consent at Thetford on April 13th. They pleaded guilty...In imposing a fine of £1 and 13s. 8d. costs on each of the defendants, the Mayor said the magistrates had decided to treat them leniently, and hoped they would be of service to the country. **Source:** *Thetford & Watton Times, 25 May 1940.*

Another man to receive a commendation and a £5 award, was PC Woods. It was during the month of September that we were ordered to one of the meres on Wretham Heath to recover the body of a man who had drowned there earlier that day. It was almost dark by the time that Inspector Dye and PC Woods got a boat on to the water and located the body, floating in some reeds. In order to get the drowned man's body onto the bank, PC Woods stripped off his clothing and jumped into the cold water; after a great deal of trouble the mission was completed. I was in the office at the Police Station, with PC

Youngs, when a very wet and cold Inspector and PC Woods returned. I felt sorry for PC Woods. In company with the Inspector he had had a traumatic experience but the Inspector was a man of great heart and character. Complaining that his trousers were wet, he just stood there in the office and took them off. You can imagine the repartee that ensued at us seeing the Inspector standing there with bare legs and the shortest of short underpants! I could see behind the laughter – the Inspector had changed the gloomy atmosphere and boosted our morale on a wet and cold evening.

Prostitutes were not uncommon in Thetford during the war and we were discouraged from reporting prostitutes in Thetford, the Inspector taking the view that they were keeping the soldiers happy. We did have one case involving prostitution, however, that I would like to mention. This happened in the little village of Great Hockham. We had received information that a house there was being used as a brothel. The Inspector gave me the opportunity to investigate the matter and I was given a certain amount of discretionary duties. After contacting the informant who lived quite near the house under suspicion, I was given permission to use the front room of his house for the purpose of surveillance. For ten consecutive nights, under cover of darkness and dressed in civilian clothes, I cycled over to Great Hockham to watch the house. Each night I was there, I saw men being taken into the house by young women. There were three women there and between them they seemed to be doing a fair bit of business. After ten days the Inspector asked me if I had gathered sufficient evidence to convict and, after reading my notes, he agreed that I had. The next day the Inspector obtained a warrant to search the house and at 1 o'clock in the morning we knocked on the front door. A man answered the

door and we walked straight into the house. Furniture was practically non-existent, but there were three beds in the house, two of these were made-up on the floor. Beside the man who opened the door, there were two other men in the house. One of these was a young, well spoken army officer who was most upset by our intrusion and demanded to know what right we had to do this at 1 o'clock in the morning. The Inspector showed him the search warrant, which soon took the wind out of his sails. The three young women, who had all come from Manchester, were convicted at East Harling Petty Sessions and each was given six months imprisonment. The local gentleman who owned the house was charged with allowing it to be used as a brothel. Despite his plea that he had no knowledge of what was going on there, he was fined £50. I doubt whether the rent he had been receiving made up the cost of the fine.

I was on duty in the Market Place one night when I was called in to quell a disturbance at a dance being held in the Guildhall. A Canadian, who was a RAF serviceman and the 'worse for wear' through drink, was the cause of the trouble. I managed to get him into the entrance hall and, after some persuasion, also managed to calm him down and make him come to his senses. Whilst I was with him, I asked one of his mates to fetch the NCO who was in charge of his party. A short Flight Sergeant came to me and said they were from Honington. I explained that if he could not control the men in his party, they would all have to leave. Whilst I was telling him this, acting Police Sergeant Emblem, who was attending the dance as a guest, came to my side and asked if every thing was alright? Whilst I assured him every thing was in control, the Canadian airman became agitated once again and wanted to know who he was and what right did he have to interfere? I told him he

happened to be my Sergeant but he had obviously taken a dislike to Sergeant Emblem. Things eventually settled down and remained quiet until I went off duty. The next day, when I reported for duty, I learnt that things had been far from quiet at the end of the dance. It appeared that the Canadian had made a beeline for Sergeant Emblem, apparently to start a fight. He obviously did not know of his boxing background. It had taken just one blow from Sergeant Emblem to knock the Canadian out cold. The Flight Sergeant, seeing what was happening, rushed at Emblem and was immediately knocked to the ground. A week after this occurrence, a complaint was received from RAF Honington accusing Sergeant Emblem of using knuckledusters. An inquiry into the incident was held, at which I attended in support of Sergeant Emblem but it transpired that that the damaged knuckles on his left hand felt like a knuckleduster when his punch struck an opponent. The airman had been silly to make this accusation and, after Sergeant Emblem had given his evidence, I had the impression that the airmen felt humiliated. After the proceedings concluded, the Chief Constable received an official apology. He had been satisfied with the outcome.

These, then, are just a few of my experiences during 5 years as a War Reserve Policeman in Thetford. There are many more incidents which come to mind, in particular the 5 days I was posted to Norwich after the city was blitzed – but that is another story.

© Doris Whalebelly

A police constable stands on duty as a Mk.1 Valentine tank roars round the Bell Corner from King Street in April 1941.
During the war years, there was at least one serious accident in the town between a pedestrian and a military vehicle. A Mrs Orford had a leg amputated after being struck by an armoured vehicle in the narrow White Hart Street.

A view of the Bell Corner taken during the war by an American serviceman. A sign fixed to the wall of the Bell Hotel reads, 'ARP Public Shelter' and an arrow points in the direction of Minstergate. Other public shelters could be found near the Guildhall and Castle Park.
[Photograph courtesy of 389th Bomb Group Collection, Hethel]

Local women and girls were kept busy throughout the war making and repairing military uniforms at this Government Ordnance factory situated in Minstergate.
Marjorie Mayes [front right] wrote on the reverse of the photograph [top], '...me at work it was taken on the day after V.E. Day. Us girls bought the trimmings, so we had some decorations we prepared for V.E. Day about 3 days before, but at least it came and you can see how pleased we all looked. This is just one bench of machines you can see the machine I work now, the one I am sitting in front of, it makes button holes'...
[Photographs courtesy of the Ancient House Museum and Marjorie Keymer]

Excitement Of A Silent Night At The 'Flicks' *Thetford & Watton Times, 16 April 1993*

Once photography became a reality in the 1840s, all sorts of experiments were made to create moving pictures - a process that eventually came to be known as cinematography. The first movie film was demonstrated in the 1880s but it was the mid-1890s before cinematography was commercially exhibited in Paris, New York and London.

Hand-operated projectors were used to show the early films, which had no sound and lasted only a few minutes. These were presented as an interlude at music halls, theatres and also at fairgrounds. In January 1897 Norfolk's first public exhibition of a movie film was presented by George Gilbert in his circus ring set-up in Norwich's Agricultural Hall - now Anglia Television.

Gilbert's Royal Cinematographe, 'The Animated Pictures', included The Derby, Boxing Kangaroo, The South Western Railway At Dover, A Prize Fight by Jem Mace and Burke, Tom Merry, and Highgate Tunnel. His enterprise was soon repeated by others including Randell Williams, a noted travelling showman who introduced moving pictures to the fairground at King's Lynn in March 1897. Another showman who helped to popularise cinematography round the village greens of East Anglia was Thurston of Norwich.

The first movie film exhibited in Thetford was most likely at a travelling fair. The late Gertrude Minett, born in 1896, remembers as a young girl entering a darkened tent of a travelling fair on Thetford's Market Place and seeing her first silent film. *'A very flickering and exciting affair it was - Charles Peace, a murderer who at the end was hanged for his bad deeds'*, she said. This no doubt was Walter Haggar's, *'The Life of James Peace'*, made in 1903 and one of the first dramatic films.

Cinematography or the 'flicks' soon developed into a popular entertainment. Before the first decade of the 20th century was over, all sorts of buildings in East Anglian towns were being used for showing the latest films. At Bury St Edmunds, Ronald Bates began screening regular shows of animated pictures in 1908. About the same time, Thetford's Oddfellows Hall in Earls Street was used for presenting films. As the film industry developed, these makeshift 'cinemas', as they came to be known, were replaced by new, purpose-built ones often displaying new forms of architecture and plush, interior furnishings.

At Thetford in 1913 a local newspaper announced, *'A picture palace is to be erected in Guildhall Street. This will supply a long felt want, and the promoters are to be congratulated on their enterprise'*. By the end of the year Thetford's new purpose-built 'Electric Cinema' in Guildhall Street was advertising *'a first class programme nightly commencing at 8 o'clock. Admission 3d, 4d and 6d'*.

Films at the Oddfellows Hall then ceased but once war was declared in 1914 and large numbers of troops were stationed in and around the town, it was again used as a cinema known as 'The Empire'. By 1919 the Guildhall Street cinema had come to be known as the 'People's Palace'. A pianist sitting at the front of the auditorium, screened from the audience by a curtain, accompanied the silent films. Not until Ben Culey took over the Palace Cinema in 1931 were new projectors capable of screening the latest 'talkies' installed. But many of the old silent films continued on the cinema circuits for several years until 'talkies' took over completely.

Further improvements continued at the Palace in 1936 with the building of a new facade which more or less survives today. And in the late 1950s a new main entrance was made from Guildhall Street and the original front entrance converted into shops.

Unlike many small cinemas, Thetford's Palace Cinema continued to be a popular night-out and survived the initial impact of television in the 1960s but sadly, because of falling attendances and increasing overheads, the last film was screened there in September 1984.

Since the publication of *A Silent Night at the 'Flicks'* in 1993, further research has revealed new evidence of moving pictures being presented in Thetford. The following is probably the very first account of the cinematograph in Thetford and appeared after the visit to the Oddfellows' Hall, in February 1899, of Norwich photographer Mr Albert. E. Coe.

... Mr. A. E. Coe, of Norwich, exhibited a very large and varied assortment of beautiful lantern views, and numerous cinematograph views of the latest kind, including the Jubilee Procession, Charge of the Lancers, Santa Claus, Cinderella, obstacle races, loading a passenger and freight vessel, launch of a warship, scenery in Devon near Ilfracombe, and other animated views, statuary, flowers, comic scenes, &c. Mr. H. Wellens sang "The bay of Biscay", and then Mr Coe exhibited one of Edison's phonographs, and gave songs, music, speeches, &c. The Rev. P.H. Davis made a speech, and Mr. W. Hannant sang "The jolly smiths," Miss Bunn presiding at the piano. Both were perfectly re-produced by the phonograph, so that, on the whole, the entertainment was one of the best of the season. **Source:** *Thetford & Watton Times, 18 February 1899.*

WAR.   **TO-NIGHT.**   WAR.

ODDFELLOWS' HALL, THETFORD.
TO NIGHT, FRIDAY, MAY 18th.

THE BOER WAR, popularly illustrated and explained by the Rev. THOMAS I. JARROTT (Member of the National Society of Lanternists).

REPEAT VISIT BY SPECIAL REQUEST.

The largest selection of Cinematograph Pictures ever shown in Thetford will be projected during an interval by the Royal American Bioscope. A large number of new slides and films have been added since the previous visit.

Doors open 7.30.   Commence at 8.

Reserved Numbered Seats, 2s. ; Second Seats, 1s. ; Admission 6d.

WAR.   **TO-NIGHT.**   WAR.

ODDFELLOWS' HALL, THETFORD.

THREE NIGHTS ONLY !
Thursday, Friday, & Saturday, May 2, 3, & 4.

Doors open at 7.30. Commence at 8 p.m. Tickets and Plan at usual places. Front Seats, 2s. ; Second Seats, 1s. ; Back Seats, 6d. Special Performance for Schools, Saturday, 3 p.m.

GRAND PATRIOTIC ENTERTAINMENT,
Our ARMY and NAVY
AT HOME AND ABROAD.

Introducing nightly 100 Pictures by the aid of the mos powerful and steadiest Cinematograph extant, vividly depicting the lives of our Soldiers and Sailors, interspersed with Songs, Recitations, and Music. Amongst other Pictures will be found Earl Roberts Landing and Reception at Cape Town. General French's Scouts having a Skirmish with the Boers. Wreck of an Armoured Train. Team of Bullocks drawing an Ammunition Waggon, and getting a gun up of a Kopje. Getting a Big Naval Gun over the drift of the De Vet River. Blue Jackets at Whale Island firing a Maxim Gun. Men of H.M.S. Powerful being Reviewed on the Horse Guards Parade by H.R.H. the Prince of Wales. Men of H.M.S. Powerful marching across London to the Agricultural Hall. Royal Engineers making a Trestle Bridge. Blue Jackets preparing for a Land Attack. Firing a 4·7 in. Gun and Hoisting into position, etc. Also Grand Selection of Miscellaneous Films, including the celebrated Spanish Bull Fight, most vivid and realistic picture ever taken, 500 feet long. "Story of a Legacy." Oxford and Cambridge Boat Race (this year's). High Diving by Men and Horses ; Fall of a Factory Chimney ; Scenes from the Paris Exhibition, etc., concluding with a grand picture of her Majesty the late Queen's Funeral.

In addition to the above a carefully selected **CONCERT COMPANY** of Refined and Clever London Artistes will appear. And a Sacred Concert will be given on Sunday.

The above event, advertised in the Thetford & Watton Times, 19 May 1900, is also amongst the first appearances of the cinematograph, or moving picture machine, to be seen in the town.

There was a great deal of local interest in the Boer War. Just a few months earlier, Thetfordians had cheered local reservists as they departed from the railway station on the start of their journey to South Africa. In March 1900, a large crowd had gathered on the Market Place to celebrate the relief of Ladysmith.

In 1901 the above advertisement appeared in the Thetford & Watton Times. The following year, William Jury of London presented his bioscope, another name for cinematograph, at the Oddfellows Hall. This was followed in 1904 with an evening performance of James Crighton's 'Imperial Bioscope'.

The 1909 Cinematograph Act required that from January, 1910, a licence be obtained from local authorities in order to show films.

The new facade of Thetford's Palace Cinema, decorated for the Coronation of George VI in May 1937. [Photograph courtesy of the Ancient House Museum, Thetford]

The Palace Cinema just a few months before closure as a cinema in 1984.

Good Deed That Saved A Stable *Thetford & Watton Times, 12 July 1991*

The Scout movement was founded by Robert Baden-Powell [1857-1941], then a lieutenant-general and a well-known Army scout, with military service in Africa and India. Reasoning that his Army training might also be useful in teaching boys good citizenship, he gathered together in 1907 a group of twenty boys, drawn from all classes of society, at an experimental camp on Brownsea Island in Poole Harbour, Dorset.

This camp proved that his scheme of Scouting for boys was not only practical but could be successful. It was followed, in January 1908, by the publication of the first part of Scouting for Boys. From then on, Boy Scout troops were formed all over the country and the world.

Thetford's first Boy Scout troop was formed in 1910 through the enthusiasm of Mr James Edgell, a retired gentleman who lived at the King's House. It was known as the No. 1 Thetford Troop, or the Thetford Grammar School Troop, as most of its thirty members were pupils there. In April or May 1910, the Thetford Troop was registered with the then Boy Scout Association. Mr W. Woods was appointed as Thetford's first Scoutmaster.

A few weeks later, Thetford's scouts were camping on Two Mile Bottom Common, enjoying many of the adventure and outdoor activities still associated with the Scout movement today. Moreover, being a uniformed organisation, Thetford's scouts were kept busy participating in local events and parades. Undoubtedly the high point of this period was the visit by Sir Robert Baden-Powell, who inspected the No. 1 Troop at Thetford railway station in October 1910.

Inspection by General Baden Powell. On Monday evening Lieutenant General Sir Robert Baden Powell, as he was on his way to London, came to Thetford, having previously sent a message that he would be pleased to inspect the Boy Scouts. He motored over from Wretham and was accompanied by Sir Andrew Noble...The Scouts assembled at King's House, where they proceeded to the station...They were under the command of Scoutmaster Woods and Assistant Scoutmaster F.M. Potter. Mr J. Edgell of King's House was also present and shook hands with Sir Robert Baden Powell and introduced him to the Scouts...Baden Powell in his address pointed out that the chief duties of the Boy Scouts was to do the same good to their neighbours, and set an example in their general conduct in life... **Source:** *Bury & Norwich Post, 4 November 1910.*

The following year, Mr Roland Palmer, a teacher at the Norwich Road Council School, founded a troop of scouts for boys at his school. Formed in June 1911, as the Thetford Town Troop, its headquarters was a building called 'The Grotto', which stood in King Street near the entrance to St Giles Lane.

It is not surprising, when there were few other organised pursuits for boys, that both troops proved popular among the boys of Thetford. Besides a small Young Men's Christian Association room in White Hart Street, children's out-of-school leisure activities centred around those organised by the many local Sunday schools and the Band of Hope.

It was probably during the 1914-18 Great War that the two Thetford Boy Scout Troops combined as the Thetford Town Troop. The local Boy Scouts had their part to play in the hostilities - patrolling the town on the lookout for incendiary devices and guarding telegraph poles against sabotage from German agents!

The year before war broke out, the Scouts helped to save the stables of the King's Arms public house from destruction by raising the fire alarm while on patrol in King Street.

Mr Palmer continued as Scoutmaster of the Town Troop until 1930, when ill health forced his retirement. The troop was disbanded but was re-formed in 1932 by Captain W. J. Short, Thetford's registrar of births, deaths and marriages.

This pattern of disbanding when the scout leader retired and reforming once a successor has been found, continues to the present day. The 1st Thetford Troop was disbanded, once again, about two years ago, so today there are three scout troops in the town: 2nd Thetford [Kimms Belt], 3rd Thetford [Admirals Way] and 4th Thetford [Abbey Farm]. Between them they have Beavers for boys and girls aged six to eight years, Cubs aged eight to ten-and-a-half years and Scouts from ten-and-a-half years upwards. There are also Venture Scouts for the older age group.

I have fond memories as a member of the Thetford Wolf Cub Pack and Boy Scout Troop in the late 1950s and early 1960s when the Scoutmaster was the late Mr Tom Anderson. Scout night was then held on Mondays in St Peter's Church school rooms - the former National School building - on the Croxton Road. A memorable event then was 'Bob-A-Job' week, when scouts and cubs scurried about the town carrying out jobs for a shilling [5p] -'a bob' - to boost scout funds. Most houses and shops displayed the 'Job Done' sticker in their windows. This event continues today as Job Week.

Thetford Town Troop of Boy Scouts, photographed in the garden of King's House 1912.

This photograph captures the 1st Thetford Troop of Boy Scouts, receiving their colours from the Mayor, Robert Tilley. The colours were also dedicated by the Bishop of Thetford, Dr Bowers. The ceremony was performed in the Castle Park, during Thetford's Coronation celebrations, June 1911. The colours were the gift of Mrs Edgell of King's House.

Thetford's Boy Scouts march along the Norwich Road, on the 14th July, 1920, as part of the funeral procession of Admiral of the Fleet, Lord Fisher, 1st Baron of Kilverstone. The Admiral's coffin was carried by rail from London to Thetford. From the railway station a horse-drawn carriage bore the coffin, draped with a Union Jack, to St Andrew's Church, Kilverstone, for burial.

In the early years of the 20th century, when picture postcards were rapidly becoming a popular form of communication, Ixworth born Roger James Bantock opened his first photographic studio at number 7 Castle Street, Thetford.

Like many other photographers of his era, when very few people owned a camera, R. J. Bantock used the picture postcard as a way of publishing and selling his photographs. As more and more people used the picture postcard [millions were posted annually], Bantock's business flourished. His sepia-coloured, photographic postcards featured a wide-range of subjects: carefully posed studio portraits of individuals and family groups; formal gatherings of people at their places of work, worship and recreation; buildings, street scenes, special occasions and events of local life.

Not only was Bantock to be seen about the town of Thetford with his camera, tripod and equipment [heavy stuff in those days] but also further afield in the counties of Norfolk and Suffolk, taking photographs for at least three national postcard publishers: Raphael Tuck and Sons, Frith & Co. and Jarrolds of Norwich. Many of these views that give us a 'fossilised' glimpse of early 20th century life, were carefully preserved in special albums and passed down to us by Edwardian postcard collectors.

About 1910, Bantock moved his business from Castle Street to larger premises at number 38 King Street, next-door to the photographic studio and shop of W. Boughton & Son, where he began his apprenticeship nearly 20 years earlier. W. Boughton & Son were Thetford's largest and most prolific

publisher of picture postcards. Their 'Britannia Series' of picture postcards, litho-printed at their Station Road works, featured many of the towns and villages of Norfolk and Suffolk. Today they continue to publish postcard views of Thetford from their old established premises.

The golden era of the picture postcard came to a close about the time of the Peace celebrations in 1919. The popularity of the postcard then declined, in response to increased postage charges, the growing use of the telephone and the post-war economic depression. Very few local views appear to have been published after 1920, compared with the pre-war years, when hundreds of different postcards could be bought from Thetford's shops. Nevertheless, R. J. Bantock's King Street studio continued, although his photographic business was supplemented by the sale of a new and popular selection of goods: fancy ware, gramophones and records, Meccano and fret-work sets.

Bantock closed his premises and retired from business in the late 1930s. While his former shop was taken over by butchers, J. K. Dewhurst Ltd, who still trade from there today, he continued to live with his wife and daughter above the old shop until his death, at the age of 72 years, in 1949.

It is only in recent years, with the loss of so many buildings that were once such familiar landmarks and our own awareness of rapidly changing life styles, that we have begun to take an interest in the work of local photographers such as R. J. Bantock, and W. Boughton & Son. Perhaps many of the old buildings and street scenes, destroyed during the last 30 years,

would have gone unrecorded were it not for these local postcard publishers. Although Bantock could not have known the extent of future changes, or that many of his photographs would become rare images of historical value, undoubtedly, he must have sensed that what he was recording would one day be history.

By the mid-1870's, most small towns such as Thetford could boast at least one professional photographer amongst its high street traders.

Thetford's earliest resident photographer was E. Marsham. In 1868 he was advertising 'carte-de-visites', from his Market Place studio, at a price of six for five shillings or twelve for eight shillings.

From the mid-1870's to the 1880's, Thetfordians could call upon the services of Signor Henri Aegena, artist, photographer and picture frame maker. He operated from the grandly named 'Thetford Institute of Photography', situated at 11 White Hart Street.

Listed in Whites Directory of Norfolk for 1888 is Walter Boughton, painter, decorator, picture frame maker and studio photographer, the Market Place, Thetford.

About 1890, Walter Boughton moved his photographic studio to 36, King Street. Whilst at these premises he took on a young apprentice, Roger James Bantock, to learn the skills of photography. After finishing his apprenticeship in the mid-1890s, R.J. Bantock left Messrs. Boughton and the area to earn his living as a photographer. In 1897 he was working in Stamford, Lincolnshire. He also worked in Yorkshire and London.

Source: David Osborne, *A View of Thetford Past III*, David Osborne [1987].

R.J. Bantock appears to have been most active about the town, photographing individuals, groups of people and street scenes in the years c.1905 - c.1914.
Many of Bantock's photographs were published on picture postcards, including this wonderful view of railway employees at Two Mile Bottom signal box in 1910.

Most of Bantock's picture postcards were printed in sepia tone, a medium that now gives us an added sense of the past. When this view of Croxton Road was photographed about 1905, most of the houses that can be seen were then modern, newly-built dwellings.

Even though many of Bantock's postcards were stamped, 'R.J. Bantock, Photographer Thetford', it is difficult to calculate just how many different picture postcards were published by him and in what numbers. Some postcards are obviously much rarer than others - presumably because only a very small number were originally produced.
This is a rare postcard view of Earls Street, circa 1905.

In the first quarter of the 20th century, many Thetfordians must have posed in front of Bantock's camera, either at home, place of work, as they went about their daily business, or even in his studio at number 38 King Street. One of those to visit Bantock's studio, about 1912, was Sydney George Cooper [1899-1970], a member of the local Boy Scouts. Sydney was to become my maternal grandfather. Numerous photographs, such as this and published on picture postcards, survive amongst family photograph albums and archives.

Before a Boy Scout troop was established in the town, boys could join a local branch of the Boys' Brigade.

This photograph of the St Peter's Boys' Brigade was taken about 1905, at the rear of the old National School, then the Sunday School rooms of St Peter's Church [now the site of the Ambulance Station] in Croxton Road.

The bespectacled gentleman on the right is the Reverend J.P. 'Pippy' Watts.

Thetford Fire Brigade.

In the 19th and early years of the 20th century, the opportunity to dress in a uniform of some description, appealed to many young men. Most uniformed groups seen parading about the streets of the town at this time were formed by volunteers. One such organisation was the Borough of Thetford Fire Brigade, formed in 1880.

This picture postcard was postally used in 1905 and the sender wrote ..."another for your collection".

The local fire brigade considered themselves really modern and up-to-date after the Borough Council purchased this brand-new Merryweather steam fire engine in February 1905. The 'steamer' was used until 1938, when it was replaced by a motor fire engine. R.J. Bantock took this photograph on the Grammar School Plains.

This photograph, of a 10 ton Burrell steam roller and sleeping van, was taken in the back garden of number 23 Croxton Road, then the home of Charles Burrell & Son's chief draughtsman, Frederick Doran. In 1896 Frederick's brother, Thomas R. Doran [1868-1940], established himself as a steam rolling contractor. In 1910 the business became a limited company known as Doran Bros Ltd.

A postcard view of Guildhall Street that has changed beyond recognition since it was taken almost a century ago.
The flint wall, in the right foreground, is where a cinema was opened in 1913. On the opposite side of the road is the shop premises of W. Gill. The signboard reads, 'W. Gill Fish Curer & Penny Cress'.

As a schoolboy football fanatic, in the late 1950s and early 1960s, one might surmise my football idols to have been some of the great professional players of the day: Tom Finney, Johnny Haynes, Nat Lofthouse and Stanley Matthews. My footballing heroes, however, turned out each week in the claret and blue shirts of Thetford Town Football Club. Players less gifted, but equally enthusiastic, come to my mind: Johnny Brooks, Dennis Carnelley, Jimmy Dowling and Percy James to name a few.

At the Recreation Ground, on the Mundford Road, Thetford Town's home ground since 1905, I would relish the visit of clubs such as Bungay, Cromer, Diss Town and C.E.Y.M.S. in the now defunct Norfolk and Suffolk League.

Although the Football Association was formed as early as 1863, the earliest account I have found of an association football match being played by a Thetford team is in 1876. In that year, a team representing Thetford lost 2-0 at Bury St Edmunds. It was probably a short-lived formation. In February 1877, Thetford played a return match with Bury; thereafter I have found no mention of football at Thetford until 1883, when a group of men from the Burrell engineering works formed a club called Thetford Wanderers, later to be known as Thetford Town F. C.

Their very first match was played in January 1883, against Feltwell, and resulted in a victory for Thetford by five goals to nil. The match was played on Thetford's Abbey Heath. The Thetford team was: J. Ollington, H. Hallis, G. Mower, H. Chandler, G. Westby, W. Watson, R. Street, E. Bullard, E. Gooch, J. Miller, W. Martin.

Newspaper reports of football matches from those early days provide a valuable insight into the sport. It was reported after the match versus Bury in 1876... *'the Thetford team did not seem to understand that handling was not allowed, and they hardly tried to dribble at all'.* After the match between Thetford and Feltwell in 1883, a *Thetford & Watton Times* reporter wrote, *'There is no amusement so exciting and economical. The football player need lay out little money, and devote little time, an hour's play on the holiday afternoon of the week being all that is expected of him'.*

Once again, when Thetford entertained Bury in 1886, the *Bury & Norwich Post* provided the following gem,... *'it was a most glaring case of hands, but at that moment the umpire was busy replenishing his pipe instead of attending to the points of the game'.* Thetford won this game 2-1, apparently, with some help from the umpire. In those days, two umpires, one nominated by each team, officiated the play.

To mark the Golden Jubilee of Thetford Town F.C. in 1933-34, a short history of the club was written by Mr G. R. Blaydon, a long-time member. A few of the original club members were then still alive. Recalled were the days when most played in their ordinary Saturday afternoon clothes and the stoutest boots they owned. Eventually, a strip of magenta coloured shirts was adopted, followed by one of yellow and black; black and white, and finally in 1905 the present club colours of claret and blue.

During its 106 year history, Thetford Town F.C. has had many ups and downs. Undoubtedly their most notable success was beating North Walsham 4 - 0 in a Norfolk Senior Cup Final replay at Carrow Road, Norwich, at the end of the 1947-48 season. Thetford's goals were scored by L. James, D. Grey, H. Eggleton [2] in front of a crowd of several thousand.

The club officials have recently overcome financial problems to secure the club's immediate future. So let us wish the Thetford Town Football Club a successful 1989-90 season - *'Up The Town'.*

One of the earliest accounts of a football match involving a Thetford team. *Bury v Thetford - These two clubs met for the first time last Saturday. Thetford won the toss and choose the lower goal. Welch kicked off for Bury and it was soon evident that the Thetford men were no match for their opponents, the ball was kept constantly in the neighbourhood of the Thetford goal, and repeated shots were made by the Bury forwards. Their kicking however was so erratic that no goal was obtained. After half-time the game continued in the same fashion, though the kicking of the Bury men was more correct, two goals were placed to their credit. Thus a pleasant though uninteresting match ended in favour of Bury. The play throughout was very poor. The Thetford men did not seem to understand that handling was not allowed, and they hardly tried to dribble at all, while the Bury men though they had decidedly the best of it, did not play well together, and seemed quite unable to avail themselves of their numerous scoring chances. Thetford:- A. G. Cronshey, Capt. and J. Houchen, backs; Emery, goal; Plows, Ladbrooke and Hill [half-backs]; M. Dewing, Crane, Haires, and Bradfield.*
Source: *Bury & Norwich Post, 16 December 1876.**

* In February the following year, a return match *'according to the Association rules'*, was played at Thetford. *'Bury for the most part kept the ball within the enemy's part of the ground; but at times Cronshey, Ludbrook, and others of the Thetford forwards ran the ball down, and were only stopped by Dewing, the Bury half-back, who played splendidly throughout'...* The result was a goalless draw.

This photograph was taken the year after Thetford Town FC amalgamated with Thetford Rovers FC to form what was known for just a few seasons as Thetford Recreation Club, hence the initials TRC on the football. It was in 1905-06 that the now familiar claret and blue colours were first adopted. Until 1898, Thetford Town FC played their home matches on the Abbey Heath, near to what is now the north end of Canterbury Way. They then moved to a new venue, a field near the Thetford Bridge railway station. Since the Recreation Ground with its new pavilion opened in 1905, the 'Rec' has been the scene of numerous footballing encounters.

Thetford Town's first XI players of are about to depart by motor coach from the Market Place for the Norfolk Senior Cup Final at Carrow Road, Norwich, on the 29th March 1948.
Left-right: K. Makins, Alan Mayes, John Middleton, Gurney Barnes, Henry Rix, Derek Grey, Percy James, John Vincent, Harry Eggleton, Jimmy Jordan, Charlie Flack.
In the 19th century, the team used to travel to away fixtures in an open wagonette drawn by two horses driven by Charlie Bye.

Throughout its history, Thetford's population has undergone varying degrees of growth and decline. These changes have been brought about by civil unrest, economic and social conditions, migration, pestilence and war.

It is probable that by the middle of the 9th century, Thetford had developed into a settlement of some significance. It was certainly a place of importance in the 11th century. From the Domesday survey it is estimated that in the reign of Edward the Confessor [King from 1042-1066] the population was at least 4,000 but by the year 1086 it was already rapidly shrinking.

Thetford Hundred...Moreover, in the Borough there were 943 burgesses before 1066; of these the King has all the customary dues. 36 of these same men belong to King Edward, their Lord, to such an extent that they could not be anyone else's men without the King's permission. All the others could be anyone else's men but always the customary dues remained the King's except the heriot. Now there are 720 burgesses and 224 empty dwellings... **Source:** *Domesday Book - Norfolk.*

How the size of Thetford's community was affected by conditions between the 11th century and 18th century is not known precisely but decline did continue. It may, as suggested by Alan Crosby in his recently published *History of Thetford*, been as low as 1,500 in 1549. This was just a few years after the Reformation and the dissolution of Thetford's numerous religious houses.

There is, however, a fairly reliable figure from the year 1801, when the first national population census was implemented and recorded thereafter, at 10 yearly intervals, except 1941. In 1801 Thetford's population was 2,246. Over the next 50 years it almost doubled to 4,074. The Census of 1851 recorded, for the first time, each individual's place of birth. A surprisingly high proportion of those then living in Thetford, gave their place of birth outside the town, although most of these were born within a 15 mile radius.

Thetford:- Houses inhabited 483 By How many families Occupied 513 Houses uninhabited 9 Persons 2246 Chiefly employed in agriculture 149 In trade, manuf. or handicrafts 367 In all other occupations 1730 Population of the County of Nfk. ascertained in consequence of the Act 41 Geo. III 1800. **Source:** Arthur Young, *General View Agriculture of Norfolk [1804].*

There was a continual migration of people. At the same time as many people were inhabiting the town, others were leaving. In 1841 Mr John Chambers at the Bell Inn sought applications from sawyers, carpenters, bricklayers, blacksmiths, shepherds and agricultural labourers for emigration to Van Dieman's Land in the Northern Territory of Australia. Emigration to the colonies continued into the 20th century.

With the opening of the railway here in 1845, travel became easier and more accessible to the people of Thetford. For the first time Norwich was linked to London by rail. The railways played an important part in the development of the nation's cities and towns during the 19th century.

At the end of the 19th century, Thetford's population had reached 4,613. This growth was accompanied by poor housing and overcrowding among the labouring classes, often resulting in a high rate of mortality.

Hundreds of troops billeted at the Thetford Camp or in the homes of local people boosted Thetford's population throughout the 1914-18 War. The war, which claimed the lives of 116 men from our ancient borough, was followed by economic depression and with it the closure of Thetford's largest employer, the St Nicholas Works of the Agricultural and General Engineers Ltd [formerly the premises of Charles Burrell & Sons Ltd]. The unemployment caused many people to leave the town for work elsewhere. In 1931 Thetford's population was 680 fewer that it had been twenty years earlier.

Hundreds of allied troops and airmen once again 'invaded' Thetford during the 1939-45 War. In addition, Thetford was also home for many families evacuated from London, before and during the blitz. Forty-three servicemen who were residents of the town were killed in the conflict.

After the war a new phase of growth developed. In 1958, the year before the first families from London arrived here under the so-called 'overspill', the population was 4,790. Now, 30 years later, it numbers about 21,000.

Thetford was little influenced by the 18th and 19th century industrial growth but a number of industries were established including a factory manufacturing steam traction engines which dominated the towns economy at the turn of the century. Between 1801 and 1851 the population doubled from 2,000 to 4,000 persons and although this rate of increase diminished, the population continued to grow and had reached a total of 4,778 in 1911. **Source:** *County Development Plan: Thetford Town Map: Report of Survey & Analysis.* [August 1962]

An unidentified family photographed about 1880, at Henri Aegena's American Institute of Photography, number 11 White Hart Street, Thetford. During the 19th century, as today and for all sorts of reasons, there was a continuous movement of people settling in the town and also moving away, both to nearby and distant places.

Thetford's Population 1801-2001	
1801 – 2,246	1911 – 4,778
1811 – 2,450	1921 – 4,705
1821 – 2,922	1931 – 4,098
1831 – 3,462	1941 – no census
1841 – 3,934	1951 – 4,447
1851 – 4,074	1961 – 5,398
1861 – 4,208	1971 – 13,706
1871 – 4,166	1981 – 19,593
1881 – 4,032	1991 – 19,901
1891 – 4,322	2001 – 21,805
1901 – 4,613	**Source:** National Census

My paternal grandparents, Herbert [1879-1970] & Emily Osborne [1886-1969] with their baby daughter Maud, photographed by R. J. Bantock outside their St Nicholas Street home in 1911.
Herbert arrived in Thetford from the Harleston area of Norfolk early in the 20th century. They were married in St Peter's Church in January 1909. Emily was born in Thetford, just a few years after her parents settled here after moving from the Bury St Edmunds area.

Denis & Peggy Keane photographed with their children in 1962. Many British and American military personnel, having served on local bases and camps, settled in Thetford during the 20th century. Among them is Denis Keane, a native of Ireland who was stationed at RAF Barnham in the early 1950s and married Thetford born, Peggy Nicholls. While the Nicholls were an old local family, Peggy's mother was a member of the Street family, skilled engineers and agricultural machine makers who had settled in Thetford from Derbyshire in the late 1850s.
Wendy, the eldest of Peggy and Denis' three children, lives in the town today, having married David Brown, one of the first settlers to arrive from London under the Town Development in the late 1950s. Wendy's sister Siobhan is married and lives elsewhere in Norfolk but their brother, Brendan, lives abroad in the Middle East.

David and Joy Osborne photographed in the mid-1980s with their daughters, Emma and Elizabeth. While many of David's ancestors settled in Thetford during the 19th century, Joy's parents arrived from Norwich in the early 1940s. Although both Emma and Elizabeth have chosen to live in Thetford, like many other residents, they commute to work at nearby towns and cities.
Already, in the early 21st century, the arrival of numerous settlers from Portugal, in particular, is a noticeable change to the structure of Thetford's population. However, it is probable that about 1,000 years ago, when Thetford was ranked amongst the largest towns in England, the ethnic origin of Thetford's population with the settlement of Angles, Danes, Saxons, and Normans, was almost as diverse as today's.

A Bibliography of Thetford History

ANGLO-SAXON

■ Davison, B. K., 'The late Saxon town of Thetford: an interim report on the 1964-6 excavations', *Medieval Archaeology,* vol. 11 [1967], pp.189-208

■ Dunmore, S., & Carr, R., *'The Late Saxon Town of Thetford An Archaeological and Historical Survey',* East Anglian Archaeology 4 [1976]

■ Dunning, G. C., 'The Saxon Town of Thetford', *Archaeological Journal,* vol. 106 [1951], pp. 72-73

■ Knocker, G. M., *Theodford The Story of Anglo-Saxon Thetford* [not dated circa 1952]

■ Knocker, G. M., & Hughes, R. G., *Anglo-Saxon Thetford,* 2 parts Archaeology Newsletter no. 2 [1950] & no. 3 [1951]

ARCHAEOLOGY [GENERAL]

■ Andrews P., *Excavations at Redcastle Furze Thetford, 1988-89,* East Anglian Archaeology 72 [1995]

■ Andrews, P., and Penn, K., *Excavations in Thetford, North of the River, 1989-90,* East Anglian Archaeology 87 [1999]

■ Davies, J. A., 'Excavations at Ford Place, 1985-86', Davies, J. A., Gregory, T., Lawson, A. J., and Rogerson, A., *The Iron Age Forts of Norfolk,* East Anglian Archaeology 54 [1991]

■ Davies, J. A., 'Excavation of an Iron Age Pit Group at London Road, Thetford', *Norfolk Archaeology,* vol. 41 [1990-93], pp.441-461

■ Davison, B. K., *Excavations in Thetford between 1964 and 1970,* East Anglian Archaeology 62 [1993]

■ Fisher, B., 'The Garden At Water Mill Green', *The Searcher* [September 1997], pp. 40-42

■ Gregory, T., *Excavations in Thetford, 1980-82. Fison Way,* East Anglian Archaeology 53 [1991]

■ Hurst, J. G., 'Saxo-Norman Pottery in East Anglia: Part 2, Thetford Ware', *Proceedings of the Cambridge Antiquarian Society,* vol. 50 [1957], pp. 29-60

■ Johns, C., 'The Thetford Treasure; a major find of late Roman gold and silver', *Gold Bulletin 14* [1981], pp. 169-170

■ Johns, C., & Potter, T., *The Thetford Treasure,* [1983]

■ Knocker, G. M., 'Excavations at Red Castle, Thetford', *Norfolk Archaeology,* vol. 34 [1967], pp. 119-186

■ Mudd, A., *Excavations at Melford Meadows, Brettenham, 1994: Romano British and Early Saxon Occupations,* East Anglian Archaeology 99 [2002]

■ Potter, T., & Johns, C., 'The Thetford Treasure', *Illustrated London News* [April 1981], pp. 54-55

■ Rogerson, A., & Dallas, C., *Excavations in Thetford 1948-59 and 1973-80,* East Anglian Archaeology 22 [1984]

■ Wells, C., 'Report on the human skeletons from Red Castle, Thetford', *Norfolk Archaeology,* vol. 34 [1969]

BIOGRAPHICAL

■ Burlingham, D., *All in a Life Time,* D. Burlingham [2003]

■ Home, M., *Spring Sowing,* [1946]

■ Howlett, J., *The Guv'nor,* John Howlett [1973

■ Sutherland, H., *They Blow Their Trumpets,* [1959]

CASTLE HILL

■ Clarke, W. G., 'Thetford Castle Hill', *Norfolk Archaeology,* vol. 16 [1907], pp. 39-45

■ Clover, R. D., *A Hypothesis on the 'Castle' Earthworks Thetford,* R. D. Clover [1975]

■ Green, B., & Clarke, R. R., *Thetford Castle Excavations 1962,* Norfolk Research Committee Bulletin 14 [1963]

■ Gregory, T., 'Excavations at Thetford Castle 1962', East Anglian Archaeology 54 [1991], pp. 3-17

■ Killick, H. F., 'The Origin and History of Thetford Hill', *Norfolk Antiquarian and Miscellany,* 2nd series, Part III [1908], pp. 1-28

CHALK WORKINGS

■ Bruce-Mitford, R. L. S., 'A Late-Medieval Chalk-Mine at Thetford', *Norfolk Archaeology,* vol. 30 [1952], pp. 220-2

■ Hewitt, H. D., 'Chalk Mines at Thetford', *Norfolk Archaeology,* vol. 31 [1957], pp. 231-232

CHURCHES, CHAPELS & RELIGIOUS HOUSES [Excluding] CLUNIAC PRIORY]

■ Andrews, P., 'St George's Nunnery, Thetford', *Norfolk Archaeology,* vol. 41 [1990-93], pp.427-440

■ Anon., *St Peter's Church Thetford,* [1953]

■ Anon., *The Salvation Army Thetford Citadel Corps Centenary 1887-1987* [1988]

■ Anon, *Thetford Baptist Church A Short History 1859-1959,* [1959]

■ Blaydon, G. R., 'History of St Mary's Church, Thetford', *Bury Free Press* [26 February 1938]

■ Brooks, E., C., *A Short History of the Parish Church of St Cuthbert Thetford,* The Church Publishers [not dated circa 1960]

■ Cooper, Rev. E. C., 'Church Plate in the Deaneries of Breccles and Thetford', *Norfolk Archaeology,* vol. 16 [1907], pp. 31-38

■ Ede, J. & Virgoe, N., (ed.), 'Thetford Union' in '1851 Census of Religious Worship for Norfolk', *Norfolk Record Society,* vol. 62 [1998], pp. 350-362

■ Hare, J. N., 'The Priory of the Holy Sepulchre, Thetford', *Norfolk Archaeology,* vol. 37 [1978-80], pp.190-200

■ Walter, J. H. F., *'Deanery of Thetford'* in 'Church Plate in Norfolk', *Norfolk Archaeology,* vol. 23 [1928], pp. 221-223

CLUBS & SOCIETIES

■ Allison, W. R., 'Thetford Mechanic Institute - The Early Story, and Later Developments', *Bury Free Press & Post,* [24 March 1934], p.13

■ Blaydon, G. R., 1883-4 - 1933-4 *A Short History of the Thetford Town Football Club* [1934]

■ Short, W. J., *50 years Thetford Lodge (Freemasons)* [1958]

CLUNIAC PRIORY

■ Corrie, G. E., 'Some Notices of Thetford Priory', *Proceedings of the Bury & West Suffolk Archaeology Institute,* vol. 1 [1853], pp. 135-139

■ Dymond, D., (Ed), *The Register of Thetford Priory Part I 1482-1517,* Oxford [1995]

■ Dymond, D., (Ed), *The Register of Thetford Priory Part II 1518-1540,* Oxford [1996]

■ Harrod, H., 'Observations on the History and Present State of Thetford Priory', *Norfolk Archaeology,* vol. 3 [1852], pp. 105-124

■ Harvey, J. H., 'The last years of Thetford Cluniac Priory', *Norfolk Archaeology,* vol. 27 [1941], pp 1-27

■ Harvey, J. H., 'Building Works for an East Anglian Priory', *Norfolk Archaeology,* vol. 35 [1973]

■ Haywood, S., 'A Timber-framed Cluniac Conventual Building', *Norfolk Archaeological & Historical Research, The Annual* [1992], pp. 40-44

■ Manning, Rev. C. R., 'Brasses of Thomas Howard, Second Duke of Norfolk, and Agnes his Wife (1524)' *Norfolk Archaeology,* vol. 8 [1879], pp.39-50

■ Marks, R., 'The Howard Tombs at Thetford and Framlingham: New Discoveries', *The Archaeological Journal,* vol. 141 [1984], pp. 252-268

■ Raby, F. J. E. & Baillie Reynolds, P. K., *Thetford Priory,* Department of the Environment Ancient Monuments and Historic Buildings [1979]

■ Robertson-Mackay, R., 'Recent Excavations at the Cluniac Priory of St Mary, Thetford, Norfolk', *Medieval Archaeology,* vol. 1 [1958], pp. 96-103

■ Wasson, J., 'Visiting Entertainers at the Cluniac Priory, Thetford 1497-1540', *Albion,* vol. 9 [1977]

■ Wilcox, R., 'Thetford Cluniac Priory Excavations 1971-4', *Norfolk Archaeology,* vol. 40 [1987-89], pp. 1-18

COINAGE

■ Carson, R. A. G., 'The mint of Thetford [959-1188 A.D.]', *Numismatic Chronicle,* 6th ser., vol. 9 [1949], pp. 189-236

■ Evans, M. M., 'A silver badge of Thetford', *Numismatic Chronicle,* 4th ser., 7 [1907]

■ Fitch, W. S., 'Notes on the Thetford Mints', *Norfolk Archaeology,* vol. 3 [1852], pp. 29-36

■ Green, B., 'Thetford Roman Coin Hoard', *Norfolk Archaeology,* vol. 37 pt. 2 [1979], pp. 221-223

■ Rigold, S. E., 'Finds of St Edmund Memorial and other Anglo-Saxon coins from excavations at Thetford', *British Numismatic Journal,* vol. 29 [1958-59], pp. 189-190

EDUCATION & CHARITIES

■ Anon., *Thetford Girls' Grammar School 100 Years of Excellence 1888-1988,* Thetford Grammar School [1988]

■ Burrell, G., *An account of the gifts and legacies that have been given and bequeathed to charitable and public uses in the borough of Thetford...also a chronological account of the most remarkable events which have occurred in Thetford from the earliest period...*[1809]

■ Heard, N., *Thetford Grammar School* [1972]

■ Seymour, D., 'Schoolchildren & Remembrance', *Despatches* The Magazine of the Friends of the Imperial War Museum [April 2000], pp. 34-35

■ Yaxley, P., 'Thetford Schooldays - Pillow Fights and Midnight Feasts', *Picture Postcard Monthly,* no. 231 [July 1998], pp. 32-34

ELECTIONS

■ Anon., The case of the election of *Thetford in Norfolk* [1685]

■ Harbord, W., *The case of the Rt. Hon. William Harbourd and Sir Francis Guybon chosen members for the borough of Thetford, to serve in this present Parliament* [1690]

■ Newson, A., *Politics and Society in Thetford 1832 - 1868,* B. A. dissertation [1973]

GENERAL HISTORIES

■ Allison, W. R., 'The Story of the Thetford Riots', *Bury Free Press & Post* [25 May 1935], p.12

■ Blaydon, G. R., *A Survey of Local Government in Thetford in the Past and the Methods by which the Borough discharges its functions Today* [1935]

■ Blomefield, F., *The History of the ancient City and Burgh of Thetford* [1739]

■ Clarke, J. W., *Thetford an Historical and Descriptive Sketch of the Town* [1894]

■ Clarke, J. W., *Guide to Thetford Norfolk,* Thetford Chamber of Trade [1931]

■ Clarke, W. G., 'A Brief Survey of the History of Thetford', *The Eastern Counties Magazine* [Nov.1900] & [Feb. 1901]

■ Clarke, W. G., *A Short Historical Guide to the Ancient Borough of Thetford,* [1908] & [1909] with variant title.

■ Clarke, W. G., *Guide to the Borough of Thetford* [1923]

■ Clarke, W. G., *In Breckland Wilds* [1925 & revised edition 1937]

■ Craig, J. S., 'The "Godly" and the "Froward": Protestant Polemics in the Town of Thetford, 1560-1590', *Norfolk Archaeology,* vol. 41 [1990-93], pp. 279-293

■ Crosby, A., *A History of Thetford* [1986]

■ Harper, C. G., *The Newmarket, Bury, Thetford and Cromer Road* [1904]

■ Hunt, A. L., *Hunt's Shilling guide to the ancient borough of Thetford, its history and antiquities* [1868]

■ Hunt, A. L., *The Capital of the Ancient Kingdom of East Anglia* [1870]

■ Mander, R. P., 'Thetford Through the Ages', *The Norfolk Magazine,* vol. 6, no. 5 Sept-Oct [1953]

■ Martin, T., *The History of the Town of Thetford* [1779]

■ Martineau, H. D., 'Ancient Thetford - the Home of Kings', *Norfolk Fair* [November/December 1967], pp. 49-54

■ Minett G., 'I Remember Thetford', in 2 parts *Norfolk Fair* [April-May 1971], pp.35-39 & 38-42

■ Osborne, D., *A View of Thetford Past* [1984]

■ Osborne, D., *A View of Thetford Past II* [1985]

■ Osborne, D., *A View of Thetford Past III* [1987]

■ Osborne D., *Thetford, Brandon & District A Portrait in Old Picture Postcards* [1990]

■ Osborne D., *Thetford A Century Remembered From 1900 - to the Present Day* [1996]

■ Osborne D., *Thetford A Century Remembered From 1900 - to the Present Day [Part Two]* [2000]

■ Various, *Thetford Antiq Burg*, Leaf Publication [1985]

■ Will Wandering, *Thetford: An Historical and Descriptive Sketch of the Town*, J. W. Clarke [1897]

LATER HISTORY

■ Anon., *Expanding Towns Thetford* Department of Architecture & Civic Design [not dated circa. 1970]

■ Anon., *Thetford Borough Council Tenants Handbook*, Thetford Borough Council [1962]

■ Anon., *Thetford town expansion: the first 500 families*, Norfolk County Council [1965]

■ Anon., *Thetford: an opportunity for industry*, Greater London Council [n.d.]

■ Davidson, C., 'Expansion at Thetford', *Building*, 27 [May 1966]

■ Bennett, H., *Thetford: further expansion study*, Greater London Council Architect's Dept. [n.d.]

■ Wallace, D. B., & Turner, D. M., 'Industrial Development of Country Towns, 4. Thetford', *Town & Country Planning*, vol. 31 [1963]

MEDIEVAL

■ Hartshorne, C. H., 'Visits of Edward I to Bury St Edmunds and Thetford', *Proceedings Bury & West Suffolk Archaeological Institute*, vol. 1 [1853], pp.91-97

■ Dodwell, B., 'The Honour of the Bishop of Thetford/Norwich in the Late Eleventh and Early Twelfth Centuries', *Norfolk Archaeology*, vol. 33 [1965], pp. 185-199

■ Williams, J. F., 'A Bailiff's Roll of Thetford 1403-04', *Norfolk Archaeology*, vol. 24 [1932], pp. 7-12

MINERAL SPRINGS

■ Accum F., *Guide to the Chalybeate Spring of Thetford* [1819]

Manning, M., *De Aquis Mineralibus* [1746]

Manning, M., 'Thetford Spa', in 'Taking the Waters In Norfolk', *Norfolk Industrial Archaeology Society Journal*, vol. 5 no. 3 [1993], pp. 157-159

PRE-HISTORIC

■ Clarke, W. G., 'Neolithic man in Thetford district', *Norfolk & Norwich Naturalist's Society*, vol. 6 [1895-99], pp. 23-36

■ Clarke, W. G., 'Remains of the Neolithic age Thetford district', *Norfolk & Norwich Naturalist's Society*, vol. 8 [1905-09], pp. 25-35

■ Clover, R. D., *Tale of an Area A Village Study and History: of Croxton, Kilverstone, and Barnham and the Infancy of Thetford* [1975]

■ Clover, R. D., 'Thetford and a tale of two hills', *Norfolk Fair* [1981]

■ Johns, C., 'Fanus and Thetford: an early Latin deity in late Roman Britain', in 'Pagan gods and shrines of the Roman Empire', *Oxford University Committee of Archaeology*, no. 8 [1986]

PUBLIC HEALTH

■ Cooke, R. & S., 'Thetford Water Works', *Norfolk Industrial Archaeology Society Journal*, vol. 2 no. 4 [1979], pp. 26-61

■ Low, Dr., J. S., *Report on the sanitary circumstances and administration of the three sanitary districts...within the Thetford registration district*, Inspectors' reports 269 [1907]

■ Osborne, D. J., *A History of the Borough of Thetford Fire Brigade* [1988]

■ Millington, F. H., *Borough of Thetford Statement with Documents Relating To The Proposed Sewerage Scheme* [1909]

TOWN GUIDES & DIRECTORIES

■ Anon., *Festival of Britain 1951 The Borough of Thetford Norfolk*, Thetford Borough Council [1951]

■ Anon., *Guide to Thetford Norfolk*, Thetford & District Chamber of Commerce [1938]

■ Anon., *Guide to Thetford Norfolk*, Thetford & District Chamber of Commerce [1948]

■ Anon., *Guide to Thetford Norfolk*, Thetford & District Chamber of Commerce [1951]

■ Anon., *Official Guide Thetford* [1967]

■ Anon., *Official Guide Thetford Norfolk*, Thetford & District Chamber of Commerce [1989]

■ Anon., *Thetford and District Illustrated* [not dated, circa. 1905]

■ Anon., *Thetford Official Guide*, Thetford & District Chamber of Commerce [1994]

■ Anon., *Thetford Official Guide*, Thetford Town Council [1999]

■ Anon., *The Thetford Almanac 1896*, W. Boughton & Sons [1898]

■ Anon., *The Thetford Almanac 1897*, W. Boughton & Sons [1898]

■ Anon., *The Thetford Almanac 1898*, W. Boughton & Sons [1898]

■ Anon., *The Thetford Book*, Regency Publicity Services Ltd [1970]

■ Anon., *Thetford & District Almanac 1912*, W. Boughton & Sons [1912]

■ Anon., *Thetford & District Almanac 1913*, W. Boughton & Sons [1913]

■ Anon., *Thetford & District Almanac 1917*, W. Boughton & Sons [1917]

■ Anon., *The Thetford & District Almanac 1923*, W. Boughton & Sons [1923]

■ Anon., *The Thetford & District Almanac and Directory 1928* [1928]

■ Anon., *The Thetford & District Almanac and Directory 1935* [1935]

■ Anon., *The Thetford & District Almanac and Directory 1936* [1936]

■ Anon., *The Thetford & District Almanac and Directory 1938*, Henry Green [1938]

■ Anon., *The Thetford Guide* [2001]

■ Astley, H. J. D., 'A Ramble round Thetford', *The Antiquary* [July-August 1903]

■ Noy, A. R., *Thetford & District Almanac and Directory 1931*, H. Green [1931]

THOMAS PAINE

■ Anon., *Thomas Paine Collection an analytical catalogue,* Norfolk County Library Norwich [1979]

■ Dixon, R.N.A., *Thomas Paine 1737-1809,* Thetford Town Council [1937]

■ Keane, J., *Tom Paine A Political Life* [1995]

■ Maddock, A., *Thomas Paine 1737-1809,* Norfolk Museums Services [1983]

TOPOGRAPHY - ARCHITECTURAL FEATURES

■ Anon., *Thetford Chase,* Forestry Commission, H.M.S.O. London [1951]

■ Anon., *34 Photographs of Thetford,* W. Boughton & Sons Ltd., Thetford [not dated circa. 1905]

■ Chamberlain, G., 'Thetford War Memorial', in 'Heraldic China and Norfolk War Memorials', *Norfolk Industrial Archaeology Society Journal,* vol. 6 no. 5 [2000]

■ Clarke, W. G., *Description of The Ancient House, Thetford* [not dated circa. 1925]

■ Ions, J., 'The Development Of The Provincial Urban Villa And Gardens Of The Eighteenth And Nineteenth Centuries, With Special Reference To Ford Place, Thetford', University of East Anglia, Master Of Arts Degree Dissertation [2002]

■ Killick, H. F., 'The King's House at Thetford, with some account of the visits of King James I to that Town', *Norfolk Archaeology,* vol. 16 [1907], pp. 2-30

■ Killick, H. F., 'The King's House at Thetford (additional notes)', *Norfolk Archaeology,* vol. 16 [1907], pp. 125-131

■ Maddocks, A., *The Ancient House, Thetford,* Norfolk Museums Services [1977]

■ Millington, F. H., *The History of the Guildhall, Thetford* [1902]

■ Ratcliffe, P., & Claridge, J., *Thetford Forest Park The Ecology of a Pine Forest,* Forestry Commission Tech. Paper 13 [1996]

■ Skipper, K. & Williamson, T., *Thetford Forest Making a Landscape, 1922-1997* [1997]

■ Tolhurst, P., *Thetford In Ruins* [1992]

■ Vincent, J., *Thetford Town Trail An Environmental Exploration* [not dated circa. 1975]

■ Wilkinson, J., *The architectural remains of the ancient town & borough of Thetford in the counties of Norfolk and Suffolk* [1822]

TRADE & INDUSTRY

■ Anon., *Boughtons Centenary 1897-1997,* Boughtons Printers [1997]

■ Anon., 'East Anglian Industries no. 5, The Patent Pulp Manufacturing Company, Ltd., Thetford', *Bury Free Press* [20 Aug. 1909]

■ Anon., 'Industries of Thetford no. 1, The Canning Factory', *Bury Free Press (Thetford Ed.)* [2 July 1938], p.12

■ Anon., 'Industries of Thetford no. 2, Lambert's Trailer Works', *Bury Free Press (Thetford Ed.)* [9 July 1938], p.12

■ Anon., 'Industries of Thetford no. 3, The Ibex Coffee Factory', *Bury Free Press (Thetford Ed.)* [16 July 1938], p.12

■ Anon., 'Industries of Thetford no. 4, Moss and Potter's Mineral Water Works', *Bury Free Press (Thetford Ed.)* [23 July 1938], p.12

■ Anon., 'Notes From Thetford', *Agricultural Gazette,* [1874], pp. 138-139

■ Anon., *Rules of the Thetford Industrial Co-operative Provision Society Limited* [1907]

■ Anon., *100 years Thetford Moulded Products Limited 1879-1979,* Thetford Moulded Products Ltd [1979]

■ Beckett, C. M., *Thomas Beckett: Master Sadler* [1994]

■ Brown, P. & Manning, D., 'Thermos Ltd., Thetford', Norfolk Industrial *Archaeology Society Journal,* vol. 7 no. 1 [2001], pp. 5-16

■ Clarke, R. H., 'The Staunches and Navigation of the Little Ouse River', *Newcomen Society Transactions,* vol. 30 [1955-57], pp. 207-219

■ Davison, A. P., 'Thetford', *Justly Celebrated Ales, A Directory of Norfolk Brewers 1850-1990,* Brewers History Society [1991], pp. 41-42

■ Farrow, C., *A Short History of the Rise and Progress of the Thetford Industrial Co-operative Society (Limited)* [1894]

■ Farrow, C., *1861-1934 A History of the Thetford Co-operative Society, Ltd* [1934]

■ Gilbert, G. F. A., *Burrell Style 1900-1932* [1994]

■ Gilbert, G. F. A. & Osborne, D., *Charles Burrell & Sons Ltd Steam Engine Builders of Thetford,* Friends of Charles Burrell Museum [1998]

■ Goodwin, C., 'Thetford Pulp Ware', *Norfolk Industrial Archaeology Society Journal,* vol. 3 no. 5 [1985], pp. 164-171

■ Helgesen, M., 'A Commercial Corner of St Nicholas Street', *Thetford Magazine, no. 21, The Magazine of the Thetford Society* [Summer 1999], pp. 8-10

■ Lane, M., *Burrell Showman's road locomotives* [1971]

■ Lane, M. R., *The Story of St Nicholas Works A History of Charles Burrell & Sons Ltd 1803-1928* [1994]

■ Maddocks, A., *Burrell's of Thetford,* Norfolk Museums Services [1979]

■ Manning, M., 'Survey of Fison's Vitriol & Manure Works Two Mile Bottom, Thetford, Norfolk', *Industrial Archaeology Society Journal,* vol. 2 no. 1 [1976]

■ Osborne, D., 'Burrells of Thetford: further research on the beginnings', *Norfolk Industrial Archaeology Society Journal,* vol. 4 no. 5 [1990], pp. 175-180

■ Osborne, D., 'The Charles Burrell Museum, Thetford, Norfolk', *Industrial Archaeology News,* The Bulletin of the Association for Industrial Archaeology no. 118 [Autumn 2001], pp. 4-5

■ Osborne, D., *'Occupations in 19th Century Thetford & Brandon',* University of Cambridge Board of Extra-mural Studies, Certificate in English Local History dissertation [1992]

INDEX [excluding A Bibliography of Thetford History pp. 124-127]

INDEX

Notes

130